A History of American Currency

with chapters on the English Bank restriction and Austrian paper money

William Graham Sumner

COSIMO CLASSICS

NEW YORK

A History of American Currency
© 2005 Cosimo, Inc.
All rights reserved. No part of this book may be used or reproduced in any manner whatsoever without prior written permission except in the case of brief quotations embodied in critical articles or reviews. For information, address:

Cosimo, P.O. Box 416
Old Chelsea Station
New York, NY 10113-0416

or visit our website at:
www.cosimobooks.com

A History of American Currency originally published by Henry Holt & Co. in 1874.

Library of Congress Cataloging-in-Publication Data
A catalog record for this book is available from the Library of Congress

Cover design by www.wiselephant.com

ISBN: 1-59605-081-0

PREFACE.

IN the autumn of 1873 I published in the ' Financier," four or five short sketches of those portions of history which are most instructive in regard to doctrines of currency. The plan was to leave the historical facts to tell their own story without comment. It succeeded so far that many persons who do not believe that financial laws vary with the period, the climate, or the continent, read them with interest, and drew the inferences of which it seemed to be important that we should all be convinced. I was asked to re-publish the sketches in permanent form. In acceding to this request, however, I desired to present these chapters of history more completely, and I determined also to incorporate with this project another plan which I had formed, viz., to edit the Bullion Report. Two of the articles referred to treated of the paper money in the American colonies, and the crisis of 1819. These have been expanded here into an outline sketch of the history of American currency. I regard the history of American finance and politics as a most important department which lies as yet almost untouched. The materials even are all in the rough, and it would require very long time and extensive research to do any justice to the subject. I hope, at some future time, to treat it as it deserves, and I should not now have published anything in regard to it, if I had not felt that it had, at this juncture, great practical importance, and that even a sketch might be more *useful* perhaps than an elaborate treatise. It follows from this account of the origin and motive of the present work, that it does not aim at any particular unity, but consists of three distinct historical sketches, united only by their tendency to establish two or three fundamental doctrines in regard to currency.

Yale College, March, 1874.

COSIMO is an innovative publisher of books and publications that inspire, inform and engage readers worldwide. Our titles are drawn from a range of subjects including health, business, philosophy, history, science and sacred texts. We specialize in using print-on-demand technology (POD), making it possible to publish books for both general and specialized audiences and to keep books in print indefinitely. With POD technology new titles can reach their audiences faster and more efficiently than with traditional publishing.

> ➤ **Permanent Availability:** Our books & publications never go out-of-print.

> ➤ **Global Availability:** Our books are always available online at popular retailers and can be ordered from your favorite local bookstore.

COSIMO CLASSICS brings to life unique, rare, out-of-print classics representing subjects as diverse as *Alternative Health, Business and Economics, Eastern Philosophy, Personal Growth, Mythology, Philosophy, Sacred Texts, Science, Spirituality* and much more!

COSIMO-on-DEMAND publishes your books, publications and reports. If you are an Author, part of an Organization, or a Benefactor with a publishing project and would like to bring books back into print, publish new books fast and effectively, would like your publications, books, training guides, and conference reports to be made available to your members and wider audiences around the world, we can assist you with your publishing needs.

Visit our website at www.cosimobooks.com to learn more about Cosimo, browse our catalog, take part in surveys or campaigns, and sign-up for our newsletter.

And if you wish please drop us a line at info@cosimobooks.com. We look forward to hearing from you.

CHAPTER I.

THE English Government made no objection to the emigration of the Puritans to New England, save that they carried money out of the realm. The earliest settlers carried very little; other forms of capital were more valuable to them, and they had no use for it, save in exchanges amongst themselves. Yet Winthrop wrote to his son, in 1630, especially to bring £150 or £200 in money. Later settlers brought money to exchange for cattle, seed, and other forms of capital which the first colonists had already accumulated. In this form, the law that every community will have so much of the precious metals as it needs for its exchanges* vindicated itself in their case.

* See p. 250.

Of the value of money amongst them we may judge from the following incidents :

A married clergyman was allowed £30 per annum.

Josias Plaistowe, having stolen four baskets of corn from the Indians, was to repay eight and be fined £5.

Carpenters, sawyers, joiners, and bricklayers (whose services were in great demand, and had a monopoly price), were forbidden to take over 12d. and afterwards 2s. per day. Penalty, 10s. to giver and taker.

Magistrates had 3s. 6d. and deputies 2s. 6d. per day.

Ed. Palmer, being found guilty of extortion in charging 13s. 4d. for the wood-work of the Boston stocks, was fined £5, and condemned to sit in the stocks one hour.

In January, 1631, the crops having failed in England, and no crop having yet been raised in Massachusetts Bay, grain was at famine prices. Including freight, wheat was 14s. per bushel, peas 10s. Indian corn from Virginia

10s.   Many cattle died.   A cow was worth £25 or £30.

The President of Harvard College was con-demned to pay an usher £20 for flogging him.

WAMPUMPEAG CURRENCY.

When exploring parties penetrated to Long Island Sound, they found along its coasts tribes of Indians far more civilized than those who had been met farther north.   The cause or indication of their superiority was that they had a circulat-ing medium.   This consisted of beads of two kinds, one white, made out of the end of a periwinkle shell, and the other black, made out of the black part of a clam shell.   These beads were rubbed down and polished as articles of ornament, and arranged in strings or belts into jewelry, being objects of real beauty when the colors were artistically combined.   These beads and belts were used by the Indians themselves as money, and were real money.   They re-garded one black bead as worth two white. This money was called wampumpeag, or wam-pum, or peag.

The colonists began to use it first for exchanges with the Indians, and then amongst themselves. It was first made legal tender only for 12d. in Massachusetts, but by custom it became the prevailing currency. The white man also proved his superiority by counterfeiting it. A fathom or belt of wampum consisted of 360 beads. One fathom of white would buy furs which were valued at 5s. sterling, and one fathom of black would buy furs worth 10s. Therefore,

360 white beads, = 60d.
6 beads, = 1 penny.
360 black beads, = 120d.
3 beads, = 1 penny.

These were the rates at which the peag first circulated among the colonists, and its operation is in many respects worthy of study. It was, for the Indians, in their limited community, a perfect money. They divided their labors, some hunting and fishing, some, who lived on the shore, making peag. They made as much as they chose or could. It was a product of labor, and subject to demand and supply. It was valued as jewelry, and when thus made up and appropriated, it passed out of circulation.   Prices must have fluctuated in it according to the active circulation which extended several hundred miles inland westward.   It was subject to deterioration by wear and use.

When the colonists, who were in exchange relations with a world which used gold and silver, began to use it, other currency laws came into operation.   It was not exportable, would not satisfy foreign debts, was not desired by the whites, save for the conventional purpose of money.

BARTER CURRENCY.

The colonists began, soon after the settlement of Massachusetts Bay, to use a barter currency,* ostensibly because they had not money enough : really because they wanted to spare the world's currency to purchase real capital, which was their true need.   The currency history of this country has been nothing but a repetition of this down to the present hour.   It has always been claimed that a new country must be drained of the

---

* In 1635 musket bullets were used for change at a farthing apiece, legal tender for sums under 12d.

precious metals, or that it could not afford so expensive a medium. The new country really needs capital in all forms. The only question is, whether, being poor and unable to get all that it wants, it can better afford to do without foreign commodities or without specie currency. No sound economist can hesitate how to decide this question. The losses occasioned by a bad currency far exceed the gains from imported commodities. The history of the United States from the landing of Winthrop to to-day is a reiterated proof of it. The best protection to native manufactures is to keep a due proportion of the national capital in a specie circulation, and do without, or find substitutes for, or learn to make, the things which the people cannot afford to buy from older and more advanced countries.

Credit, in its legitimate forms, is priceless to a new community, but when used in illegitimate forms, as in a pure credit currency, or in a currency into which credit enters as an indefinable element, it makes legitimate credit impossible. This history will do little more than to expose the errors involved in mistaking credit currency for money, and money for capital—errors which are repeated to-day by the new States—and to show the bad results of those errors.

The barter currency was inferior to gold and silver in cost. When corn and beaver, and, in fact, all other products, were made legal tender, no one would pay debts in specie. It was hoarded and paid away for imports.

A barter currency is also the most rapid of all currencies in its depreciation. If a cow will pay taxes, the leanest cow will be given. If corn will pay a debt, the corn which is of poorest quality, or damaged to a certain extent, will be given.

If a large number of commodities are made legal tender, the poorest quality of the commodity, which may be cheapest at the time of payment, will be given. Credit operations are therefore made almost impossible.

Some ludicrous complaints, on the part of the tax-gatherers, scattered up and down in the records, bear witness to the fact that this was all experienced in New England. The more barter currency was used " because money was scarce," the scarcer money became.   Prices rose to fit the worst form of payment which the seller might expect.

Accordingly, in 1640, prices having risen so much that the nominal "penny" in the barter currency had fallen, we find the Massachusetts Court re-rating wampum at four of the white and two of the black for a penny, to the amount of 12d.   Interest was 8 per cent.

During the ten years, then, from 1630 to 1640, the specie brought over, and that gained by trade with the West Indies and Virginia (not yet great) had been steadily exported.   Merchants had found the colony a good market.   In 1640, Winthrop tells how the merchants came and drained off the people's cash.   That he should not have understood the case is not strange, but that people nowadays should not have learned from the experience of two centuries and a half, and the teachings of science, any better than to repeat the same theory, is astonishing.

DISTRESS.

Meantime silver prices had, of course, fallen enormously. Now came other circumstances to prostrate the colony. The emigrants ceased to come, on account of the prospect of a new state of things favorable to them at home. Merchants came, but no longer found a market. The project of moving away was broached and earnestly debated in the colony. This tended to still further depress the price of all fixed improvements and stock. Cows were valued in taxation, in 1646, at £5; horses four years old, £6.

In the first years, 1630–1640, 22,000 people came over. For some time after 1640 more went back than came. The settlers had gained by sales of stock, etc., to successive new arrivals. A farmer had clothed his family on one cow sold annually from his stock. £192,000 had been spent on the colony, "a dear purchase, if they had paid nothing to the Council of Plymouth and nothing afterwards to the sachems of the country."

NEW INDUSTRIES.

Under the new circumstances they turned to new industries, and, so far from being ruined, were far better off. In 1641 corn would buy nothing, but was legal tender for debts. They turned to ship-building, carrying between Virginia and the West Indies, fishing, seal fishing on the Isle of Sable, and lumbering. These industries all prospered. In 1643 the crop failed, and corn was sold only for ready money or for cattle, at 12d. more per bushel than for cash.

In 1648 it was necessary to order that only such peag as was unbroken and of good color should pass—legal tender up to 12d.

In 1649 the colony treasurer was forbidden to take peag. The inhabitants began to reject it, but the court then ordered that peag should be legal tender for 40s., the white at eight and the black at six for a penny. Disputes arising about the barter currency for taxes, three appraisers were provided for, one to be chosen by the treasurer, the second by the owner, and the third by the marshal.

THE "PINE-TREE" COINAGE.

Coin was now coming in freely by the trade with the West Indies. The buccaneers also spent a great deal of their booty in the colonies, but it all just as steadily went out. In 1652 Massachussets set up a mint at Boston to coin this metal and try to keep it in circulation. They coined shillings, sixpences, and three-pences, and continued to do so for many years, but, as it was a breach of the prerogative to coin, they dated all the coins 1652. The coins were to be of sterling alloy, $\frac{11}{12}$ fine, and the shilling worth 10d. sterling. The mint master had 15d. in 20s. for coining. As silver was worth 5s. 2d. sterling per oz., if the New England shillings had been equal to 10d. sterling each, silver should have been worth 6s. 2½d. New England currency per oz., but as the mint master kept 15d. out of every 20s., silver was worth 6s. 7d. New England currency per oz., if the coin was up to its own standard. It would therefore have been 22 per cent. worse than sterling. The English Mint declared it not of even weight or fineness, and it was taken in England only at 25 per cent. discount. The normal rate, therefore, was 6s. 8d. per oz. The law forbade exportation on penalty of forfeiting all visible estate. Of course this restrained but it did not prevent it. This currency, known as the "pine-tree" currency, forms the standard by which calculations were made from this time on.

Meantime the barter currency was continued, and another act passed in 1654 provides that all contracts in kind shall be so satisfied. In 1655, a constable brought cattle to the treasurer for taxes which were so poor that he would not take them. In 1657 another prays for relief because, having taken boards for taxes, the treasurer would not allow him as much as he allowed for them. In 1658 it was ordered that no man should pay taxes in "lank" cattle. In fact the barter currency continued general.

In 1655 the colony accounts allow for £35 10s. peag burned with the treasurer's house, and contain an entry of eighteen strings of peag at six a penny.*

---

* For this, and many other citations from the Colonial Records, I am indebted to Felt's Mass. Currency.

Accordingly, the silver money no sooner appeared than it was either smuggled out of the country or clipped. The principle laid down by Sir Thomas Gresham in Queen Elizabeth's time, that a better and a worse currency cannot circulate together, but that the worse will drive out the better, was the only secret. If the better currency could not be exported, it was clipped down to the rate of the inferior currency, or rather below it, in order to be on the safe side, and pay rather less than more than one need.*

The silver which came to the colony consisted for the most part of Spanish pillar coins. On account of the heavy mint charges these were not taken to the mint. They were not allowed to be circulated. The dollar, or piece of eight, was worth 4s. 6d. sterling, or 6s. New England currency. In 1672 a law was passed allowing these pieces to circulate at 6s. and other pieces in proportion. In 1675 the mint was leased again, in spite of prohibitions from England. In the

* In 1873 the United States coined a "trade dollar" with the purpose of getting a share of the China banking and exchange business. The project was in every way fallacious, but the dollars were made worth $1.03 in gold, and, coming into circulation in Nevada, were clipped.

same year, 25 per cent. discount on barter taxes was allowed for cash, and afterwards 50 per cent. In the same year, it was provided that, instead of transporting barter payments of taxes to and from the treasury, the transfers should be made by paper orders. Meantime, the coin was sent to England and to the other colonies, and was extremely scarce in Massachusetts.

In 1686 a bank was proposed, to issue notes. Its history is obscure, and though it seems to have made issues, they soon disappeared. Andros stopped the mint about 1688. It formed one of the chief charges against the colony on account of which the charter was revoked in 1691.

THE FIRST EXPEDITION AGAINST CANADA, AND PAPER MONEY.

In 1690 an expedition was fitted out against Canada, the payment for which was to come from the booty. It came back not only without booty, but in great misery. The soldiers were clamorous for pay, and it was to satisfy their demands that the first paper money was issued. This expedition cost the colony £50,000.

£7,000 were issued in notes from 5s. to £5, receivable for taxes, and for goods paid into the treasury for taxes.

Sir William Phipps tried to sustain the paper by giving coin for some of it, but the soldiers disposed of it at one-third discount. The issues were limited to £40,000, and £10,000 in the treasury were ordered burned in 1691. In 1692 it was ordered that the bills be received at 5 per cent. advance over coin at the colonial treasury, and the Court promised to redeem them in money within twelve months. This kept the paper at par for twenty years. In the same year legal interest was reduced to 6 per cent. The barter currency now ceased for a time, or at least became less common. Felt and Bronson both quote Madam Knight's letter that, in Connecticut, there were four prices : " pay," " pay as money," " money," and " trusting." The merchant asked his customer how he would pay before fixing the price. " Pay " was barter at the government rates. " Money " was Spanish or New England coin, also wampum for change. " Pay as money " was barter currency at prices ⅓ less than the government rates. "Trusting" was an enhanced price, according to time. A sixpenny knife cost 12d. in pay, 8d. in pay as money, and 6d. in coin.

Paper was now issued to pay the annual charges of the colony of Massachusetts, but it was also drawn in by taxes, and it does not appear that the amount in circulation at any one time was excessive. In 1702, money being scarce, taxes slowly paid, and government affairs hindered, £10,000 were issued, secured on the import and excise, and £6,000 taxes were voted. By this tax all the bills out were to be withdrawn and destroyed. In 1704 a royal proclamation fixed the value of Spanish and other foreign coins, not at sterling rates, but apparently on the basis of the New England coinage. Little heed was paid to it. The current rates of the coins obeyed other than royal laws.

SECOND EXPEDITION AGAINST CANADA— DEPRECIATION.

In 1709, another expedition against Canada being intended, £30,000 in bills of credit were issued, and £10,000 of the old were reissued. The preparations dragged on for two years, and, in 1711, £10,000 more were issued to pay military expenses. New Hampshire, Rhode Island, Connecticut, New York, and New Jersey joined in this expedition, and now began to issue bills of credit. The Massachusetts bills had hitherto been held close, and provisions for redemption by taxes in a year or two had always been made. They had been put out in payment of government expenses, and had thus been a kind of exchequer bills.

In 1709 the time for redemption was set at 4 years; in 1710 at 5 years; in 1711 at 6 years; this injured the credit of the bills at the same time that they became redundant. The depreciation now began. The paper was legal tender, its acceptance being enforced from time to time by more and more stringent enactments.

COLMAN'S BANK.

The mystery of banking was now attracting attention the world over. The Land Bank in England about 1685, the Austrian enterprises of 1700, John Law's scheme of 1715, the South

Sea Company founded in 1711, bear witness to it. The Massachusetts people were not behind the age. In 1715 John Colman and others proposed a bank based on land and issuing notes. They proposed to build a bridge over Charles river, which was scouted as impracticable. The Council (upper house of the General Court, always conservative) forbade them to make public proposals or print notes until the General Assembly could act on their plans.

LOAN BANK.

There was a great clamor for more paper money of some sort, and those who opposed all paper joined those who opposed the Bank in carrying a scheme for a public issue. This was the first of the loan banks * which were created in nearly if not quite all the colonies before the Revolution. In the process of time certain new de-

---

* "Bank," as the word was used before the Revolutionary War, meant only a batch of paper money, issued either by the government or a corporation. The impression seems to have remained popular; that the essential idea of a bank is the issuing of notes. Gouge, accepting this definition, assailed all "banking." The notes issued in banks, or masses as loans, were pure paper money, and may be distinguished from the Treasury notes issued for the current expenses of government.

velopments were added, which were supposed to perfect the system. To take one of the most perfect specimens, which enjoyed the approval of Franklin,* and which was made in Pennsylvania in 1723, the plan was as follows: the issue was for £15,000, put in the hands of commissioners in each county, according to the taxable assessment. The commissioners loaned the bills at 5 per cent. on mortgage of land. The loan was for 16 years, payable $\frac{1}{16}$ annually, and the interest was to defray the expenses of government. Instalments repaid during the first 10 years of the period were to be loaned out again only for the remainder of the period.

Rhode Island was the most unfortunate of all the colonies in her currency legislation. She kept peag longer than any of the others, and plunged into paper issues more recklessly than any. The loan bank system she tested to the bitter end.

---

* The great philosopher was not unbiassed in his judgment. He printed the bills, having written a pamphlet in favor of them, and he says, " It was a very profitable job and a great help to me." Looking back upon it later, he argues that it was a good thing, " though I now think there are limits beyond which the quantity may be hurtful."—*Works, II.* 254.

The first "bank" in that colony was for £30,000, issued in 1715, for 10 years. In 1728 the time was extended to 13 years, and then 10 years more were allowed for the repayment, without interest beyond the first 13 years. In 1721 a second bank was issued of £40,000 for 5 years, extended in 1728 to 13 years, interest payable in hemp or flax. It was intended to act as a bounty on those articles. In 1631 the same colony laid a bounty on flax, hemp, whale oil, whale-bone, and codfish.*

As this system of public loans is now advocated by the so-called "labor-reformers," it is especially worth while to know that it has been subjected here to a full experiment, and what its results were. Hutchinson says that the people of Massachusetts must have wondered that no one had before hit upon this marvellous expedient for paying the expenses of government. The persons who obtained loans in the ninth and tenth year of the bank period, complained that they must pay back in seven or

---

* Potter, R. I. Paper Money in Phillips' Colon. and Contin. Paper Currency, I. 100.

six years, whereas others enjoyed the loan for sixteen years. The banks were accordingly "continued," or renewed continually. New claimants who desired to come under this shower of wealth clamored for new banks on the ground of "justice" and "equality." All who had received loans joined as a compact body in favor of further issues. All new issues to others depreciated the currency, and enabled them to pay back more easily. However, they did not in many cases pay at all, either principal or interest. Having accumulated large arrears they decamped, and, when process issued, could not be found. The mortgaged estates were found entangled in inextricable confusion. The legislatures, composed largely of men in the system, would allow no extreme measures. Foreclosures were rare, and did not pay for the trouble and excitement they caused. The paper became a political issue, and Douglas says the parties were no longer Whig or Tory, but Creditors and Debtors—the latter in the majority. Felt says that some of the loans of 1714 in Massachusetts, made for five years, were out over thirty years.

In 1715 there was a petition from Boston merchants for more paper, which was laid over.

Governor Shute recommended the Assembly to take measures to revive the low state of trade. They issued £100,000 of bills, "because bills were scarce." These were issued on loan. Silver rose to 12s. per oz.

South Carolina had issued bills in 1712 for war expenses. "This emission fell a third the first year, a half the second, and continued to depreciate."

Felt quotes a writer who said: "The evils of litigation abound. People of estates cannot raise money, unless they dispose of them at half their value. Individuals depending on their labor are forced to take for their toil from one-half to two-thirds in goods, while their creditors imperiously demand cash of them. The private bank* does not receive encouragement from the legislative authorities. £50,000 ought to be laid out for building a bridge over Charles river, so that workmen might be employed and currency

* There are hints that it had made issues.

enlarged, as well as the public accommodated, and ruin will come unless more bills of credit are emitted." This was in 1719.

In 1720 trade was stagnant, and there was a great cry for more bills. Let it be observed how this complaint is heard again every four or five years, although the amount of paper was continually increasing. It is the best instance in history of the way in which a country "grows up" to any amount of currency. Here was a sparse population in a new country with untouched resources, and it seemed to them necessary to have recourse to artificial issues of currency to "make business brisk;" to get up enterprises for the sake of "making work;" and to lay bounties on products in order to enable the people to carry on production. The distress was real, but it came from turning their backs on what nature offered them gratuitously, and violating the laws by which they might have profited by these gifts.

The commissioners of the New England colonies passed a resolution deprecating further issues of paper, but it had no effect. Widows, orphans, and salaried men suffered greatly from the depreciation. Hutchinson, referring to the temptation to trustees, says: "The influence which a bad currency has on the morals of a people is greater than is generally imagined. Numbers of schemes for public and private emissions were proposed as remedies. The only effectual one, the utter abolition of the bills, was omitted." Expeditions were favored for the purpose of bringing about issues of paper, and public works were advocated for the same reason. In 1721 Massachusetts issued £100,000, and forbade buying and selling silver. Hutchinson says: "Such an act can no more be executed than an act to stop the ebbing and flowing of the sea." £500 in paper were now equal to £180 sterling.

In 1720 Parliament passed an act forbidding any companies to carry on banking without a charter.

In the same year the treasury of Massachusetts ceased to allow 5 per cent. premium on bills. £5,000 were issued in this year, redeemable from 1726 to 1730.

The royal instructions forbade the governor to

sign any acts for emitting bills, and the history of the next twenty years is a story of long conflicts between successive governors and the Lower House on this question. Governor Shute gave it up and went home. Lt.-Gov. Dummer signed a bill issuing £30,000 in 1724.

In 1727 Wood's patent for coining pennies of English value was issued. They were to be so rated in the paper as to circulate. They were very unpopular because they reflected on the paper and marked its depreciation. In this year £50,000 were issued to help redeem the issue of 1716. On this ground Dummer signed it. The council also wanted to redeem the £30,000 issue of 1724, but the House would not agree. In 1728 the redemption of the £100,000 loan being enforced by orders from England, £60,-000 more were allowed, "because bills were scarce."

Hutchinson comments on this: "It would be just as rational, when the blood in the human body is in a putrid and corrupt state, to in-crease the quantity by luxurious living, in order to restore it to health." Interest was now charged on the loan at 4 per cent., because low interest encourages business. The natural rate was 8 per cent. A great speculation in unoccupied lands had sprung up in the last year. Enough new towns were laid out for the whole existing population.

During the administrations of Burnet and Belcher the war over paper issues went on, but the restriction was enforced to issue only for government expenses. The injunction was also to reduce the outstanding amount to £30,000, but this was not obeyed.

BANKS.

The colony being no longer allowed to issue, bank projects revived. As a concession, £76,500 were allowed in 1733 for public expenses, and the year 1741 was fixed as a terminus for all outstanding issues. This year (1733) was one of great distress throughout New England. Trade was stagnant and "money scarce." Rhode Island issued £100,000. The Boston merchants agreed not to receive them, and themselves issued £110,000, redeemable in silver at 19s. per oz., one tenth of the issue each year for ten years, without reissue. Some of them broke the engagement and received the Rhode Island bills, and all the notes flowed in together. Silver rose to 27s. per oz. The merchants' notes were hoarded.

In 1734 Governor Belcher recommended the withdrawal of paper money and bounties on hemp and naval stores, so as to turn the balance of trade.

In 1737 "new tenor" bills were issued, to circulate at the rate of one for three of the old. Felt quotes an act showing that a system of counterfeiting had grown up by which a counterfeit part was pasted on a mutilated bill, raising its denomination. £170,000 of outstanding bills must, by law, be redeemed before 1742.

THE LAND BANK.

In 1739 the Land Bank scheme was revived. The scheme was this: a number of land owners formed a company and mortgaged their estates to it for its notes, giving 3 per cent. per annum interest in merchandise, and 5 per cent. per annum on the principal in the same currency. A mechanic, with two sureties, might have £100 stock. The notes were payable after twenty years "in manufactures of the province." The preamble of the schedule of this bank recites that it is organized "in order to redress the existing circumstances which the trade of this province labors under for want of a medium." This bank was the most prominent factor in the political movements of the next ten years, and even later it turns up, from time to time, a cause of perplexity and distress to the government and the surviving stockholders.

THE SPECIE BANK.

Another bank was proposed to counteract the Land Bank. It was called the Specie Bank, and was to issue £120,000 in notes redeemable in fifteen years, in silver, at 20s. per oz. Both went into operation, but, in 1740, Parliament declared the old Joint Stock Companies' Act, passed after the South Sea bubble (1720), to be of force in the colonies. Both banks were therefore forced to wind up.

The Land Bank resisted its fate by social and political intrigues, and became a political issue between its friends and its enemies. The large merchants had refused its notes, but the small dealers had taken them, and £35,582 were out. For a thorough-going application of the paper theory, nothing has ever been proposed anywhere, much less put in operation, which could equal this. A note for $1 payable twenty years hence in gold without interest, when interest is 3 per cent., is worth 55 cents, or, if interest is 6 per cent, 31 cents. If payable in any one of a dozen commodities it is payable in that one which twenty years hence may be the cheapest. At what rate, then, ought a man who to-day gives wheat for the note to make the exchange? These notes were based on nothing, floated on nothing, and represented nothing definable. The system of money which consists in "basing," "floating," and "representing" was, therefore, here in perfection.

The governor made war on this bank with all his energy, as unlawful and pernicious, contrary to the act of Parliament and to his instructions. Finding that some civil and militar officers were engaged in it, he removed them. This called forth a protest from Samuel Adams and John Choate, as an invasion of personal liberty. There can be no doubt that the bitterness engendered by this conflict was one great cause of the Revolution. Two great economic errors were amongst the causes of that war. One, the attempt of the colonies to issue paper in which they were in error as to the question of political expediency; the other, the attempt to carry out the "colonial system," by which the colonies were used as means of aggrandizing the mother country, in which the latter was at fault. There is no tribunal to decide such questions. They work themselves out in history.

The instructions forbidding the governor to allow paper issues contained one exception. He might issue for the expenses of government. This was the gap through which the issues were still continued, though more moderately. In 1741 all outstanding notes were to be cancelled. As that year approached, it was found impracticable to call in all in one year by tax, no steps in that direction having been taken. Taxes were provided for retiring them in 1741, '2, and '3. At the same time the governor was allowed to approve issues beyond £30,000 for expenses, to tide over the withdrawal of the old. A new set of bills was now issued to circulate at the "ideal" rate of 6s. 8d. per oz. silver. These now became the "new tenor," and those of 1737, "middle tenor." Subsequently it became necessary to distinguish "new tenor first," and "new tenor second." Similar stratification existed in the paper of Rhode Island and Connecticut. If the new tenor bills depreciated they were to pass at current rates, that is, were not legal tender for their face. The depreciation was to be ascertained and published by commissioners, but these persons were restrained by public opinion from ever stating the depreciation at its true amount. One commissioner who did rate it truly was overwhelmed by a storm of abuse. The new tenor bills fell to 7s. 9d. per oz., but were hoarded. In 1741 old tenor were at 29s. per oz.; new tenor Massachusetts, 9s. 8d.; new tenor Connecticut, 8s.; new tenor Rhode Island,

6s. 9d.; old Specie Bank of 1733, one-third better than colony bills; Specie Bank of 1740, issued at 20s. per oz., were at that rate; Land Bank not quotable. Mr. Hutchinson, the historian, and subsequently governor of Massachusetts, very wisely advised Governor Belcher to try to put down the Land Bank in some other way than by invoking the authority of Parliament. Colonial independence was enlisted on the side of the bank, and insurrection was feared.

In 1743 Massachusetts proposed to the other New England colonies to appoint commissioners to agree on joint action for doing away with the bills. They refused to do so. "Money" was now scarce as ever again, the better kinds of paper being hoarded, and only the worst paper of all the colonies circulating in any. The governor of Massachusetts, in 1744, said that of £400,000 Rhode Island bills in circulation £380,000 were in Massachusetts. The people of the latter colony had lost £25,000 on this sum in nine months. In 1744 the amount of bills in Massachusetts was scarcely diminished.

EXPEDITION AGAINST LOUISBOURG.

The governor now took it into his head to capture Louisbourg, on Cape Breton, from the French. The New England colonies joined in this enterprise. Nothing more was heard of the royal instructions, but bills were issued as they were needed to prepare this expedition. It was popular, as all expeditions against the French were popular. It appealed to the love of adventure—always great in a new country, and it met the wishes of those who wanted more paper.

All the authorities agree that the enterprise was wild and reckless, and that it only succeeded by a succession of strange and lucky accidents. However, succeed it did; the town was captured, and the colonies were greatly elated by their military glory.

As a result of this expedition the paper issues of the colonies in 1749 reduced to old tenor, were :

Massachusetts	£2,466,712
Connecticut	281,000
Rhode Island	550,000
New Hampshire	450,000

RESUMPTION IN MASSACHUSETTS.

Parliament voted to ransom Louisbourg from the colonies. The sum coming to Massachusetts was £138,649 sterling, which at eleven for one, the ruling exchange, would nearly cancel the paper. Hutchinson proposed that they should ask Parliament to ship to them their share of the payment in silver dollars and copper coins, and that these should be used to cancel the paper as far as they would go, the rest to be called in by tax. After considerable opposition this course was adopted. The silver was sent over and exchanged. Prices were adjusted to this new measure, and the silver remained in circulation when it no longer had a meaner rival. The "shock" which was apprehended did not occur. The only shock was to Rhode Island and New Hampshire, who found their trade transferred to the "silver colony," and their paper suddenly and heavily depreciated. The West India trade of Massachusetts had been largely done through Newport. It was now transferred to Salem and Boston. In 1752 a Newport merchant, Joseph

Whipple, who was deputy governor at the time, failed. Failures "had been almost unknown in Newport," and Mr. Whipple was constrained to resign his office.

The apprehensions of loss and danger from the change in Massachusetts led to some demonstrations of riot, but the change took place so quietly and easily that these fears were not realized and the tumult subsided. Trade had been immediately before (1749–50) at the lowest ebb. Ship-building and fisheries had declined, and people were moving away. Trade now revived steadily and rapidly, and we hear no more of "scarcity of money" until the next violation of the laws of circulation.

The following table shows the depreciation of Massachusetts paper:

	EX. ON LON- DON.	SILVER PER OZ. IN THE CURRENCY.	
		s.	*d.*
1702	133	6	10½
1706	135	7	
1713	150	8	
1716	175	9	3
1717	225	12	
1722	270	14	

	EX. ON LON-LON.	SILVER PER OZ. IN THE CURRENCY.	
		s.	*d.*
1728	340	18	
1730	380	20	
1737	500	26	
1741	550	28	
1749	1,100	60	

The following table shows the depreciation of the paper of the several colonies:

	1740	1748
New England	525	1,100
New York	160	190
Pennsylvania	160	180 and 190
Maryland	200	200
North Carolina	1,400	1,000
South Carolina	800	750
Virginia		120 and 125

Douglas, though bitterly opposed to paper money, opposed violently the plan of Hutchinson. His own history shows that he was irascible and impracticable. He thought the measure too sudden, and wanted to use the English payment by drawing bills of exchange on long time and selling them for the bills of credit. If a contraction had been practicable it ought certainly to have been gradual and careful, but this was out of the question with a currency sunk to $\frac{1}{11}$ of its denomination, and a bankruptcy could not be too sharply and definitely accomplished when resolved upon.

ACTION OF CONNECTICUT.

His plan was followed in Connecticut, the bills being drawn at three years' date, and the consequence was that the paper was not withdrawn before the next war called for new issues.

ACTION OF RHODE ISLAND.

Rhode Island went on upon the paper system. In 1750 the paper-money party were in the ascendant, and the ninth bank was issued for £25,000. It was for the purpose of giving bounties on manufactured wool, and whale and cod fisheries. "In June, 1751, the act was amended. The bounties were abolished; that on manufactured wool as being displeasing to England, the others as useless." Rate in 1750: Notes of ninth bank, 6s. 9d.=13s. 6d. new tenor

=54s. old tenor.   Rate in 1757: 6s. 9d. of ninth bank=16s. new tenor=64s. old tenor.   In 1756, new bills were issued at 6s. 8d. per oz., payable in two years, called "lawful money," and some efforts at reform began to be made.   The notes were no longer legal tender, and in 1763 a scale of depreciation was fixed for the settlement of old debts by the courts.   It put one Spanish milled dollar, of the value of 4s. 6d. sterling, at £7 in old-tenor notes in 1763.*

LEGAL-TENDER PAPER ABOLISHED.

In the year 1751 Parliament passed an act forbidding any more legal-tender paper issues, and allowing no issues, save in the form of exchequer bills, redeemable by taxes in a year, bearing interest, or, in case of war, similar issues redeemable in four years.   The colonies now set to work earnestly, though with only partial success, as above shown, to retire their old issues.

A new war with the French in 1756 involved them once more in war expenditures, and bills of

---

* See Potter *l. c.*, and Arnold's Rhode Island.

the above description were issued. They were of small denominations, bore interest, and circulated only until the interest accumulated so much as to make them worth hoarding. Remittances were continually received from England to partially reimburse the colonies for their expenses, and by these funds, and by taxes, the bills were redeemed to such an extent as to save them from great depreciation.

Early in the eighteenth century Virginia adopted tobacco as a currency. It was deposited in warehouses, and the receipts for it passed as currency. It was a true money, but not a good one, as it naturally fluctuated considerably in value. In 1755 Virginia issued paper money.*

North Carolina issued paper to build a palace for the governor. A similar project was started in New Jersey, but it never passed the legislature.

* Phillips' Colon. and Continent. Paper Money. Vol. I.

DOUBLE STANDARD TRIED IN MASSACHU-SETTS—OTHER COLONIAL ISSUES.

Scarcely had specie come into circulation in Massachusetts when it was found that, although the remittance had been in silver, gold from the West Indies began to stay in the colony. The question of making it legal tender as well as silver soon began to be agitated. It circulated of course, not being legal tender, at its weight. An act was passed in 1762 to make gold legal tender at 2½d. per grain. At this rate it was more profitable for the debtor to pay in gold than in silver. The currency was depreciated five per cent. by this operation, and, as Hutchinson declared at the time must follow, this drove silver out of circulation. Some hints also show that barter currency was still allowed in the payment of taxes. Silver now became scarce, and the next stage was a new agitation in 1767 for paper money.

In 1768 the House resolved that "in order to prevent the unnecessary exportation of money, of which this province has of late been so much

drained," they will do without foreign superflui-
ties, and encourage the manufactures of this
province. The same doctrine has been preached
and avowed ever since, as the sum and essence of
political economy, but it has been a signal failure.
The colony was drained of money (silver) because it had adopted another legal tender, gold,
which, though the best money for large exchanges, was so rated that it was the cheapest means
of payment. It alone therefore remained, and the
other metal was exported. It was not, however,
exported for nothing, and no resolutions could
make the people desist from using foreign super-
fluities which came back to pay for it. The same
violation of coinage laws was twice repeated under
the federal constitution, as we shall see below.
In the same year (1768) the Massachusetts Council petitioned the House of Commons for relief
from the new tax laws, pleading the great scarcity of money, which they ascribe to the balance
of trade being against them.

Mr. Hickcox, writing on the New York paper
money,* says that the colony traded in 1720 with

* Albany, 1866, page 21.

Madeira, the West Indies, and England. He expressed still more explicitly the theory underlying the above view on the subject. The trade " to the West Indies was wholly to the advantage of New York, while that to Madeira was to our loss, the province consuming more wine from thence than could be purchased with its commodities. The money imported from the West Indies was not sufficient, however, to preserve a specie currency, a large amount being necessary to balance the exchange with England."

The errors involved in this way of looking at the matter were most clearly exposed in connection with the " Bullion Report," and will be found noticed in Chapter II.

In 1763 Parliament declared any colonial acts for issuing paper money void. Franklin wrote a pamphlet in opposition to this act. He said that gold and silver owe their value chiefly to the estimation in which they happen to be among the generality of nations and the credit given to the opinion that they will continue to be so held. " Any other well-founded credit is as much an equivalent as gold or silver." When exchange rose he thought that this was only an advance in ex change, not a fall in paper. In 1773 Parliament allowed any bills issued by any colony to be a tender at its treasury. In 1774 Massachusetts was out of debt.

In 1775 representatives of the colonies of Connecticut and Rhode Island met the Congress of Massachusetts to concert measures for the war.

It was agreed, as their money was paper and they could not offer anything else, that this should be allowed to pass in Massachusetts.

CONTINENTAL PAPER MONEY.

The colonies now went into the Revolutionary War, many of them with paper already in circulation, all of them making issues for the expenses of military preparations. The Continental Congress, having no power to tax, and its members being accustomed to paper issues as the ordinary form of public finance, began to issue bills on the faith of the "Continent," Franklin earnestly approving. The first issue was for 300,000 Spanish dollars, redeemable in gold or silver, in three years, ordered in May and issued in August, 1775.

Paper for nine million dollars was issued before any depreciation began. The issues of the separate colonies must have affected it, but the popular euthusiasm went for something. Pelatiah Webster,* almost alone as it seems, insisted on taxation, but a member of Congress indignantly asked if he was to help tax the people when they could go to the printing-office and get a cartload of money. In 1776, when the depreciation began, Congress took harsh measures to try to sustain the bills. Committees of safety also took measures to punish those who " forestalled " or " engrossed," these being the terms for speculators who bought up for a rise. The tyranny of the government was of course only a stimulus to the private committees. It is natural to suppose that malicious and criminal persons assumed the duty of public regulators, and committed those acts of violence and wrong which equal or surpass anything of the kind under any despotism, but such an error as a legal-tender act, enforced by

* Political Essays. Philadelphia, 1791.

pains and penalties, is responsible for the secondary evils which are sure to flow from it. Webster says of the paper : "We have suffered more
from this cause than from every other cause or
calamity. It has killed more men, pervaded and
corrupted the choicest interests of our country
more, and done more injustice than even the arms
and artifices of our enemy." The enemy, perceiving the terrible harm the Americans were doing
themselves, thought it well to help on the movement. They counterfeited the bills and passed
them through the lines.

At the end of 1779 Congress was at its wits'
ends for money. Its issues had put specie entirely out of reach, and the cause was in danger
of being drowned under the paper sea.

Webster says : "The people of the States at
that time had been worried and fretted, disap-
pointed, and put out of humor by so many tender-
acts, limitations of prices, and other compulsory
methods to force value into paper money, and
compel the circulation of it, and by so many vain
funding schemes, declarations of promises, all
which issued from Congress, but died under the

most zealous efforts to put them into operation and effect, that their patience was all exhausted. I say these irritations and disappointments had so destroyed the courage and confidence of the people, that they appeared heartless and almost stupid when their attention was called to any new propositions."

The French alliance helped more by giving means of procuring loans in Europe than by military assistance. Congress promised to limit its issues to $200,000,000, and tried a new form of note ; also loan offices and lotteries. Over 350,-000,000 were issued in all, but it is doubtful if more than 200,000,000 were out at any one time.

In the spring of 1780 the bills were worth two cents on the dollar, and then ceased to circulate. Specie now came into circulation, being brought by the French, and also that expended by the English passing the lines. The paper was now worth more for an advertisement or a joke than for any prospect of any kind of redemption. A barber's shop in Philadelphia was papered with it, and a dog, coated with tar, and the bills stuck all over him, was paraded in the streets.

On account of the peculiar character of American society, there are few family traditions of the Continental currency; but the contemporary literature shows that the suffering it caused was wide-spread and intense. It fell most heavily on the most patriotic and most helpless. Phillips quotes a letter addressed by a lady to the "Pennsylvania Packet" in 1779, saying that her father had left her a competence which her guardian had invested in real estate six years before. He now proposed to pay her fortune in paper. It is only a single instance.

"The gradual depreciation was urged as a reason why the notes should not be redeemed at par. It was said to operate as a tax; as a most equal tax, because it acted in proportion to the amount held. The rich suffered largely on their vast sums; the needy but slightly on their scanty pittances. How fallacious these reasonings, with which the Congress and the people solaced themselves, are, must be apparent. Poor consolation it was to those who had been beggared confiding in the honor and in the honesty of their country, to hear that their ruin had merely been a gradual tax; to know that from the operation of tender laws their property had been taken away and given to others; to see the wealth accumulated by the dishonest multitudes of contractors and the many defrauders of that unhappy period, and to feel that it had been plundered from their own coffers for the aggrandizement of such people." *   The trouble is that the government cannot make a forced loan by legal tender issues, without giving the opportunity for private individuals to take "forced loans" from their neighbors.

"If it saved the State, it has also polluted the equity of our laws, turned them into enemies of oppression and wrong, corrupted the justice of our public administration, destroyed the fortunes of thousands who had most confidence in it, enervated the trade, husbandry, and manufactures of our country, and went far to destroy the morality of our people." †

---

* Phillips: Colonial and Continental Paper Currency, II. 175.
† Webster *l. c.* 175, note.

It ought to be noticed that this paper was vaunted as "the safest possible currency," which "nobody could take away."

BANK OF NORTH AMERICA.

December 31, 1781, the Bank of North America was chartered with a capital of $400,000. It took its origin in a union of citizens of Philadelphia, formed in the preceding year, to supply the army with rations. They were allowed to form a bank, and, as it seems, issue notes to buy the articles required. Congress ordered bills drawn on American ministers abroad to be deposited in the bank as a guarantee of payment. $70,000 in specie were subscribed in 1782 by individuals, and the remainder by the government out of the proceeds of a foreign loan. It issued convertible notes, redeemable in Spanish dollars; but the people were slow to take them. According to the story given by Gouge, the Bank was not over strong, and tried to keep up its credit by parading and handling over its stock of silver. However, it made large dividends, and was attacked by a rival which it was obliged to absorb, and secondly by an effort to have its charter repealed. The latter effort was successful so far as the state charter was concerned. It went on under the charter of the Continental Congress until 1781, when it was re-chartered by Pennsylvania. It exists yet.

RENEWED AGITATION IN FAVOR OF PAPER MONEY.

In 1785 and 1786 an insurrectionary movement, known as Shay's Rebellion, broke out in New England. It was an insurrection of debtors who were suffering from the collapse of the currency and return to specie values. They clamored for paper.

" No desperately indebted people can long endure a regular, sober government." This insurrection was put down by force, but Massachusetts passed a law delaying the collection of debts.

In Rhode Island this movement was not riotous, but took the form of a political movement. The paper money party carried the elections in 1786, and began a new period of this mania for their colony. £100,000 were issued by a vote of the rural districts against the cities. The bills were to be loaned on mortgage of land for fourteen years. They depreciated at once. Merchants refused to deal, and closed their shops. The farmers retaliated by refusing to bring produce to the cities, and thus the urban and rural populations were pitted against one another in a ridiculous warfare which brought business to a stand-still. In Providence it was agreed to enter into intercourse for necessaries so far as parties could agree, and to borrow $500 to send abroad for grain. The farmers met and petitioned the Assembly to enforce the penal laws in favor of the paper money. By these laws cases involving legal tender took precedence of all others, and must be tried within three days after complaint entered, without jury, and with three judges a quorum. The decision was final. The fine for the first offence was from £6 to £30, and for the second offence, from £10 to £50. A protest by the representatives of the large towns against this law was not allowed to be recorded

John Trevett, of Newport, complained of John Weeden, a butcher, for refusing bank paper. The five judges agreed that the act was unconstitutional. A special session of the Assembly was convened, before which the judges were summoned to "assign the reasons and grounds" of the late decision. Three judges came. Two were sick. The hearing was postponed. A test act was prepared and sent to the towns for approval, but it went *too* far. Only five towns approved. It proposed to disfranchise any one who refused the bills at equality with metal. With all this, money was so scarce that land rents were paid in corn, and barter became common.

It was now determined to pay off the debt of the colony, except the 4 per cents, one quarter at a time, in the bills received for taxes. Any holder of colony securities who did not come up to take his notes within a set time forfeited his securities. The whole debt was paid off in this way within two years. Three months after it was issued, the paper stood six for one gold. The question of ratifying the new constitution now coming up, the paper money party was for state rights, and the specie party for the federal constitution.

In the spring of 1787 there were twenty bills in equity filed in court for the redemption of mortgaged estates. "The suitors came prepared with paper money in handkerchiefs and pillow-cases to redeem their lands." It was moved to have the bills counted, and the tender recorded, but the court held that it had nothing to do with the money before rendition of judgment, nor was it for them to be instrumental in proving a tender. They refused to entertain any motion with the latter intention. The Assembly next removed four of the judges who declared the legal-tender act unconstitutional. In June, 1787, the paper was at eight for one. In 1789 it was at twelve for one. In September of that year the action of the legal-tender act was suspended; October 12 the depreciation was legally fixed at eighteen for one, and debtors were allowed to pay in produce.

If paper-money issues, tariff laws, and bounties on exports can make a nation great and prosperous, Rhode Island ought to have been the first

State in the union in point of wealth, though the last to enter it.

The historian, Arnold, apologizes for her dilatoriness in joining the union by the extraordinary degree of liberty her citizens had enjoyed, and their jealousy of having it curtailed. They may have had *la Liberté* in Rhode Island; they did not have liberty.

It appears that all the provinces were struggling with paper issues during the period of the old confederation. Specie was scarce in some, and plentiful in others, according to the amount of paper outstanding. The Congress of the confederation had not the power to tax, and its efforts to obtain the consent of the States to its fiscal legislation failed. Its certificates of indebtedness were worth only twelve or fifteen cents on the dollar. A coinage law was passed in 1786, but no coins of gold or silver were struck. Copper coins were made, but they were below standard and depreciated.

ASSUMPTION OF THE STATE DEBTS.

One of the first acts of the Federal Congress was to provide for the settlement of the outstanding accounts. $21,500,000 were apportioned to the States to assume their indebtedness, subscriptions being received in their paper at a discount, but as the federal debt at once rose in value, the transaction was very favorable to the holders of State obligations. The amount actually assumed was $18,271,814. At the same time the States were credited with advances made to the confederation, and charged their quota of its expenditure. Thus some appeared as creditors and others as debtors. The debtor States never settled the account. The creditor States were paid. The whole transaction was criticised by Mr. Gallatin * as unwise and wasteful. It met with much opposition, especially from the South, and there were always rumors of bargain in connection with this act and the removal of the capital to Washington.

---

* Sketch of the finances of the United States. 1796.

BANKING ON CONVERTIBLE CURRENCY.

We come now to the period in which the currency consisted more or less of bank-notes, nominally convertible, issued by chartered banks. The system to which it has most analogy is that of the Scotch banks, although of these latter only three are chartered, the others being joint-stock companies and partnerships. We shall have abundant proof that this system of free banking requires, as its indispensable conditions, moderation, sagacity, and scientific knowledge on the part of the bankers. Without these qualities in the managers, it is as wild as any scheme of paper money. Men who believe that "banking" consists in making paper issues and loaning them, making them as large as possible and stimulating them by all artificial means, and discouraging conversion as much as possible, may, as we shall see, bring down more ruin on the community by this engine than by any other.

The Bank of North America had already been founded. Its success in earning dividends led to other similar enterprises. Massachusetts chartered the Massachusetts Bank in 1784. Soon after, a bank was chartered in New York and another in Maryland.

PAPER MONEY AND THE FEDERAL CONSTITU-TION.

In 1787 the Federal constitution was framed. It contains a clause that no State shall "coin money, emit bills of credit, or make anything but gold or silver coin a tender in payment of debts." The framers of the document thus fixed their condemation of the old paper system, and the people, smarting under recent experiences, acquiesced.

It was proposed in the constitutional convention to give to Congress the right to emit bills of credit, but the proposition was defeated nine States to two. (Madison Papers, III. 1,344.)

Two questions have been raised under this clause: 1. Can a State authorize banks to do what it cannot do itself? As the confederation had already chartered the Bank of North America, it does not seem that the "bills of credit" were understood to cover bank notes. The courts have held that a State may authorize bank issues when itself owns all the stock, the legislature appoints the directors, the faith of the State is pledged for the redemption of the bills, and they are receivable for public dues, provided the capital is paid in and the bank may be sued. (Story, 4th ed., I. 227, note.)

2. Can the national government do what the States cannot do under this clause? The legal-tender cases have recently decided this question in the affirmative. Mr. Gallatin said, in 1831, of Congress: "*As this body has no authority to make anything whatever a tender in payment of private debts*, it necessarily follows that nothing but gold and silver coin can be made a legal tender for that purpose, and that Congress cannot authorize the payment, in any species of paper currency, of any other debts but those due to the United States." This is only important as showing the belief of prominent public men on this point in earlier times. For them it was a simple matter of course that Congress could not pass a legal-tender act of any kind, how much less one which should apply to existing contracts. The legal-tender decision did as

great a wrong as the Dred Scott decision, and the latter instance shows us that it is not useless to discuss a constitutional question, even after the court has decided it. It will not probably take a war to overthrow the principle of the legal-tender act, but it may take a national bankruptcy.

THE FIRST BANK OF THE UNITED STATES.

The first United States Bank was chartered by Congress in 1791. Its capital was $10,000,000, to be paid, one-fourth in cash, the rest in bonds of the United States. The charter was to run for twenty years. It issued no bills under $10.

Other banks were now formed very rapidly. The following list is given by Gouge, though he says that it is not full:

	Banks chartered.		Banks chartered.		Banks chartered.
1792	8	1799	3	1806	4
1793	3	1800	2	1807	9
1794	0	1801	3	1808	1
1795	5	1802	4	1809	3
1796	1	1803	15	1810	8
1797	0	1804	10	1811	11
1798	0	1805	4	1812	19

COINAGE.

In 1794 the first silver was actually coined, the dollar weighing 416 grs., 1485 parts pure to 179 parts alloy. Its pure contents were, therefore, 371.25 grs. Gold was first coined in 1795, the eagle weighing 270 grs., $\frac{11}{12}$ fine, so that one dollar contained 24.75 grs. pure gold. It will be observed that where two metals are thus made legal tender, and there is both a silver " dollar " and a gold " dollar," the question of relative value of the two metals is involved. It was assumed in the above rating that silver was to gold as 15 to 1. We have had one instance before us already when Massachusetts, in 1761, overrated gold in the coinage and drove out silver. If the rating should be correct at the time of passing the coinage law, yet the fluctuations which are continually taking place in the relative value of the two metals would in time disturb the relations, and only one metal would circulate, viz., the cheaper one. France has changed to a silver currency only, and then to a gold currency only, by these fluctuations since her mint law fixed the relation in the coinage. The ratio of 15 to 1 was, at this time, unjust to gold. The actual market value being $15\frac{1}{4}$ to 1. We shall have occasion to notice the operation in this case.

BANK ISSUES IN NEW ENGLAND.

The development of banking took place first in New England. It was of the kind later known as " wild-cat" banking. The new financial machine seemed so powerful and beneficent that all that was necessary was to work it to the utmost. Notes under $5 were not allowed in Massachusetts until 1805, but after that smaller denominations were allowed, and finally notes were issued as low as 25 cents, and, by the law that paper drives out specie to the lowest denomination to which it is issued, there was no specie in the New England States. The stock of specie in bank was insignificant, and was moved from bank to bank to meet the inspectors' visits. The downfall came in 1809. One bank in Massachussetts had $40 in specie; another nothing. The system of subscribing to capital by notes was, as it appears, universal. The Farmers

Exchange Bank of Gloucester, R. I., founded in 1804, was probably the worst case. Its capital was $1,000,000. Only $19,141.86 were ever paid in, and of this the directors withdrew what they paid in, leaving $3,081.11. One Dexter bought out eleven of the directors for $1,300 each, paid out of the bank's funds. He borrowed of the bank $760,265. When it failed it had $86.46 in specie; bills out unknown; the committee estimated them at $580,000. South of New England banks were fewer, and there was no disturbance. Silver was plentiful in the West. The exportation from Mexico was through the United States.

After this crash, the New England States passed severe banking laws, with penalty of twelve per cent. interest on all notes not redeemed on demand. In 1813 the New England Bank was chartered as a bank of redemption at Boston, in order to keep the paper of banks in the adjacent country at par. It accomplished this object, but was exceedingly unpopular with its country clients. This was the origin of the Suffolk Bank system.

BANK ISSUES IN THE MIDDLE STATES.

The banking mania now broke out in the Middle States. In 1810 Pensylvania found it necessary to forbid the issue of notes by incorporated companies — bridge companies, etc. The charter of the Bank of the United States expired in 1811, and its renewal met with such vigorous opposition that it was defeated. The constitutionality of the charter by Congress was doubted from the outset. This bank, so far as we can judge from the information we have in regard to it, was soberly managed, successful, and beneficial in restraining the issues of the smaller banks. It was on this latter account especially, and also because others desired to form small banks, that a strong party was formed against the renewal of its charter. The same influence defeated its efforts to get a charter from the State of Pennsylvania. Great fears were entertained that a severe crisis must follow the winding up of the United States Bank, but they were not realized.

The note circulation of the banks of the country in 1811 is estimated by Gallatin at 46,000,000.

The field being thus cleared, twenty-five charters were passed through the Pennsylvania legislature in 1812–13, but all vetoed. In the following session forty-one banks, with $17,000,000 capital, were chartered by Pennsylvania over the veto. In a report to the Pennsylvania Senate made in January, 1820, by a committee of which Condy Raguet was chairman,* it is stated that at this time prices were low in New England, and specie was flowing thither.

The country being now at war, Mr. Eppes, of the Ways and Means Committee, thus explained the financial measures by which it was proposed to carry on war (Winter of 1813—1814).

There were $75,000,000 bank capital, and $100,000,000 circulation and discounts (deposits). Deduct forty-seven millions circulation required; there remain fifty-three millions, "of which we propose to borrow thirty millions." In 1812 the government borrowed six millions from

---

* Abstracts are given in the appendix to Raguet's Currency and Banking. Philadelphia, 1840.

banks, and four millions from individuals at par. In 1813 it borrowed twenty millions, allowing one hundred and thirteen for one hundred paid. In 1814 it borrowed fifteen millions ; twelve millions nett, allowing one hundred and twenty-five for one hundred received. No more was to be had. No tax was laid until January 1, 1814. The loans nearly all came from the Middle States, the New England States being strongly opposed to the war, as foolish, unnecessary, a help to Napoleon, and completing the ruin begun by the embargo.

The revenue for 1812, '13, and '14 was twelve millions. The peace expenditures had been eight millions. Treasury notes for one year were issued in 1812 to the amount of three millions, interest at five and two-fifths per cent., receivable in taxes. Six millions were issued in 1813 ; eight millions in 1814. By 1814 prices were rapidly advancing, business was brisk, and importations were great. Pennsylvania notes were at fourteen per cent. discount. It was complained at Philadelphia that silver flowed to New England and was there exported. The importations came through New England. There was, therefore, now an " adverse balance of trade," between the Middle and New England States. It was also claimed that the New Englanders were buying bills drawn for the supply of English troops in Canada with their surplus silver.

The New England Bank having collected over $100,000 worth of the New York bills which flooded New England, sent them home for redemption. The silver was loaded and on its way to Boston, when the Collector of New York stopped it at Chester, and ordered it to the Manhattan Bank, of which he was a director. He said he suspected that it was to be sent to Canada. The President of the United States ordered it to be given up.

On the 30th August, 1813, the directors of the chartered banks of Philadelphia published a circular, in which they said that, on account of the blockade, exportation of produce was impossible. Hence specie had been exported, and " as the im portation of foreign goods in the Eastern States has been very large, it has for many months past occasioned a continual drain from the bank."

They also refer to the English bills of exchange. For a time they had been able to draw from the Southern States (the New Orleans banks suspended because " a contraband trade was drawing off the specie "), but this was no longer possible. " It became a serious consideration whether the banks should continue their exertions to draw within their vaults the specie capital of the country, and thus facilitate the means of exporting it from the United States, or whether they should suspend the payment of specie before their means were exhausted."

This plausible explanation appealed to the popular prejudice against exporting silver, but evidently concealed the true relation of facts. The silver went to New England unquestionably. On the 1st June, 1811, the banks of Massachusetts held $1,709,000 in specie;

1812	$3,915,000.
1813	6,171,000.
1814	7,326,000.
1815	3,915,000.
1816	1,270,000.

It went thither because there was a sound currency and low prices there, and went away from the Middle and Southern States because displaced by redundant paper and consequent high prices. It was because the Pennsylvania banks had issued paper until it was at a discount, that, when they got the silver into their vaults, they could not keep it there, but it was demanded of them and exported. When the New Englanders took it they gave something for it, and there was an unusual importation from New England. They also used it. Having far more than they needed, they exported it either directly to Europe or by buying bills payable in London, and increased their imports. I know of no more complete illustration of the true doctrine, and of the error by which it is beclouded

There was at the same time a movement of specie to Ohio, Kentucky, and Tennessee, where there were no banks.

SUSPENSION OF 1814.

In 1814 all the banks, save the New England banks, suspended. In the year 1815 the Pennsylvania banks increased their loans $10,000,000.

Business was active and prices high. The merchants agreed to the suspension if specie payments should be resumed after the war. Small coin disappeared and tickets were used. Notes were depreciated from twenty to fifty per cent. Importations, especially of articles of luxury, increased. Credit was great and expanding, prices continually rising.

The Secretary of the Treasury now began to be engaged in the money-market. He tried to get the banks to come to some agreement which should bring about a uniform currency, but he failed. He then ordered that taxes should be received only in specie, Treasury notes, or notes of banks which received Treasury notes at par. The banks received them at par when they were at or above par in the market, but not otherwise. The banks which took Treasury notes issued bills for them, so that the issues of the Treasury stimulated those of the banks. The notes of the latter when issued accumulated in the banks which did not take Treasury notes, so that the Treasury received the notes of debtor banks when it would not receive those of creditor banks. At the same time, while loans increased three per cent. on capital, there was $3,000,000 less mercantile discount, the rest being on governments, and the government Treasury held bank notes instead of. Treasury notes. These bank notes would not pass thirty miles from the place at which they were issued. The paper prosperity was now in full tide (1815). Gouge quotes a pamphlet of Mr. Matthew Carey, in which he called this the " golden age " of Philadelphia.

The ideas about money and currency which had prevailed in England in 1810 and 1811 now appeared here, as they always appear where paper money is in use. It was said that silver had risen (though the Pennsylvania Senate Committee say this notion was abandoned by the end of 1815), and that a dollar was an ideal unit. Dr. Bollman proposed a scheme for a National Bank to issue notes redeemable in six per cent. government stock, which would keep them from depreciation and tie them to a fixed value. State banks were to issue notes and redeem them in

this paper.   Carey said it was a " magnificent "
plan.

Madison recommended another national bank,
but vetoed the first bill because it allowed the
bank to begin under a suspension.   Peace was
ratified in February, 1815, and the Conservatives
now held that a national bank was necessary
to hold the State banks in check.   They did
not want it to begin under a suspension.   A
second charter was passed.   The capital was to
be $35,000,000.

There were immense importations in this
year.   The English merchants exported enormously* after peace ·was declared, anticipating
demand.   These goods were forced to sale here
as well as elsewhere.   The prices proved un-
remunerative to the foreign owners, and also ruinous to the injudicious enterprises which, having
been undertaken here under the protection of
war, had taken permanent form.   These · were
by no means so numerous or extensive as is
sometimes asserted and generally believed, but
there were such.   This brought us the boon

* See Chapter II. p. 283.

of our first strong protective tariff, though the average duties were only about thirty per cent. on dutiable. The principle of protection had been adopted in 1789, and the rates of duty, very low at first, had been steadily increased by successive enactments. The tariff of 1816 was avowedly carried as a realization of the " American system," but afterwards it came to be referred to, in the retrospect, as a British free-trade tariff.

The great importations gave the government a large surplus revenue. It had $22,000,000 nominal balance in the Treasury, but it consisted of bank-notes which could only circulate in a small district around their place of issue, and the places where the government was creditor and held the notes were not the places where it wanted to pay its floating debt. New seven per cent. notes were issued to pay the quarterly interest, and, to pay the interest at Boston, January 1, 1817, the government was obliged to borrow $500,000 of the United States Bank before it opened. Banks which were government depositories refused to pay government drafts, save for current expenses, and they controlled other banks because they held government deposits in the bills of the latter.

SECOND UNITED STATES BANK.

On January 1st, 1817, the Second United States Bank opened. By the charter its capital was to consist of $7,000,000 government subscription, 7,000,000 specie, and $21,000,000 government stock or specie. It began business with $1,400,000 in specie, $14,000,000 in stocks, and the rest in stock notes. $2,800,000 were soon due on the second instalment, but this would come for the most part from notes or discounts of the bank itself. Only $32,400 of it were paid in specie. The third instalment was still worse. The bank discounted its own stock at par to enable the instalment to be paid. " The discounts, the payment of the second instalment, the payment of price to the owner, the transfer, and the pledge of the stock were, as it was termed, simultaneous operations." In August, 1817, the bank discounted its own stock at 125. The facilities for stock-jobbing were excellent, and they were used.

RESUMPTION.

Congress resolved that after February 20th 1817, only specie, Treasury notes, and notes of specie-paying banks ought to be taken by the national Treasury.   The banks refused to resume before July, 1817.   New York passed a law imposing twelve per cent. interest on notes not redeemed, and the banks finally agreed to resume on February 20th, if the United States Bank would extend its discounts as they contracted. This was agreed to.   The bank allowed $30,000,000 discounts the first year, and the Committee of the Pennsylvania Senate say that it more than made up for the contraction of the State banks, and that the resumption was only nominal.

The Western banks were still comparatively sound, silver being at six per cent. premium there, and fourteen per cent. in Philadelphia. The Southern banks had joined the inflation.   There were fourteen banks in Virginia, North and South Carolina, and Georgia, in 1814, and twenty-three in 1815.

In 1817 a case at Richmond, after specie payments were resumed, gives an insight into the state of things. A man having presented ten one-hundred-dollar notes for redemption was refused. He could not get a lawyer to take a case against the bank for a long time. Finally, having obtained judgment, the sheriff was sent to collect. The president of the bank was taken before the court, but refused to pay. The bank was closed by the sheriff, but soon after opened and went on.

The inflation during this year was increased by the government paying off eleven millions of the public securities held by the bank. The note circulation at this time is estimated at one hundred millions. It is to be noticed that the banks were as recalcitrant about giving statistics, either to the Secretary of the Treasury or private investigators, as about any of their other duties, so that we have no trustworthy statistics.

CONDITION OF THE UNITED STATES BANK.

In March, 1818, the discounts of the United States Bank were forty-three millions, eleven millions on stock. The notes could not be signed fast enough.   It had two millions in specie.   Our knowledge of its affairs at this time is derived from the report of Mr. Cheeves, who became its president during this year, and three years afterwards delivered a report stating how he found the bank, and what he did to save it.   It now had eighteen branches, but never over $3,000,000 specie in them all.   Its operations in the West drew that region into the prevailing mania. Its branches paid out their own notes and held those of the State banks as far as possible.   They redeemed their own notes by drafts on the East. They thus obtained the specie of those States, and the States had credits at New York for the value of the same, which they used for enlarged purchases.   The West therefore now entered on the " golden age."   There were forty-three banks in Kentucky, ten in Tennessee, and eight in Ohio in 1818.

The bank now bought seven millions bullion in the West Indies at a cost of $800,000 expenses.   It was exported as fast as it was imported.   In April, 1818, fifteen months after the bank started, it was doubtful whether it was solvent. Energetic measures of contraction were adopted. It was ordered that discounts be reduced by November 1st, $2,000,000 at Baltimore, $2,000,000 at Philadelphia, $700,000 at Richmond, $500,000 at Norfolk. $4,500,000 contraction was accomplished, but more was urged, as silver was yet at ten per cent. premium.

The parent bank refused the notes of its branches, and they of each other, and called on the State banks to pay balances in specie. It was proposed that the government should issue Treasury notes, and a meeting was held at Philadelphia, Mr. Carey in the chair, which appointed a committee to petition Congress to pass a law forbidding the exportation of specie. The committee refused to serve.

In November, Congress appointed a committee of investigation, which reported a resolution that a *scire facias* should issue for the forfeiture of the charter of the United States Bank. This was lost, forty members of Congress being stockholders. John Randolph said a man might as well go to Constantinople and preach Christianity, as to go to Congress and preach against banks.

Mr. Cheeves now became President, *vice* Mr. Wm. Jones. The total contraction this year was six millions, all in the North and East. The issues in the South and West were increasing.

On April 1, 1819, the state of the bank was: specie, $126,745.28; notes, $6,000,000; due other banks, $79,125.99; due government, $500,000; due Barings, $900,000. There were $267,978.09, in the mint, and $250,000 specie on the way from the West. The New York and Boston branches were in worse condition. The Baltimore branch had given $3,000,000 discounts, of which the parent bank had no knowledge, apparently from corrupt motives. $1,671,221, were lost there. The total losses to date were $3,500,000. Dividends for $4,410,000 had been paid, of which $1,348,553 had been gained by interest on public securities. Net loss over $500,000. The bank now took the most energetic measures to save itself, and in seventy days was once more solvent, but it had ruined the community. The "golden age" was now far in the past, and was seen to be only a gilt-paper age after all. The ruin was almost universal.

CRISIS OF 1819.

In August, 1819, 20,000 persons were seeking employment in Philadelphia, and there was a similar state of things in New York and Baltimore. Thirty trades which employed 9,672 persons in 1816, at Philadelphia, employed only 2,137 in 1819. Trades which employed 1,960 persons, at Pittsburg, in 1815, employed only 672 in 1819. The papers were filled with advertisements of sheriff's sales.

All this was used as an argument then, and has been so used since, to prove that we needed "protection to American industry."

The committee of the Senate of Pennsylvania, already referred to, ascribed the distress to abuses of banking, and a similar committee of the House traced it back to the expansion of banking in 1814. "In consequence of this most destructive measure, the inclination of a large part of the people, created by past prosperity, to live by speculation and not by labor, was greatly increased. A spirit in all respects akin to gambling prevailed. A fictitious value was given to all kinds of property. Specie was driven from circulation as if by common consent, and all efforts to restore society to its natural condition were treated with undisguised contempt."

Niles' Register, quoted by Gouge, says of the prevailing extravagance: "The prodigality and waste of some of these [speculators] were almost beyond belief. We have heard that the furniture of a single parlor possessed (we cannot say owned) by one of these cost $40,000. So it was in all the great cities—dash—dash—dash—vendors of tape and bobbins transformed into persons of *high blood*, and the sons of respectable citizens converted into knaves of rank—through speculation and the facilities of the abominable paper-money system."

Land in Pennsylvania was worth on the average, in 1809, $38 per acre; in 1815, $150; in 1819, $35. The note circulation of the country in 1812 was about 45,000,000; in 1817, 100,000,-000; in 1819, 45,000,000.

The newspapers of 1819 contain numerous ac-

counts of riots, incendiary fires, frauds, and robberies. The House committee spoke of the
" change of the moral character of many of our
citizens by the presence of distress." The distress extended to New England, but was less
severe there than elsewhere. In the West it
was intense. In Kentucky stay laws were
passed which were distinctly unconstitutional,
but, the court having so decided them, a new court
was appointed which reversed the decision. Old
Court and New Court became political issues.
The New Court party carried the State until 1826,
when the disorganization and misery occasioned
by the laws led to a revulsion, and the laws were
set aside. Similar laws were passed in Tennessee, Gen. Jackson vigorously opposing. The
banks of the South pretended to pay specie, but
Gouge quotes an eye-witness in regard to the
proceedings of the Darien Bank, Georgia.
One who presented a bill must make oath in the
bank before a justice of the peace that the bill
was his own, and that he was not an agent for
any one. He must also make this oath before
the cashier and five directors, and must pay

$1.37½ on each bill. The United States Bank protested $500 of the bills of the Bank of Georgia, and sold them at auction. When specie was demanded, cents were counted out at the rate of $60.00 per day.

Stagnation and distress lasted throughout 1820. Prices were at the lowest ebb and liquidation went slowly on. Wheat was at 20 cts. per bushel in Kentucky. A man in Western Virginia stopped Niles' Register because one barrel of flour used to pay a year's subscription ; now three barrels would not. At Pittsburg flour was $1 per barrel, boards 20 cts. per hundred, sheep $1. Imported goods were at old prices. The banks settled down to quiet regularity. Notes were for the most part brokers' merchandise, but others circulated at a discount only equal to the cost of transporting specie from the place of issue to the place of circulation. Money was plentiful in the hands of those who had no debts to pay, where of course it must settle whenever the social machinery comes to a stand-still. They would not lend or invest, though the papers were filled with advertisements. Rent of a given house in Philadelphia fell from $1200 to $450, fuel from $12 to $5.50, flour from $10.00 to $4.50, beef from 25 cents to 8 cents per lb. Printing was little done. School-books were a drug. Niles says that five years before, stores on Market Street were cut in two and then not enough. Dwelling-houses were in great demand. The stores were now reunited, and houses more than enough. The population of Philadelphia decreased 10,000 between 1815 and 1820. Rents on Market Street were $250,000 less in 1820 than in 1815. Wages were low on half time.

In 1820 Virginia forbade notes under $5.

During 1821 the general stagnation continued. Liquidation went on slowly. Investments were only gradually taken up as confidence revived. In April of that year Kentucky notes exchanged for silver 210 for 100. Tennessee notes were at 10 per cent. discount until 1830. Comptroller's warrants were issued in Alabama, which, in order to make them more attractive, were printed on silk paper. The tariff on iron was raised. In June an expansion began, and by October there was a well-marked upward movement, but in the fall of 1822 there was a reaction, woollen and cotton goods falling 50 per cent. in a few weeks in December.   In 1823 the circulation of the United States Bank was very low—$4,081,842, but there was a great creation of banks, and insurance and other companies at New York.   Later in the year the United States Bank received the notes of all its branches, and began to expand.

CRISIS OF 1825.

In 1824 all the banks expanded.   Pennsylvania re-chartered the banks of 1814.   A new tariff was obtained raising duties to 35 per cent., and a grand era of prosperity was expected.   In the spring of 1825 fifty-two charters were petitioned for in New York for banks and insurance companies.   When charters could not be obtained of New York, they were obtained in New Jersey, and the banks were established on the west bank of the Hudson.   In Kentucky there was anarchy. Alabama and Tennessee notes were at a discount. Indiana, Illinois, and Missouri were still suffering from the "relief" system (stay laws against the collection of debts, etc.).   The New York and

Boston city banks were fighting the country issues, which, being current and depreciated, drove out the better notes of the city banks. The Bank of the United States increased its issues over 3,000,000.

In the meantime business was reviving in England, manufactures especially being very prosperous, and creating a great demand for raw materials.* Heavy orders for cotton ran its price up here to 27 cents. Corn was pulled up to plant cotton, and an active speculation in it began. The excess of exports over imports of specie in 1825 were $2,646,290. The excess of exports over imports of merchandise were $549,-023. In July the fall in prices in England brought a fall here. Fifty failures took place in New York before December. Banks failed in large numbers. The United States Bank was in trouble. The government wanted to pay off seven millions through the bank, but delayed this operation at the request of the latter, giving occasion to one of Jackson's subsequent charges against it. When it was done the bank

* See Chapter II. p. 302.

became debtor to the State banks and could not redeem its notes, explaining that bills drawn to pay English troops in Canada and for the formation of a bank in New Orleans had shortened specie supplies. It will be observed that the outflow of specie must always take place in that *form* which at the moment gives greatest profit, though the *cause* is always the same, and the usage is to explain the *cause* by the form of the export. The causes mentioned could have had no effect whatever unless there had been over-issues.

In 1826 there was dulness and reaction throughout the year. The cotton crop was poor. There were applications for charters for 123 banks and insurance companies in New York, which were refused. In April, 1826, ten or twelve failed and a run followed; but the banks held out. In this year the importations of merchandise exceeded the exportations by $5,202,722; the importations of specie exceeded the exportations by $2,176,433. The method of importation was to buy bills, get long credit for duties, and send the cargos, as soon as received, to auction. The auctioncer's notes were discounted, new bills bought, and the transaction repeated as long as rising prices and easy credit made it possible.

The crisis of 1825 was by no means so great in this country as in England. The country was not yet recovered from the convulsion of 1819. The Western States especially had, as yet, not escaped from the effects of that crisis. The speculation here was led off by the excitement in England, especially in cotton. The joint-stock-company mania seems also to have broken out here by contagion or sympathy. The banks, instead of applying any check to the unhealthy movement, or using any conservative measures, joined freely in the excitement. The crisis was not a bank crisis. Suspensions were not in fashion, and the few banks which did suspend failed. The prudent refusal of the New York legislature to grant the charters asked for during the last two years was amply justified.

In 1827 money was plentiful. In 1828 it was plentiful until May, when there was great scarcity, renewed in September. In May, 1828, the highest protective tariff before 1864 was passed. The percentage of duties on total imports in 1830 was 30.93, and on dutiable, 47.46. In 1829 money was scarce until July, when it became plentiful. President Jackson opened the attack on the United States Bank in his first message in December of that year. In 1830 money was plentiful. An English writer of the period speaks of specie as flowing to America from all parts of the world, and Niles' Register quotes a contemporary as complaining of the over-abundance of silver, and wishing some gulf might open to swallow it. The Bank of the United States increased its loans. During 1831 it continued this movement, increasing its loans from forty to sixty millions, as President Jackson charged, in order to manufacture popularity. In October, 1831, the money-market became stringent. In 1832 the United States Bank still further extended its discounts to seventy millions.

INVESTMENTS OF FOREIGN CAPITAL.

About the year 1830 American securities began to attract English investments. Some stock of the United States Bank had been held by foreigners from still earlier date, but large transfers of it occurred late in the twenties. State and canal stocks were also sold abroad in 1828–1832. The opportunities for remunerative investment of capital in this country waited only for improved transportation to present themselves. Canals were the first movement in this direction, and steamboats the next; but, in the decade from 1830 to 1840, railroads being introduced, the industrial development of the country went on with gigantic strides. At the same time the old restrictive system was partially broken down, first by the freeing of some raw materials in England under Mr. Huskisson's administration, then by the modification of the Navigation Acts, extorted from England by Prussia in 1825, by which the trade with the British West Indies was opened—an advantage which did not accrue to the United States, on account of diplomatic mistakes (this country claiming as a right what was offered as a privilege) until 1830, and thirdly by our lame compromise tariff.

The interesting period whose history we have

next to pursue, cannot be understood if observed from a narrow standpoint, and interpreted by subordinate incidents. The introduction of the new means of intercourse produced a development of industry so great as to amount to a revolution, so sudden as to create a convulsion. It required for its guidance, above all, financial skill; for it caused a strain upon the existing capital of society beyond what it was able to bear. This led to the usual resort to credit, and to credit in its most explosive forms, bank discounts and paper currency. The downfall at the end of the decade was the result of too headlong a career of prosperity, or of the intoxication which comes to men when they find themselves in control of undreamed-of powers of production. The two greatest commercial nations, England and the United States, were naturally the first to avail themselves of the new inventions, and they felt the crisis the most severely. They were tied together by the capital loaned by the elder to the younger nation. Some asserted at the time that specie currency would hold the two together, and render every circumstance of the one important to the other; others affirmed the same of paper currency. Neither party was on the right track. Evidently the bond which bound them was the credit extended to America by England, and the crisis in either country cannot be understood without reference to the events and movements in the other.

CURRENCY AND TARIFF AS POLITICAL ISSUES.

Unfortunately during this period—the period in which financial and fiscal questions were studied and understood by the American people better than at any other time in our history—those questions were made issues in party politics. I see no reason why they should not be political issues. Indeed, I am convinced that such questions never will be settled until they become political issues. But the reason why the struggles of the thirties proved so fruitless in the end was that parties did not divide according to intelligent conviction in regard to tariff and hardmoney, but parties already formed took sides on these questions. President Jackson, elected as

much for military prestige as anything, had im-
bibed from what he had seen of paper money in
Tennessee and Tentucky a fierce, but not too intelligent, detestation of it. He committed his
friends and the democratic party to hard money.
Thus thousands of men who were democrats on
previous issues became hard-money men without knowing why. Mr. Clay committed himself
to protection without any thorough knowledge
or true conviction of the principles involved.
He carried the Whig party (proper exceptions
being understood) into the support of protection.
Mr. Webster, originally free trader and hard-
money man by the convictions of a sober and
clear reason, gave his support to protection because Massachusetts had been turned from a
commercial into a manufacturing State, and, as
he thought, could not go back. He advocated
the bank originally for the purpose of checking
paper issues by hundreds of petty banks. In
the party contest he found himself committed to
the bank so far that he could not draw back even
if he wished. Mr. Calhoun, a protectionist in
1816, when it was thought that cotton needed

protection, turned free trader when the South came to bear the burden of protection without any benefit. Thus it appeared to be a mere question of interest. If Thomas H. Benton's story is correct, the compromise tariff of 1833 was made to save Mr. Calhoun from a trial for treason, and to enable Mr. Clay to retire from a position from which he found it impossible to advance on account of his enemies, or to retreat on account of his friends. Looking at the history of these three men, one is forced to believe, that if any one of them had been less politic and more honest to his convictions, he might have been far more successful. It remains yet for some statesman to show that the commonplaces about " yielding to circumstances " and " doing what you can " are only a petty wisdom ; that, so far from being the grand principles of politics in a republic, the latter is just the place for that man to succeed who, by showing that he understands himself, and knows whither he wants to go, proves to the mass that he is fit to lead. The time must come when the people will learn that to rule by the small men is the most expensive and ruinous of all methods of government. History will, moreover, set its verdict upon the position of the South in 1832, selling their product in a free market and buying their manufactures in one loaded by obstructive taxation; that, although the means they employed were unlawful, and their conversion to free trade was due to self-interest, yet their grievance was great and their protest was just. Probably this will come about when the farmers of the West, who have inherited the grievance of the South, shall have learned, as they will learn, what it is which really afflicts them, and shall have broken the system to pieces. The history we have now to follow will show that when existing political organizations take up scientific questions as party capital, they use them only to support ambition, and the questions reach no satisfactory or permanent solutions. It is a vital question for the republic whether parties shall form and reform around issues as they arise, or whether the issues shall arise under and inside of permanent party organizations.

WAR BETWEEN THE ADMINISTRATION AND THE UNITED STATES BANK.

In 1832 the bank petitioned for a renewal of its charter which was to expire in 1836. In speaking in favor of a renewal, Mr. Webster said :

" A disordered currency is one of the greatest political evils. It undermines the virtues necessary for the support of the social system, and encourages propensities destructive to its happiness. It wars against industry, frugality, and economy, and it fosters the evil spirits of extravagance and speculation. Of all the contrivances for cheating the laboring classes of mankind, none has been more effectual than that which deludes them with paper money. This is the most effectual of inventions to fertilize the rich man's field by the sweat of the poor man's brow. Ordinary tyranny, oppression, excessive taxation, these bear lightly on the happiness of the mass of the community, compared with fraudulent currencies and the robberies committed by depreciated paper. Our own history has recorded for our instruction enough, and more than enough, of the demoralizing tendency, the injustice, and the intolerable oppression on the virtuous and well disposed, of a degraded paper currency, authorized by law, or any way countenanced by government."

The bill passed both Houses, and was vetoed by the President on the 10th July.   It being now evident that the bank must expire unless some influence could be brought to bear to change the President or win two-thirds of Congress, a violent warfare was begun by the bank.   The power of its interest at the time is attested by any amount of evidence.   Mr. Wm. Gouge published his work on the History of Paper Money in 1833, in which he bears the strongest testimony to the power of the bank corporations throughout the country. The expressions used now in the West in regard to railroad corporations are not stronger than those used by many writers at the period under review in regard to " banking "—by which they meant the issue and loan of notes nominally convertible but really inconvertible, and thus subject, in their expansions and contractions, to nothing but the will of the bankers themselves. It is certain that the banks paid no more heed to the laws of the State than they did to the laws of prudence or of banking science, and that they paid very little heed to either. This veto was the cause of some genuine anxiety and of some manufactured fears in regard to the business future, and played a prominent part in the political canvass of 1832. Jackson defeated Clay, the latter representing bank, tariff, and internal improvements, by 288 to 49 in the electoral college.

The President, in his message in December, 1832, recommended the sale of the seven millions stock of the United States Bank which was owned by the nation, and the appointment of a committee to investigate its affairs. Bank shares fell from 112 to 104, but on a favorable report by the Treasury agent they recovered to 112. This report showed over seventy-nine millions assets ; liabilities, thirty-seven millions ; leaving forty-two millions : thirty-five millions capital, and seven millions surplus. But when the Government desired to pay the three per cents., in July, 1832, the bank agreed to pay the interest on them until October, if the payment might be delayed so long. It then negotiated a loan of five millions from Barings to make the payments of drafts on government deposits held by it, which would be made to carry out the payment of this stock. The reason given for negotiating this loan was fear of cholera. These operations raised questions of the safety of the public deposits, but the Committee of Ways and Means (Polk dissenting) offered a resolution that the deposits were safe. It was passed, 109 to 46. The motion to sell out the public shares was lost, 102 to 91, through the influence of the bank, which, as was afterwards discovered, had a large number of debtors, attorneys, and stockholders in the House.

THE COMPROMISE TARIFF.

In 1833 was passed the compromise tariff, by which duties were reduced gradually to 20 per cent. in 1842. This tariff was deceptive and complicated. It had no principle of economic science at its root—neither protection nor free trade. It was patched up as a concession, although it really

made very little, and its provisions were so intricate and contradictory that it produced little
revenue.   Specific duties were unaffected by it,
and these included books, paper, glass, and
sugar.   It did not run its course without important modifications in favor of protection, for it
could not bind future Congresses, and the doctrine of the horizontal rate of 20 per cent.—a
doctrine which has no scientific basis—produced
an increase on many articles.   It raised the cost
of cheap woollens, much worn, and, as it did not
provide for any other source of revenue, it was
certain that it could not last.   It was a compromise between Clay and Calhoun only, but it gave
Calhoun the chance to say, as he did often, that
the warlike attitude of South Carolina, in 1832,
coerced national legislation.   It taught Southern-
ers to believe that a warlike *attitude* was all
which was necessary; and the violation of the
act in 1842 was used with immense force to jus-
tify the repeal of the Missouri Compromise.   It
would lead me away from my present subject to
unravel the effects of the tariff, but I insist
strenuously upon this, that the political and finan-

cial history of the country are interwoven throughout, and that neither the currency nor the tariff nor the politics can be satisfactorily treated, save as a whole. Take the statistics, and review them in view of the tariff only, and your inferences are vitiated by the currency. Take the same data, and look at the currency only, and you go astray because you neglect the tariff. Neglect the political intrigues which wove the two together, and you cannot explain the motives of legislation. You argue from the authority of common conviction, when the true explanation is log-rolling.

REMOVAL OF THE DEPOSITS.

After Congress adjourned, September 22, 1832, the President ordered Mr. Duane, the Secretary of the Treasury, to remove the public deposits from the United States Bank. He refused to do so, and was displaced by Mr. Taney, who did it. The order was that collectors should send no more money to the bank, but to authorized depositories, to be chosen amongst the State banks. There was no positive and sudden transfer of the amount in bank, but it was proposed to draw for it at the proper intervals.

The war was now in full blaze. The bank had circulated documents during the canvass of the previous year, showing its services and merits. Against this proceeding I see no valid objection. The documents were " political," because the question of the bank's existence had become political. It was justified in defending itself. But in August, 1833, it altered its policy. It rapidly contracted its loans, giving as a reason the necessity of providing for the transfer of the deposits, a reason which the facts did not warrant.

On the assembling of Congress, December, 1833, the message announced the step taken, giving as grounds the misconduct of the bank in attempting to control the election, and the unsoundness of the institution. The President also charged the bank with now creating an artificial stringency in order to make itself appear necessary to the community. The bank question occupied a great part of the session. Mr. Clay attacked the President for removing the Secretary. The

Senate resolved (28 to 18) that the reasons for removing the deposits were unsatisfactory, and that the President had usurped unconstitutional power over the Treasury by removing the Secretary. The House never noticed the resolution, but resolved (134 to 82) that the bank ought not to be rechartered nor the deposits restored.

DISTRESS OF 1834.

The recharter of the bank being now definitely refused, a number of small banks were organized to take its place. But before they could get into operation the contraction of the bank had time to operate upon the market. Many deputations came up to Congress to complain of distress, and many memorials were sent up. The excitement was great throughout the country. It was asserted, however, on the other side, that all this distress was manufactured by the bank interest, in order to gain a recharter, and that loans were refused to some and granted freely to others, who used them to charge usurious rates. Benton asserts that two cases were discovered, one in which a broker received $1,100,000 to use in this

way, for which he charged $2\frac{1}{2}$ per cent. per month.
Prices did fall very slightly in 1834 as compared
with 1833, taking them over 80 articles, but some
advanced, and the fall on none was great.

The aggregate amount of loans and of circulation in the country increased steadily all these
years.*   I have not been able to find any statement of the loans of 1833, but the circulation, even
of the United States Bank, was not contracted in
1834, and, taking the whole number of banks, there
was an increase.   The business of the country
was increasing quite as rapidly, and it is impossible to ascribe the fluctuations of prices to the sole
action of the currency.   The fears, real or manufactured, of a crisis on the winding up of the national bank, account for the decline which took
place.

CHANGES IN THE COINAGE.

By the law of 1789 the exchange of sovereigns
($\frac{30}{21}$ of a guinea) for American coin was fixed at
4.44\frac{4}{9}$.   It is not known how this ratio was de-
termined.   The old exchange of a Mexican dol-

* See table, p. 107.

lar was 4*s.* 6*d.* sterling, but Gallatin says that there was no specimen of that coin which was worth this estimate. The coinage law under which coins were first struck in 1794 and 1795 fixed the ratio of gold to silver at 1 to 15, the silver dollar being 416 grains, 371.25 grains pure, and the gold dollar 27.0 grains, 24.75 grains pure, the alloy counting for nothing. The actual rate of gold to silver was at that time different in different countries, but in England it was 15.2 to 1. Gold was therefore underrated in the coinage, and it was easier for a debtor to get silver to the amount of one dollar than gold to the amount of one dollar. Silver accordingly became the real measure used, and gold bore a premium.

The contents of a sovereign are 113.001 grains (full weight 123.274), supposing it to be up to standard, 916⅔ in the 1000 fine. Our mint, in 1839 and again in 1863, declared it to assay only 916.5 in the 1000. At the ratio of 15.2 to 1, 371.25 grs. pure silver would be equal to 24.424 grs. pure gold, and a sovereign would be worth $4.626 of American silver. In American gold the same coin would be worth $4.565. In 1831 Gallatin took 15.6 to 1 as the existing ratio in England, at which rate a sovereign was worth \$4.75 in our silver. The difference between the coinage rating and the true value of the metals was thus greater in 1830 than in 1795, and gold was at a premium, on the average, in 1830, of five per cent. selling price.

The figures above given show the par of the coins grain for grain, but coins are worth more than bullion, being manufactured, that is, an ounce of gold in coin must buy more goods than an ounce of gold in bullion. The difference is the cost of manufacture. Gallatin says that it took two months to coin bullion left at the mint, which involved a loss of one per cent. interest. There was no seigniorage or charge for coining. In England there was no seigniorage, and the loss of interest was represented by the difference between the mint price of bullion, £3 17*s*. 10½*d*. per ounce, and the market price, which was then generally £3 17*s*. 6*d*.,* that is, it cost 4½*d*. to get an ounce coined. If coins are exported they lose

* Since 1844 the Bank is obliged by law to give its notes at £3 17*s*. 9*d*. for all bullion offered, reducing the difference between coin and bullion.

5*

the value of their own coinage, and must pay that
of the country to which they go. Freight and
insurance must also be paid. The cost of coining here being one per cent., the cost of freight
etc., one per cent. more, and the cost of English
coinage a slight addition, coin could not be exported unless exchange was a fraction over two
per cent. above par. When an American had to
pay $4.656 to discharge one pound sterling debt,
he would ship gold. He could not ship silver to
profit until he had to pay $4.845 for a pound
sterling. From 1795 until 1821 exchange was
almost always favorable to this country. After
1821 it often ruled adverse. Gold was shipped.
The following table from Senate document 290,
1st Ses. 26th Congress, shows the movement from
1824–1833, the gold and silver not having been
separated before 1824 in the returns. The figures are in thousands :

	GOLD BULLION.		GOLD COIN.		SILVER BULLION.		SILVER COIN.	
	Excess of Imports	Excess of Exports.	Excess of Imports.	Excess of Exports.	Excess of Imports.	Excess of Exports.	Excess of Imports.	Excess of Exports.
1824	11.9		34.9	. . . . . .	319.4		998.9	. . . . . .
1825	151.0		62.5	. . . . . .	357.9		. . . . . .	3,127.8
1826	100.5		127.9	. . . . . .	436.9		2,116.7	. . . . . .
1827	82.4		199.0	. . . . . .	419.3		478.9	. . . . . .
1828	55.9		. . . . . .	189.8	422.4		. . . . . .	349.3
1829	85.3		. . . . . .	229.0	623.2		2,612.8	. . . . . .
1830	104.6		231.0	. . . . . .	1,025.1		5,553.5	. . . . . .
1831	144.5		. . . . . .	133.5	482.7		. . . . . .	144.1
1832	94.4		. . . . . .	16.1	480.9		1,102.6	. . . . . .
1833	21.4		67.6	. . . . . .	297.8		4,438.4	. . . . . .

The following table shows the amount of both
metals coined in the same years, two figures being omitted :

	GOLD.	SILVER.
1824	$93.2	$1,752.4
1825	156.3	1,564.5
1826	99.2	2,002.0
1827	131.5	2,869.2
1828	140.1	1,575.6
1829	295.7	1,994.5
1830	643.1	2,495.4
1831	714.2	3.175.6
1832	798.4	2,579.0
1833	978.5	2,759.0

The strong movement of metal to this country

is apparent. In great part it was a real transfer of capital. Of all the gold which came in and was coined the Secretary of the Treasury said, 1836, that not over $1,000,000 remained in the country in 1834, "and of that small amount only a very diminutive portion was in active circulation." The fact is certain that the law of the mint gave the country a silver currency only, and that gold was exported or melted.

The par of exchange with Great Britain remained at $4.44, and this being taken as 100, exchange was quoted at 105, 106, etc.

These circumstances had attracted attention at various times, and efforts had been made to change the law. Congress, however, hesitated to touch so delicate a matter as the coinage, especially as even experts could not tell accurately what the real ratio of gold to silver was. President Jackson, being determined to introduce a specie currency, the matter was necessarily taken in hand. By an act of June 28th, 1834, the gold eagle was made to weigh 258 grs., standard .899225, that is, its pure contents were 232 grs., or 23.20 grs. to the dollar. Under this regulation silver was to gold as 16 to 1. This ratio was fixed upon in a blaze of exultation about the recent discoveries of gold in North Carolina, which, though known to exist since 1801, had only been developed since 1828, and extravagant hopes were entertained of finding "a new Peru" in the mountains of Georgia and the Carolinas. It was thought by some that it would "encourage the miners" to overrate gold in the coinage. In 1837 silver and gold were both made exactly nine-tenths fine, but the pure contents of the silver dollar remained the same as before, the gross weight being reduced to 412.5 grs. The gold dollar now contained 23.22 grs. fine.

There were two different dollars after these changes, as much as before. The silver dollar remained as before, but the gold dollar was now worth less than before. The gold dollar had formerly been worth in the silver coinage $1.038, taking the true ratio to be 15.6 to 1, which was asserted by the best authorities to be the true one at that time. The new gold dollar was worth, at the same ratio, in the same coin, 97.5 cts. As before no one would pay a debt with gold dollars, so now no one would pay with silver dollars. Silver went out of circulation and became the better metal to export, while, for the same reasons, gold became the better remittance this way. The only silver which could circulate here was that which was worn or clipped until it was not worth more than silver was rated at in our coinage. All the worn-down Spanish pillar pieces came here, because they had a value here higher than anywhere else in the world. While the mint was coining fine American pieces, scarcely one was to be seen in circulation. The people were obliged to use the smooth shillings, which produced a quarrel at almost every exchange as to whether you could "see the pillars," until somebody "crossed" them, and they sank into unquestionable dimes. They were generally overrated at that.

Thus, according to the great principle which has governed our fiscal legislation down to the present time, the discovery of gold in the United States was made, as far as the intention of the legislators could do it, to render gold more expensive to the people of the United States than it had ever been before. The absurdity of attempting to influence the price of gold must, however, be plain to every one. We might as well attempt to gain time for the American people by passing a law that all clocks should lose an hour a day.

Prices of goods adjusted themselves to the new dollar. The relations of gold to silver and to goods the world over remained unaltered, and the adjustment of values by the exportation of silver and importation of gold went on in spite of all laws. The experiment cost every creditor 2.5 cts. on every dollar due, and the wrong bore immense interest when this action of the government was made a basis of argument, in the legal-tender cases, to prove that Congress had the con-stitutional right to issue legal-tender paper, and interfere with existing contracts, because it had already debased the coinage—that is, in the middle of the nineteenth century the United States had committed the greatest wrong charged against the tyrants of the middle ages, and one which no modern despot had dared to repeat, and therefore it had a right to perpetrate another folly which is not yet quite so thoroughly exposed.

The pound-sterling, being now reckoned in the current gold of this country, was worth $4.8665, if of full weight and standard. This dollar, 23.22 grains of gold, ninth-tenths fine, remains still the definition of " one dollar" in the United States. Other coinage laws, to be mentioned below, have never touched this. The par of exchange for the sovereign has also remained unchanged, but, as the coinage expenses must be lost by export, light coins which cannot be current in England are sent here as bullion. The mint, in 1863, reported sovereigns worth, when new, $4.8391 ; on the average, $4.8206. The old par $4.44, being retained, actual par was $1.09\frac{7}{10}$. The Chamber of Commerce of New York petitioned, in 1839, that this system of reckoning might be changed, and the exchange quoted in dollars and cents. This was never done until 1873, and January 1, 1874, the method of quoting 4.86, 4.87, etc., came into use. In 1853 the law imposed a seigniorage of one-half of one per cent for coining. The par of $4.86 is "ideal." If the sovereign weighed and assayed up to this, the seigniorage in this country for recoining would reduce its value to $4.84. If the cost of transporation was one per cent., no sovereigns could come until they were down to $4.80. If the mint assay is to be taken, they could not come until they were worth only $4.78. For the same reasons American gold coin is worth one-half of one per cent more in coin than as bullion. This is lost when it is shipped. Shipment costs something over one per cent. Taking these expenses all together at two per cent., if $4.866 of our coin is worth £1, no one will pay more than $4.957 for exchange before shipping. If $4.84, are worth one sovereign, coin will be shipped at $4.936, gold.

In 1873 Congress fixed the Custom House valuation of a sovereign at $4.86. It will be seen that while we charge a seigniorage of one-half of one per cent., the sovereign cannot be worth over $4.84, the old Custom House valuation. This change added one-half of one per cent. to the invoice valuation of all English goods subject to ad valorem duties.

WAR WITH THE BANK CONTINUED.

In the message, December, 1834, the President made known to Congress that the bank had retained dividends due the nation on its stock, to reimburse itself for a draft on the French government which it had negotiated, and which had not been honored because the treaty had not been ratified by the French Chambers. The bank was forced by suit to pay the dividends.

He also said that the bank, after contracting its loans from August, 1833, to June, 1834, had as suddenly extended them. The amount was seventeen millions. He took this as proof that the previous curtailment had been wanton and unnecessary, and placed the bank in the position of having manipulated the money-market solely to carry its own point.

In fact the bank, finding that other banks were taking its place, and that it was robbing itself without coercing the public, had changed its course.

The deposits were now put in designated banks which issued no small notes, and which kept one-third of their circulation represented by specie. Many banks bought or imported gold in order to meet this latter requirement. The general government also used its influence successfully with nearly all the States to have laws passed forbidding small notes.

SMALL NOTES.

The prohibition of small notes is a measure which is simple, but very important for the results it effects. The principle is that paper issues displace coin of equivalent denominations. If paper is issued for sums of $ o and above, it may be issued to the amount of the coins of that and higher denominations which the public require, and no more. If issued for $5, the paper may be increased by the amount of half-eagles, which the public formerly used, and no more. Therefore, if it is desired to use paper to a certain extent, but not to displace specie entirely, the simplest way to accomplish this is to limit the paper to a certain denomination, say $10. Then half-eagles, and pieces of $3.00, $2.50, and $1 would circulate, and would form a stock, which, in the absence of any usury law, might be drawn into bank in a crisis. At the same time, this restriction goes far to make convertibility genuine. Convertibility in the currency is like conscientiousness in a man—it has many grades, and is valuable in proportion as it is strict and pure. The prohibition of small notes does more than any other arbitrary rule to ensure convertibility. It also secures to the poor the use of a value currency for their exchanges, and to the whole community the same currency for the exchanges which are made for consumption. These principles were recognized in England in 1827,* when the notes under £5 were abolished, and President Jackson's administration sought to put them in operation here. The Scotch banks still issue £1 and £2 notes, but they manage them very conservatively, and their example furnishes no argument. They seem to be such sagacious bankers as to need no limitations; therefore they do not need this one; but when limitations are needed, this is the simplest and most efficacious.

Such were the movements up to 1835, to

* See page 302.

which the subsequent developments must be traced as their origin. The lowering of the standard caused a rise in prices. The easy credit obtained in England for stocks and securities, the low rates for money here on account of the multiplication of small banks and increase of capital devoted to banking, the actual strong and great development of the country, combined to encourage a spirit of speculation and enterprise which, in this country, have never needed urging.

RAILROAD BUILDING.

To show the actual development which was in progress, it is sufficient to notice the number of miles of railroad built in these years. Railroad building was not a subject of unhealthy speculation, and the crisis did not, as it appears, stop an unnatural development in this respect, but rather checked a species of enterprise which, without it, might have gone on to produce great and healthy prosperity.

	MILES BUILT.		MILES BUILT.
1830....	none built. 23 in operation.	1837....	224
1831......	72	18_8....	416
1832......	134	1839....	389
1833......	151	1840....	516
1834......	253	1841....	717
1835......	465	1842....	491
1836......	175	1843....	159

SPECULATION.

The object on which speculation fixed especially was real estate, either in the Eastern cities or the Western States. The improved communication with the East by the Erie Canal (built in 1817–1825) had done wonders for the development of the territory bordering on the lakes. The advance in values there had been of the kind to produce a speculative mania. In 1835 the canal was enlarged and its benefits increased in a far greater ratio, but the speculative mania outstripped all reason. It did not follow, from any of the facts of the case, that mere speculative holders in the East could realize quick and solid gains from Western lands. The advantage of improved communication fell suddenly on those already settled in the West, and promised sure and steady development to those who should settle there and wait, but nothing more.

The progress of this mania is best shown by the returns of sales of public lands. (Sums in millions.)

$$
\begin{array}{lr}
1833 & \$3.9 \\
1834 & 4.8 \\
1835 & 14.7 \\
1836 & 24.8 \\
1837 & 6.7 \\
1838 & 3.0
\end{array}
$$

City real estate, especially in New York and some of the Southern cities, was also a favorite subject of speculation. New York gained by the canal, becoming from that time the emporium of the country, but, according to a table given by Grosvenor, New York city real estate was assessed at 309,000,000 in 1836, and it did not again reach 300,000,000 until 1851.

The advance in the Southern cities was due to the advance in cotton, and that had its causes in England.

AFFAIRS IN ENGLAND.

After 1832 the monopoly of the Bank of England was restricted to a circle of 65 miles around London. Within that circle strong joint-stock banks were formed, on unlimited liability, to do a true banking business, discount and deposit, but without issues of notes. Beyond that limit joint-stock banks were formed, which did issue notes on the American or Scotch plan. They called it the Scotch plan, but they managed it more in the American fashion. This extension of banking fell in with the industrial development already noticed, and with a great prosperity of cotton, silk, and iron manufactures, and with a series of good crops. The natural consequences followed —rising prices of manufactures, cheap food, demand for raw materials, easy credit, and hopeful speculation. The rapid increase of capital encouraged railroad building and American investment.

COTTON.

The effect on cotton is the one which most interests us.

The average prices for the year 1833 were, 11½ and 13½ cents, and for 1834, 11⅛ and 13¾. For 1835 the prices were:

Jan.	Feb.	March.	April.	May.	June.	July.
15–18	15–17	15–17	15–18	16–19	17–19	17–20

Aug.	Sept.	Oct.	Nov.	Dec.	Average.
17–19	17–19	15–18	14–18	14–16	15½–18

This was at a time when the supply was increasing both from this country and from India, but it was now certain that cotton was to be the great American staple until the abolition of corn laws in Europe. Even at this time there was a duty of 3 cents per lb. on cotton, levied in 1790 to secure the " home market."

It therefore appeared that the Southern cities were to see great prosperity as cotton markets, and at Mobile especially the speculation in real estate was great. To borrow Grosvenor's figures once more, real estate in Mobile was assessed as follows :

	REAL ESTATE.		POLLS.
1834	$4,000,000		980
1835	6,000,000		788
1836	18,000,000		617
1837	27,000,000		836
1838	20,000,000		1,487

In 1848, with 1,217 polls, the assessment was just under nine millions. The cotton culture does not require nor build up great cities.

BANK EXPANSION.

The following table shows the bank expansion throughout this period. It is taken from Condy Raguet's " Currency and Banking," and the circulation of specie is added from the report of the Secretary of the Treasury, 1837 (sums in millions) :

Date.	No. of bks. of which ret's rec'd.	No. of banks estimated.	Total No.	Loans.	Specie.	Circulation.	Capital.	Specie in circulation.
1820	213	95	308	....	19.8	44.8	137.1	....
1830	282	48	330	200.4	22.1	61.3	145.1	Oct. 1833, 4.
1834	406	100	506	324.1	....	94.8	200.	Jan. 12.
1835	515	43	558	365.1	43.9	103.6	231.2	" 18.
1836	559	8	567	457.5	40.	140.3	251.8	" 23.
1837	632	2	634	525.1	37.9	149.1	290.7	" 28.
1838	663	..	663	485.6	35.1	116.1	317.6	....
1839	662	..	840*	492.2	45.1	135.1	327.1	....
1840	661	61	901*	462.8	33.1	106.9	358.4	....

(It will be observed that the banking capital went on increasing. The banking capital of this country in 1854 was only 332 millions.)

It will be evident, from the facts already stated, that the movements of this period had their origin in a number of natural and legitimate causes. The removal of the deposits from the United States Bank gave a great stimulus to the creation of small banks, which could not go on in safety save under a strict system of convertibility. The administration thus pulled down with one hand what it built up with the other, by trying to introduce a specie currency. The bank ex-

---

* Branches counted separately.

pansion, however, was not properly a cause. It simply went along with and sustained a movement whose causes were independent. It is a very easy method of explaining mercantile and industrial movements to ascribe them entirely to expansions and contractions of the currency, but, on a currency even nominally convertible, the currency inflation does not lead off.* The mania for sudden riches gets possession of the community, and the banks fall in with, aid, and stimulate it. The blame cannot be simply thrown upon the banks for "causing" the trouble. They have a certain function to perform, and they fail to be faithful to it, and this failure takes off the legitimate check to over-speculation. Banks collect the capital of the country from the hands in which it lies idle, and transfer it to those who lack capital, but could use it to advantage. Over-speculation is speculation which outstrips the capital of the country. It is the pitfall which stands always open in a new country. The banks being thus the transfer agents through whose hands the capital passes,

* See page 253.

are the ones to know and give warning when it is used up. This they should do naturally by raising the rate of discount, and the usury law, which makes this impossible, is fairly chargeable with a large share of the mischief which is usually ascribed to bank expansions. For, the capital passing out of the bank in the form of discounts and bank-notes, the bank has no means of profiting by the increased demand for, and value of, capital save by increasing these items, that is, passing over to the most perilous forms of credit, while the public, obtaining the notes which represent capital and those which are credit, precisely in the same form, and, at first at least, on the same terms, has no warning when the line is passed.

Condy Raguet gives descriptions of ordinary bank operations in the period before us, which were reckless in the extreme, but they were nearly all devices for evading the usury law. Men who had embarked in speculations clamored for increased issues on any terms; in a manner which has become very familiar to our experience. They formed a public opinion which forbade any one to test the foundations of credit. The enhanced prices and expanded credit continually absorbed the new issues, and no depreciation occurred until a shock to credit and prices from outside causes produced a collapse. The banks suspended, escaped the results of their share of the folly, and loaned their irredeemable notes at high rates; but the public, conscious that it had been humored in its wish by the excessive issues, could not be severe with them. It is idle for either party to blame the other. They went hand-in-hand in folly.

Affairs on the other side of the water were in much the same condition. There was a new demand for capital there also. The new joint stock banks in England, and similar institutions in Belgium and France, pursued much the same course, though not to the same degree, as our banks. The note issues of the Bank of England and of the joint-stock banks were not excessive and did not increase, but the methods of banking pursued by the latter were such as to call down blame from those who had favored joint-stock banks most zealously, and the rule observed by the Bank of England at this time did not prove sound in practice.

"DISTRIBUTION" OR "DEPOSIT" OF SURPLUS REVENUE.

The session of 1835-6 was not marked by financial legislation, save by one plan proposed this year and carried out the next, which added a new element to the financial situation. If there is any property which is of little value, real estate or stocks, some plan is sure to be proposed for selling it to city, town, State, or nation. If the nation or any subordinate body holds any property, stocks or real estate, which is valuable, some one raises the question what to do with it? The answer is : Why do anything? If the public owns good property, why not keep it? But an intrigue for bringing about the sale is very sure to be planned by those who want to buy, or for dividing by those who want to receive. The lands owned by the general government have always been subject to such intrigues, and at the period under review many schemes were proposed for dividing them among the States, though none of them actually received shape in Congress. A still more attractive object for distribution appeared in the surplus revenue. The public debt was now nearly extinguished. It stood on the 1st January in each year as follows, in millions.*

1832	24.3
1833	7.0
1834	4.7
1835	.037
1836	.3
1837	3.3
1838	10.4
1839	3.5
1840	5.2
1841	13.5
1842	20.6

There was a surplus in the Treasury, and it was anticipated that there would be a surplus until the compromise tariff was in full effect, of nine millions a year on the average. Mr. Clay wanted it divided. Mr. Calhoun introduced the subject. He at first wanted the Constitution amended to satisfy certain scruples of his, but soon dropped this notion. Mr. Webster favored the division. The administration opposed it, and

* Finance Report, 1872, p. 374.

wanted the lands surveyed and sold at $1.25 per acre, with a homestead provision for actual settlers, surplus revenue to be spent on national defences. The bill for distributing the income from lands sold to the States passed the Senate, but never came up in the House. The Senate passed a bill in 1836 for "depositing" the surplus revenue (being regarded as the part which came from land) with the States, subject to call. The plan for distribution found no chance in the House, but that for "depositing" was passed by a large majority. It was declared that the name only was changed and that the "deposits" could never be recalled, and so the event proved, but the protest was unheeded. The President unwillingly signed the bill, this being the session before the Presidential election. In his next message, December, 1836, he expressed his fears of the measure, but that whole session was agitated by schemes for distributing land and revenue, and a second "deposit" scheme for the surplus of 1837 was passed by the House as a rider on an appropriation bill. The Senate not concurring, the entire appropriation bill was lost.

PUBLIC CLAIMS.

Several outstanding claims of the United States for embargo damages and blockade captures against France, Spain, Portugal, Naples, and Denmark were settled at this time, and the payments were imported in specie in 1837, in furtherance of the plan for a specie currency. The coin was used in public payments, and in the first instalment of the distribution.

THE "SPECIE CIRCULAR."

On the 11th July, 1836, the President issued the famous "Specie Circular," by which he ordered agents for the sale of public lands to take in payment only specie. It was based on the old law of 1816, mentioned above, by which the Secretary was ordered to receive only specie, *or* Treasury notes, *or* notes of specie-paying banks. The notes of Eastern banks were carried West for a "good circulation," and "coon-box banks" were set up in the Western States, which issued notes in easy loans to land speculators. These notes were practically inconvertible, and might be issued in any amount. The consequence was that the title to land was passing to speculators, and the Treasury was being filled with worthless paper. The best justification of this measure was, as Benton says, that ten millions of paper on its way to the Land Office was arrested by this circular.

When Congress met (December, 1836) it passed an act rescinding the specie circular, after a long and acrimonious debate. The bill was not sent to the President until the day before the close of the session, and he did not sign it, so that it did not become law. In the course of the debate there were abundant prophecies of coming trouble. Mr. Calhoun did not vote on the bill, and in giving his reasons said: " He believed the state of the currency was almost incurably bad, so that it was very doubtful whether the highest skill and wisdom could restore it to soundness, and it was destined at no distant day to undergo an entire revolution. An explosion he considered inevitable, and so much the greater the longer it should be delayed."

THE PENNSYLVANIA BANK OF THE UNITED STATES.

The Bank of the United States, whose charter had now expired, obtained a charter from the legislature of Pennsylvania in a section of a road bill, "by bribery, as subsequent legislative investigation proved." It had not yet paid back the government stock or the government dividends, and it continued to reissue the notes of the old United States Bank which it received.

THE CRISIS.

One effect of the changes in the coinage in 1834 had been to make gold the better remittance this way. This being the metal on which English banking was based, the movement had importance for the English banking and commercial world which silver remittances had never had. In April, 1836, the gold reserve of the Bank of England began to be lowered. This went on all summer. The speculation had also reached a point at which the rise was stayed. The Bank rate was raised to 4½ in July, and 5 in September.

American bills were refused discount. Prices fell and money was withdrawn. A Parliamentary report, which criticised the joint-stock banks severely, added to the prevailing uneasiness.*

In November, 1836, the Agricultural Bank of Ireland and the Northern and Central Bank of Manchester were in difficulties which forced them to call on the Bank of England for aid. They received it on condition of winding up. This was the first blow of the crisis which convulsed Europe and America. The shock upon the London Exchange developed weakness in three houses doing large business with, and giving extended credit to, this country.† The importations here had been very rapidly increasing, and had been extraordinarily large in 1836. Taking merchandise only, the excess of imports over exports had been very large from 1831 on. The following table shows the excess of imports or exports of coin and merchandise during this period :

* Gilbart's " Banking " ; Macleod's Dictionary, art. " Banking in England " ; Tooke's " Prices," Vol. II.

† Wilkes, Wilde, and Wiggins, celebrated at the time as " the three W's."

	MERCHANDISE.		SPECIE.	
	Excess of Exports.	Excess of Imports.	Excess of Exports.	Excess of Imports.
1830	8,900,000	....	....	5,900,000
1831	....	23,500,000	1,700,000	....
1832	....	13,600,000	.. ..	200,000
1833	....	13,500,000	....	4,400,000
1834	....	6,300,000	....	15,800,000
1835	....	21,500,000	....	6,600,000
1836	....	52,200.000	....	9 000,000
1837	....	19,000,000	....	4,500,000
1838	9,000,000	....	....	14,200,000
1839	....	44,200,000	3,100,000	....
1840	25,400,000	....	....	400,000
1841	....	11,100,000	5,000,000	....
1842	3,800,000	....	700,000	....
1843	40,400,000	... .	....	20,800,000

Thus there had been imported, according to the statement, during the six years ending Jan. 1st, 1837, over 130,000,000 more merchandise than had been exported, and a net import of specie in the same time of over 34,000,000. The movement of the metals I reserve for another section. It is evident here that the imports had not been paid for in coin, exported either by the balance of trade or by the depreciated currency. Allowance must be made for the error in all statements of export and import due to the method of estimating them. The excess of imports contains freights and profits. American shipping at this time was steadily increasing. It increased in spite of this crisis without interruption, and it did the larger part of the American foreign trade.

The freights, therefore, added little to foreign payments.

Due allowance being made, it remains true that the imports had not been paid for in merchandise or metal. They had been balanced by securities exported—in other words, they had been bought on longer or shorter credits. It does not appear from the above figures, or from any evidence, that any considerable amount of securities was sent back during the panic; rather the contrary. Outstanding business obligations were, however, called in by English creditors.

The revulsion in England had also acted disastrously on the price of cotton. This ran for the year 1836 and the beginning of 1837 as follows :

	Jan.	Feb.	March	April	May.	June	July.	Aug.	Sept.	Oct.	Nov.	Dec.
1836	14-16	14-16	15-19	16-19	16-19	16-19	15-18	15-20	12-20	12-20	12-20	18-19
1837	15-17	14-17	14-17	11-15	8-12	.	...	...	...	...	...	...

It remained at the latter figures throughout 1837.

Nowhere had the paper-money mania raged worse than in Mississippi, where the banks operated as cotton factors, manufacturing money to carry cotton, as they needed it. In March several New Orleans houses were in trouble, and were forced to apply to the banks there for extra aid. Next the pressure was felt in New York, and by April the crisis was general throughout the country. There were one hundred failures in New York in March, and the losses were fifteen millions.

The New York and Philadelphia banks, including the Bank of the United States, made advances to the merchants to the amount of $1,500,000; the Bank of the United States loaning bonds payable in London, Paris, and Amsterdam. These bonds sold well, but at rates which made the loans cost the merchants two per cent. per month, and the United States Bank held all the best paper which was running to maturity. *

* Macleod. I have not met with mention of this elsewhere.

The rule of the Bullion Committee, * that banks should discount freely in the face of panic, seems to be here obeyed after a certain fashion, but the committee contemplated the loan of notes by a bank whose credit cannot fail in the wildest panic ; not the loan of post notes (as these " bonds " were), on which the merchants must pay a second discount ; nor the loan of notes of suspended banks, on which the merchants must suffer a loss. Their rule cannot be obeyed by banks which work up to the utmost verge of capital and credit in the best times, and have no margin for safety in a crisis. The latter can only suspend, escape all the results of a folly in which they had full share, and then loan their notes at exorbitant rates to the merchants who are yet out in the financial storm. This has been the process here in every crisis, and probably will be as long as people stand it without complaint. †

* See page 250.

† There is a very erroneous opinion prevalent, that the English government allows the Bank of England to suspend in a crisis. There is never any question of the kind. The run on the Bank in a panic is not for gold, but for notes, that is, for discounts. If, however, there is an export of gold at the time, the notes are taken to the issue department and gold demanded. According to the charter, the Bank can circulate only fifteen mil-

In March a meeting was held at New York, which was addressed by Mr. Webster. He ascribed the distress to the interference of the government with the currency, and to the "specie circular." A committee of fifty was sent to Washington to ask for the rescinding of the circular. In the address to the President (Van Buren) they said : " The value of our real estate has, within the last six months, depreciated more than forty millions." " Within the last two months there have been more than two hundred and fifty failures." " A decline of twenty mi'lions of dollars has occurred in our local stocks." " The immense amount of merchan-

lions in notes on government security, and for all other notes it must have gold, sovereign for sovereign. If, therefore, there is a drain on its bullion, it must contract, or keep all notes handed in for gold. This heightens the panic. The action of the government is to recommend the Bank to disregard the clause governing circulation. It promises to ask Parliament for indemnity. The Bank then discounts freely for solvent parties, but at high rates. This always kills the *panic* as panic. The crisis runs its course. Erroneous assertions have been made to the effect that the whole crisis comes to an end. This is not the case. Also that the Bank never has to avail itself of the permission. This also is an error. In 1847 and 1866 there was no over-issue. Prices fell, the exchanges turned, gold came in, and the trouble died out in two or three days, but in 1857 the bank issued £900,000 more than the law would have allowed. They were retired again within a week. Evidently when a bank has over thirty million pounds' circulation, of which fifteen millions are secured on government debt, and the rest by coin, then £900,000 over-issue cannot affect its credit. It has a reserve strength which it can put forth in a panic.

dise in our warehouses has, within the same period, fallen in value at least thirty per cent." "Within a few weeks not less than twenty thousand individuals, depending on their daily labor for their daily bread, have been discharged by their employers, because the means of retaining them were exhausted." They ascribe all this, as they say, not to undue extension of mercantile enterprise, but to the attempt to substitute a metallic for a paper currency, the removal of the deposits, and the specie circular, "which withdrew the gold and silver of the country from the channels in which it could be profitably employed." "We therefore ask whether it is not time to interpose the paternal authority of the government, and abandon a policy which is beggaring the people." In a subsequent meeting, at which the committee reported that they could obtain nothing from the President, a resolution was passed in which the defeat of Mr. Clay's land bill was alleged as another cause of the trouble.

In May a run began on two New York banks, of which one failed. Three banks in Buffalo failed next. The New York banks then suspended in a body May 10th, a law being passed by the legislature to allow them to suspend for one year. Amongst the direct causes of suspension was the demand upon the government deposit banks for the first two instalments of the 40,000,000 surplus to be paid in specie into the State treasuries, under the deposit-distribution act. These banks having now stopped payment, the government deposits were locked up, or must be taken in depreciated notes. The other banks throughout the Union followed the example of the New York banks, the New England banks holding out longest. The notes of all the banks fell to a discount, specie disappeared, and notes of every description were issued. The New York banks began to contract in order to be ready to resume, but the actual diminution of the circulation throughout the country was very small. Nearly all the banks made money out of the suspension, and paid large dividends during the year.

Two instalments of 10,000,000 each having been paid in specie to the States, one in January and one in April, under the distribution act, and a deficit in the revenue being probable, a special session of Congress was called for September, the government still attempting to continue specie payments.

The message at the opening of the extra session proposed that the Treasury keep its own deposits (the plan afterwards adopted), and that a bankruptcy law for banks and corporations should be passed. Neither was passed. The President made known an estimated deficit of 6,000,000, and proposed to meet it by retaining the fourth instalment of the surplus to be distributed, and to issue Treasury notes to provide for immediate necessities. The third instalment had been paid on the first of June to the States in notes. As for demanding back the " deposit," no one spoke of it. The States were generally demanding the fourth instalment.

The Treasury notes were issued, bearing interest, and running as low as $50. As for the fourth instalment, the payment of it was put off until January 1, 1839, and then made imperative on the Treasury. When the appointed day came, however, the Treasury had a deficit and could not pay it, and it was abandoned by the States.

Some States were led by this distribution into expensive improvements and debt, others distributed it per capita, a few shillings per man, " which was received with contempt by some, and rejected with scorn by others ; " others divided it amongst the counties, and others refused it. As a measure of popularity-hunting, it failed.

We hear a great deal of wailing about the national debt, and English history is full of such lamentation, but nations go on prospering while the debt stands still, and a forty-million surplus works demoralization far and wide. Where the carcass is, there will the eagles be gathered. Recent experience shows us that, even under a great debt, when there is a surplus revenue wrung from the people by taxation, it is more likely to increase the appropriations than to lessen the debt. The project for giving back to the people money taken from the people by taxation, was opposed to all sense and reason, and the idea of distributing the proceeds of sales of public lands in largesses was unstatesmanlike to the last degree.

The distresses of 1837 were aggravated by a failure of the wheat crop. In that and the following year this country imported bread-stuffs from the Mediterranean.

MEASURES FOR RESUMPTION.

In January, 1838, several Boston banks were insolvent. The Massachusetts country banks were in bad condition. The best of them had $1 in specie for $11 in circulation, and the worst (Berkshire) 1 to 25.

A meeting of bank delegates was called by the New York banks for November 27, "for the purpose of conferring on the time when specie payments may be resumed with safety, and on the measures necessary to effect that purpose." The convention did not meet, on account of the refusal of the United States Bank.

Meantime the New York banks had been vigorously contracting to prepare for resumption. Their issues were reduced from $25,480,000,

January 1, 1837, to $12,920,cco, January 1, 1838. The exchanges turned and gold flowed in, the Bank of England sending £1,000,000, an act which Macleod vehemently condemns, seeing that the exchanges were adverse.*

Early in 1838 Congress passed an act to forbid the Pennsylvania Bank of the United States from using old notes of the United States Bank: penalty, on the president or agents, fine not to exceed $10,coo, and imprisonment not less than one nor more than five years. Meantime, the bank, finding that it could sell its post notes in Europe, had issued more of them and made a business of it.

April 15, 1838, a convention of 143 bankers met at New York, by invitation of the New York banks, to discuss resumption. The majority wanted to resume January 1, 1839, but the New York banks were under the compulsion of State law to resume May 10, 1838. They resumed on

---

* In a sketch of the life of James G. King in the *Merchants' Magazine* for January, 1854, it is said that he negotiated this loan from the Bank of England to enable the American banks to resume; and the object was the ultimate advantage from setting American business once more in operation.

that day, and nearly all the other banks in the Union, except those of Philadelphia, followed. Philadelphia bills were at a discount in New York, and prices were higher in Philadelphia than in New York. A balance of trade adverse to Philadelphia arose between the two cities, with a movement of specie from Philadelphia.* The New York legislature passed a bill in this year providing for securing bank-notes by a deposit of stocks.

A committee of New York merchants now gave a statement of the causes of the suspension far more correct to the facts than the one made in the first heat of excitement. " The immediate causes which compelled the banks of the city of New York to suspend specie payments on the 10th of May last are well known. The simultaneous withdrawing of the large public deposits, and of excessive foreign credits, combined with the great and unexpected fall in the price of the principal articles of our exports, with an import of corn and bread-stuffs, such as had never before occurred, and with the consequent inability of the

* Condy Raguet, Currency and Banking.

country, particularly in the South-western States, to make the usual and expected remittances, did, at one and the same time, fall, principally and necessarily, on the greatest commercial emporium of the union."

In July, 1838, the United States Bank called a convention of bankers at Philadelphia, at which it was agreed to resume August 13. The example of the banks which had resumed made it necessary for others to follow. Thus, at the end of 1838, the great majority of the banks throughout the country had resumed, at least nominally. The Bank of the United States had given as a reason for not resuming with the New York banks, that it was bound to consider its weaker brethren. All the questions between this bank and its enemies must be decided now in view of subsequent developments, which all went to show that the bank was at this time in no condition to perform its functions, but was working mischief.

REVIVAL OF BUSINESS.

During the year 1838 there had been a general revival of trade. The Bank of England rate was from 2½ to 3½ per cent. during the whole of that year. This led to increased investments in American securities. " Bonds of all kinds issued by the Bank of the United States, by the various States in the Union, and by numerous private undertakings, were poured upon the English market, and found eager purchasers." * This served as a further extension of credit on American debts carried over by the operations of the Bank of the United States and others from the previous crisis. It is important, as showing that besides the strenuous efforts made by Americans to pay (a fact to which there is the best testimony), and the amount lost in bankruptcy, the time for liquidating the debts of America to Europe was greatly extended.

Towards the end of the year there were symptoms of further trouble. The exchanges became adverse, and the stock of gold in the

* Gilbart, " Banking," 218.

Bank of England declined until October. In that month the Bank had £2,525,000 in bullion; notes, £17,612,000; and deposits, £6,734,000. In May the rate was 5 per cent.; June 20, 5½; August 1, 6; September, 6½. In the autumn the Bank of Belgium failed, and there was a run on the banks at Paris. * The Bank of England borrowed £2,500,000 of the Bank of France through Barings. After October gold began to flow into England, and the pressure subsided.

These incidents again reacted on this country. The suspension had not been followed by any great reduction of paper here, but had rather enabled the banks to go on without reducing; only at New York, where they were most exposed to the action of an adverse exchange, and where the legislature had taken prompt measures of compulsion, was there a thorough reduction.

THE BANK CRASH OF 1839.

The Bank of the United States during the year 1838 became involved in cotton specula-

* Macleod.

tions, assuming the troubles to be over, and buying for a rise. On the revival of business in England in that year cotton did rise, and in May, 1839, it was at 16 cents, but from that time it declined again. It was not above 12 cents in 1840 (September), not above 11 cents in 1841 (February), not above 9 cents in 1842 (March), and not above 8 cents in 1843 (October). It did not reach 12 cents again until February, 1847. To the bank this course of the market was ruinous. It made the utmost exertions to sustain itself by the sale of bonds in Europe, and by issuing post notes which were sold in New York and Boston at 18 to 24 per cent. discount. Several banks failed in different parts of the Union, and the struggle to sustain specie payments became very severe. Throughout the Western States, especially in Michigan and Illinois, the failures were numerous. The banks of Mississippi, which, as above stated, had become extensive dealers in cotton, of which they were carrying large quantities, were nearly all ruined, and their notes, and those of the various joint-stock companies which had issued notes, were at from

25 to 60 per cent. discount. The State of Michigan was engaged in building railroads, and was involved in debt. The roads were sold to incorporated companies at a loss of almost their entire cost. Alabama had created a debt of fifteen millions to found a banking system. This was nearly all lost. In 1838 Mississippi borrowed seven millions in bonds to found banks. This debt was repudiated.

It afterwards came out that the Bank of the United States was carrying on operations at this time for which no condemnation could be too severe. As the New York banks were staggering under the effort to avoid new suspension, which the United States Bank eagerly desired, it took the step of selling exchange in New York, and using the notes and checks obtained in order to make a run on the New York banks for specie, which it shipped to meet the exchange when it fell due. This almost incredible action is stated and described in detail by Mr. Cowperthwaite, formerly assistant cashier of the bank, in a report of a committee of stockholders in 1841, which is quoted at length by Benton,

" Thirty Years' View," II, 370. It, however, met a fit reward. The United States Bank was deeply in debt to Europe, and relied on the success of its manœuvre to meet the bills, but it drew so rapidly and recklessly that it could not send notice of the drafts, and on the 16th of September, 1839, one of its drafts was refused at Paris. It then tried to effect loans in Holland, and, failing, it applied to the Bank of England, where the rate was now 6 per cent. This Bank was itself in as severe straits as at any time in its history, but it loaned a small sum. Macleod quotes the New York *Evening Post* on the operations of the bank at home, showing that it owed from ten to twenty millions in New York and $800,000 in Boston. It appears that the prestige of the bank was not broken until this time, and that the question between it and its opponents was held open. On the 10th of October, 1839, it closed its doors and was followed by nearly all the banks in the South and West. The New England and New York banks held out bravely, but, taking the country over, this was the real collapse of the banking system which had been growing up. 343 out of 850 banks closed entirely, and 62 partially. Of the government deposits some two millions were lost.

The second suspension lasted in Pennsylvania until June 15, 18;1, being limited by statute. As soon as the Bank of the United States opened a run upon it began, and it closed finally on February 4, 1841. This led to a third suspension, and specie payments were not definitely resumed until March 18, 1842.

The London Bankers' Circular * said that four million pounds sterling of the stock of the United States Bank was held by Englishmen, £20,000 by the people of Guernsey. Its capital was a total loss, and the seven millions United States stock subscribed into the capital of the bank by the government is mentioned by the Secretary of the Treasury (Finance Report, 1872, p. 18) among the items of the debt for which no cash ever came into the Treasury, *i.e.*, it was created for this purpose.

The speculation in Western lands and city lots burst in 1837, but the banks escaped by

* Quoted by Benton.

suspension. As will be seen by the table given above,* the currency was not greatly reduced in 1837 and 1838, and, as will be seen by the diagram opposite p. 227, prices *of staple articles* were arrested in their fall in 1838. The blow fell upon speculative investments, articles of luxury, and imported articles, the prices of which always feel paper inflation most. Nor was the fall of prices from 1839 to 1843 due to any forced contraction of the currency. The more correct explanation of the phenomena is that the destruction of the banking system brought with it a collapse of the industry of the country. The revulsion was so complete that it could not be arrested until industry came almost to a standstill and took a fresh start. 1841 was considered comparatively a year of prosperity, but on January 1, 1844, the banks held forty-six millions in specie against forty-four millions of circulation,† and money was easy at 3½ and 4 per cent. The year 1843 was one of the gloomiest in our industrial history. The grand promise of ten years

---

* Page 107.

† Hunt's Magazine, July, 1844. The returns were probably incomplete.

before was now entirely obscured. Mortgaged property was passing into the possession of mortgagees. Factories were idle. Trade was dull, investments slow. All the natural advantages of the country were present unimpaired, but the haste to realize them had brought ruin which time only could repair. The year 1843 was one in which the ideal of some economists was realized. We exported forty millions more merchandise than we imported, and we imported twenty millions more specie than we exported, but the significance of these facts was simply this : we were paying up for the grand times of the years before. It was like the spendthrift living low to recover his position, and we were doing it by producing mainly for export, at prices low enough to suit the creditors. The patient being in this low state the doctors gave him another dose of protective tariff, and, as he got better, they have published the case in their almanacs ever since.

MOVEMENTS OF SPECIE, 1830–1840.

The cases we have had to deal with hitherto have presented us with the simple phenomenon of the export of the precious metals and increased importations of commodities, due to the repetition of the grossest error possible in currency—the attempt to use two kinds of circulating medium, one inferior to the other. In no other way than this can a country be " drained of its specie," and in no other way can a permanent and heavy " balance of trade" against it be brought about.* It may indeed send money abroad to support armies, or to buy food, or for foreign investment, but these are arbitrary acts, not effects of the laws of trade. Their influence is also slight and temporary, for the specie tends at once to return, if it is needed, to where it was. The United States do not need to contemplate either of these contingencies.

The case now before us is different. We have here a large excess of imports over exports, a vitiated currency, and at the same time a flow of specie towards the country.

* See p. 263.

The Secretary of the Treasury speaks of the movement of specie which escapes the Custom House. He does not seem to place implicit reliance on his statistics, and it must be understood of them that they are not trustworthy, either as to goods or specie, save for general results. The fact, however, may be accepted as true, that the movement was as here shown.

There were certain arbitrary interferences with the natural movement. The banks were induced by government regulations to import specie, and the government itself caused payments this way to be made in coin at every opportunity. By altering the rating of gold to silver also it made gold a profitable remittance to this country until the metals and prices had adjusted themselves to the new arrangement. The operations of the Bank of the United States in 1839 were of a character to traverse all natural laws, and render scientific inferences extremely difficult.

None of these things, however, could have kept the specie in the country, if there had not been other causes at work.

Condy Raguet says that there were but very

few small notes in the country until after the suspension of 1837. The habit of calling for specie had never been formed, and it was sternly discountenanced by public opinion. It is indeed extraordinary that, as the currency increased so rapidly, it should not have depreciated, for the fact, as shown by public documents, is that it did not depreciate more than the cost of transporting specie from the place of issue to the place of circulation; but this fact is a strong support of the opinion stated above, that the bank expansion only kept pace with the speculative expansion and rise of prices, and that the issues, although opposed to all sound rules of banking, and sure in the end to prostrate banks and dealers together, were not made faster than they were called for.

Beyond and below all these circumstances we must look for a more permanent law of the movement of the metals, and we find it in the scientific principle which these things only modify more or less. The metals move away from the country in which prices are high to the country in which prices are low, that is, they go from the countries where they have low value to the countries where they have high value. Evidently in a natural state of things there would be some things in each country (those for whose production that country has the best advantages) which would be lower in price, would be given in larger quantity for a given quantity of the precious metals, in that country than in others. The movement of metal from country to country would in that case be very slight, but whenever the average of prices in one country rose above the average in others, an outflow of specie would bring them down to the level, and whenever they fell below the average, an influx would raise them. Some argue that high prices make prosperity: others that low prices make prosperity. High and low prices are only relative terms, and in fact have no meaning when we embrace the production of the world. The true place for prices in each country to occupy is in their due relation to the general average the world over, for then *each country gets the utmost possible gain from its relative advantage in those things which it can produce best.* The movement of specie would therefore be, if the whole world used the metals and regulated prices by them without interference, as regular, as self-controlled, and as beneficent as the movement of the tides. This, too, is the grand fundamental reason why inconvertible paper is a suicidal folly in the country which adopts it.

In the case before us prices were unduly inflated by speculation and over-issues in nearly all the countries of Europe, as well as in this country. Hunt's *Merchant's Magazine* for July, 1844, gives a table of English prices showing that if the prices for fifty articles in

1833 be taken as	....	1,000
1834 would be	....	1,099
1835 "	....	1,150
1836 "	....	1,346
1837 "	....	1,133

This relative inflation in the countries with which our relatious were closest, shielded us from the effects which must have followed if their finances had been in a sound condition.

There was one thing, however, which was dearer here than in Europe, and which therefore made this the best market for those who wanted to sell or lend it, and that was capital.

As has been said above, the country was new, its natural advantages undeveloped, and only just made available by improved means of commmunication. The remuneration for all sorts of investment was high. In the crisis of 1837 the crash was not in *production*, but in those real estate investments which were to become profitable by the results of productive labor. Even in 1837, and especially in 1838, the European investments in American securities were, as we have seen, very large in amount. When the Bank of the United States finally failed it owed the Bank of England twenty-three millions. Its failure, with the total loss of its capital, much of which was owned in Europe, the failure of many injudicious enterprises, and, above all, the repudiation of indebtedness by several of the States, ruined American credit abroad. Up to 1840, however, that credit had been high, and it was acknowledged that in 1837 the American merchants had generally exerted themselves to the utmost to meet their obligations. These continual loans and investments from Europe kept down the exchanges. They were transferred, as far as it was profitable to do so, in goods, for the rest, in specie, and the surplus import of merchandise and specie, was, in great part, a real transfer of capital highly advantageous to all parties concerned. The same may be said in general of that "increasing indebtedness to Europe" which has been going on more or less ever since, and has caused so many good people great anxiety.

FINANCIAL MEASURES FROM 1840 TO 1850.

The second suspension of the United States Bank in 1839, and its operations of that year, cost it a great many of its friends. The administration of Mr. Van Buren clung to the hard-money policy, and opposed any national bank. But the fight was not yet over; in fact, the few next years were full of financial legislation and of battles over bank or no bank.

In 1840 the Independent Treasury Act was passed, by which the government was to take the custody of its own funds. It was not passed without fierce opposition, especially from those who saw in the specie circular the beginning of all the woes of the country. As that had withdrawn the support of the government acceptance from the bank issues, so this would withdraw the public funds from use as banking capital. The specie circular did indeed withdraw powerful support from the bank-notes, which enjoyed credit while the government received them, which they did not possess when refused at the Treasury, but if A is a man of doubtful credit, and gains confidence by being supposed to be a friend of B, an honest man, and if B declares that he is not a friend of A, A may lose the credit he enjoyed, and be ruined ; but who except A will lay the blame of that ruin on B ? The Independent Treasury Act accomplished the "divorce of bank and State," and we, who have that battle to fight over again, can see in it only wise statesmanship.

It was proposed in England that the holders of State bonds should try to get Congress to assume the State debts as had been done in 1791.* Sydney Smith wrote a letter to Congress petitioning that this might be done,† and represent-

---

* See page 55.
† The text of it is in McCulloch's Dict., Art. "Funds."

ing that he and other liberals had staked both their word and their money on the honor of the American Republic. After a strong contest resolutions were passed to crush any hopes of success in such an attempt. The opposition was based, not on the impropriety of the assumption of State debts by the general government, but on the necessity of resisting the dictation of foreign bankers. The foreign bankers were only trying to collect their debts, and this story, colored by tradition, still injures American credit, especially in England.

In 1841 Mr. Harrison became President, and called an extra session of Congress for May 31st of that year. This session was held under Mr. Tyler, and was marked by some of the worst legislation ever passed since the Constitution was adopted. Mr. Tyler had become a whig, though formerly a democrat. To this he owed his place on the ticket, and it soon seemed to the whigs that with President Harrison they had lost the victory, for which they had waited so long and worked so hard.

The first act of the session was the repeal of

the Independent Treasury Act. Mr. Clay had proposed three other important measures for the session: a national bank, an increase of duties, and a land distribution bill. Before any of these latter could be acted on, a Bankruptcy Act was introduced by the Senator from Mississippi. This act was bargained off for the Bank Act and the Distribution Act, and the three went through together.

Benton says of the Bankrupt Act: " It applied to all persons in debt—allowed them to commence their proceedings in the district of their own residence no matter how lately removed to it—allowed constructive notice to creditors in newspapers—declared the abolition of the debt where effects were surrendered and fraud not proved." He says that the number of men who had failed and wanted to get clear of encumbrances for starting anew was estimated at one hundred thousand.

The Land Distribution Bill was the new form of the bill for assuming the State debts. The income from public lands (less than one and a half millions in 1846) was to be divided amongst the States to help them pay their debts ($200,000). It contained a proviso that if duties above 20 per cent. should ever be laid, this act should be suspended. When the tariff was passed it contained a proviso that it should *not* suspend the Land Distribution Act, but it was vetoed.

The Compromise Tariff had cut down the revenue from customs without providing any other resource. During its first years it had produced a surplus, but its last years, falling in with the "hard times," had left a deficiency. The debt increased as follows :

<pre>
Jan. 1, 1840 .... $5,125,077.63
Jan. 1, 1841 ....   6,737,398.00
Jan. 1, 1842 .... 15,028,486.37
July 1, 1843 .... 27,203,450.69
</pre>

From this time it decreased until 1847.

As for the bank, President Tyler took a whim in regard to the word "Bank." He wanted it to be called the Fiscal Agent, or something "fiscal." He vetoed two bills passed for incorporating such an institution, the relations of which to the

Treasury promised great mischief, if either had gone into operation.

The Treasury, being still unable to pay specie by the failure of a loan authorized at the special Session, began to pay congressmen in Treasury notes. Benton caused one of the checks to be protested in January, 1842. Specie payments were soon after resumed by the government, and did not cease until 1862.

Two tariffs having been vetoed in 1842, because they provided for the distribution of the revenue from public lands, a third was passed, which raised duties above twenty per cent., and so suspended distribution.

In 1843 the Bankruptcy Act was repealed, having been found in its operation to be worse for debtors than for creditors. The man who availed himself of it could obtain no further credit.

Thus the legislation of these years came to nothing but the new tariff, and the excitement of party contests only served to keep the country anxious, and to restrain it from entering on the new career. The government was now, however, fixed in the hard-money system, and the sub-treasury system. by which it was so entirely severed from the money-market that, fortunately, the bankers and merchants could afford to laugh at the insignificance of the government on their arena. Its position was never so strong or sound as when, in this point of view, it was most ridiculous.

The nation had too much energy and too vast opportunities to long remain inactive. From 1844 on, things began to mend. Banks began to expand once more with the growth of trade. Prices advanced, and in 1846 a new tariff once more relaxed the restrictions of trade. In 1847 the failure of the crops in Europe gave a market for bread-stuffs, of which nearly $37\frac{1}{2}$ million dollars' worth were exported. The total exports of that year were larger than for any preceding year, 158,000,000. The imports of specie exceeded the exports by more than 22,000,000. The abolition of the corn laws in England opened a permanent market for the surplus product of the West, and the settlement of that portion of the country took new form. As soon as the famine was felt in Ireland, its population began to apply the only true cure of the trouble—emigration— and the revolutionary struggles on the continent in the year 1848 contributed to increase emigration to this country by their failure.

IMMIGRATION.

	FROM IRE- LAND.	TOTAL.
1845	44,821	114,371
1846	51,752	154,416
1847	105,536	234,968
1848	112,934	226,527
1849	159,398	297,024

The extension of railroads kept pace with the other developments, which it in turn helped to multiply.

MILEAGE OF RAILROADS.

	WESTERN STATES.	TOTAL.
1845	374	4,633
1846	419	4,930
1847	608	5,578
1848	679	5,996
1849	727	7,365
1850	1,276	9,021
1851	1,846	10,982

Finally, the discovery of gold in California in 1847 added another powerful element to the industrial development of the time.

PERIOD FROM 1850–1862.

The outlook in 1850, with abundant emigration, a new empire arising on the Pacific, the prospect of becoming the granary as well as the cotton-field of the world, ship-building increasing year by year, and no cloud of war or political disturbance visible, was very flattering. The only hindrances to a speedy realization of these golden dreams were want of capital and want of technical and scientific training. Railroad building at the West must, in the nature of things, outstrip the settlement of the region. It is the chief form in which capital is applied to the settlement of the country, but evidently it is a case in which the returns from the investment cannot be immediate, and in every such case in which the supply goes ahead of the demand there is especial need of care, foresight, and judgment.

For the supply of capital there was recourse

naturally to the older countries. The injury done to American credit in 1837–40 had hardly yet been healed, but in 1854 it was estimated by the Secretary of the Treasury, on reports called for by him, that there were 200,000,000 dollars worth of State, railway, and other bonds and bank-stock held abroad.* In 1857 the amount of English capital invested here was estimated at 400,000,000. While naturally turning to the older countries for supplies of capital, there has always been a certain prejudice here against foreign investors. Our "foreign indebtedness" has been a cause of serious and sincere anxiety to many, but the more we can borrow, so long as we know how to invest it productively, the better, and our credit—our power to borrow abroad—is the possession which it is most essential for us to preserve intact.

CAPITAL AND CURRENCY.

Our other resource when straitened for capital, the one to which we had betaken ourselves before, was now also employed—a multiplication of

---

* He said that the amount was not greater in 1853 than in 1829.

the paper representatives of capital. Capital is that portion of all the previous product of a nation which at any given time is available for new production. This will be a certain amount of tilled land, houses, buildings, stock, tools, food, clothing, roads, bridges, etc., etc., which have been made and are ready for use in producing, transporting, and exchanging new products. These things are all the product of labor, and require time for their production. Nothing but labor spent upon them can produce others, and time is required for this labor to issue in new and increased possessions. Currency only serves to distribute this capital into the proper hands for its most efficient application to new production. Banks, it must be repeated, only facilitate the transfer of capital from hands where it is idle, or is distributed in too small quantities, into hands by which it will be usefully employed, being collected in the necessary amounts. Currency, therefore, is not capital, any more than ships are freight; it is only a labor-saving machine for making easy transfers. Banks do not create wealth, they only facilitate its creation by distributing capital in the most advantageous manner. If, therefore, currency is multiplied, it is a delusion to suppose that capital is multiplied, or, if "money is plenty," by artificial increase of its representatives, it is only like increasing the number of tickets which give a claim on a specific stock of goods—the ticket-holders would be deceived and could, in the end, only get a proportional dividend out of the stock. If banks not only lend capital but also lend " coined credit," some time or other a liquidation must come, there must be an effort to touch the capital which the notes pretend to convey. Then it is found that they represent nothing ; then " credit breaks down," and there must be a settlement, a liquidation, a dividend, and a new start. We do not get away from the facts at all. The real amount of capital which we possess is divided up, and we have to make up our minds that we possess only 50 or 75 per cent. of what we thought we possessed. We put smaller figures for everything, and reconcile ourselves to smaller hopes, but the experience is soon forgotten, and the old process of inflation and delusion begins again.

Some have wondered that we go on in this way with a grand crisis only once in twenty years, while the oldest and most prudent nations have one every ten years. The explanation no doubt is, that the future which we discount so freely honors our drafts on it. Six months' restraint avails to set us right, and our credit creations, as anticipations of the future product of labor, become solidified. So long as we understand that we have anticipated future production, and must apply that production to make good the anticipations, we run on without very great risk, but whenever we lose our heads in the intoxication of our own achievements, look on the credit anticipations, which are only fictitious capital, as if they were real, use them as already earned, build other credit expansions upon them, do away with our value money and export it to purchase articles of luxurious consumption, then we bring a convulsion and a downfall. The mistake is then realized, the lesson is taken to heart for a little while, but a new generation grows up which forgets or never knew the old experience, and the mistake is repeated. The relations of trade are often spoken of as a machine, and such indeed they ought to be—a complex machine, with parts so regulated that it can go on at any speed and for any length of time, without danger of anything more than an occasional and temporary derangement; but this reckless, although skilful, extension of groundless credit is more like the performance of the juggler who keeps first three, then four, then five, and so on, balls in the air at once. If he goes on continually increasing the number, it is physically certain that he will sooner or later miss one of them, and the whole will fall to the ground in confusion.

BANK EXPANSION.

The bank expansion from 1848–1851 was as follows:

	CIRC.	DEP.	SPEC.
1848	128,500,000	108,200,000	46,300,000
1849	114,700,000	91,100,000	43,600,000
1850	131,300,000	109,500,000	45,300,000
1851	155,100,000	128,900,000	48,600,000

These figures are not as trustworthy as one might wish. They represent the status on January 1, or as near that date as possible, and minor fluctuations are not represented. A well-defined movement, however, was apparent before 1851. The currency set towards the financial centres, country banks keeping their balances generally in New York. These balances were required in the fall, and the withdrawal of them produced con traction and stringency at that season. Weekly bank statements were not made by any banks until August 6, 1853, when the New York banks began the custom, and others gradually followed.

In 1851 there was an export of gold with unfavorable exchange, and a drain upon the banks. As no reports were published, the extent of this drain was not known, but a writer in 1857 states that it amounted to twelve millions in June and July, and that the stock remaining in the New York banks was only six millions. The consequence was a sharp contraction and great suffering, which finally caused the Secretary of the Treasury to buy bonds for the relief of the market.

The same course of events, more or less marked, occurred throughout this period. Currency flowed to New York during the summer, was loaned on call (interest being paid for deposits), was withdrawn in the fall, producing contraction of loans and stringency.

It was asserted at the time that the worse the currency the more mobile it will be, and the assertion is true; but it is still more true that when the currency is *unequally* bad it will flow to the financial centres. Gold was being exported as a commodity all the time, but the exchanges showed the pressure of the redundant paper at New York, and caused a demand of gold for export with chronic overtrading. This was, according to the doctrines of the Bullion Report (discussed in Chapter II), a warning that the issues were excessive. The New York banks of course felt the weight of the evil. The warning came to them in actual experience, but the pressure of the country issues, which were never regulated by the exchanges at all, continued, and the metropolitan banks do not seem to have taken measures to restrain them.

The usury law, although disregarded in private practice, made it impossible for the banks to *publish* a usurious rate, and thus control discounts by this means. They could only exert a direct contraction on their issues and loans whenever the drain upon them made it necessary, and the pressure of this was, of course, most severe in the city itself.

STATE OF AFFAIRS IN 1853-4.

In 1853 the fears of war in Europe produced anxiety with regard to financial affairs both in England and here. The bank rate was at 5 per cent. throughout the autumn in London. Railroad building here amounted to 2,452 miles in that year. Stock speculation was unusually active throughout the winter and spring, and prices were high. Undefined fears of the effects of a European war led to greater restraint in loans during the summer, and stocks suffered a fall. Many of the earlier speculations in exports to California had proved disastrous, and their results now accumulated. The discovery of a fraudulent issue of two millions of New York and New Haven Railroad stock was followed by similar discoveries in regard to some other stocks, and the result was a panic on the exchange.

	CIR.	DEP.	SPECIE.
Jan. 1, 1854.....	$204,600,000	188,100,000	59,400,000
" 1855.....	186.900,000	190,400,000	53,900,000

" The prosperity which prevailed almost universally up to the middle of last year [1853] had made our business men so confident in their own strength that all classes had expanded their engagements far beyond the protection of their own resources, and were exposed to the storm which began to gather on every side. The first great shock to credit was the discovery of the Schuyler fraud, which brought to a stand nearly all those works of internal improvement for whose successful completion a large share of public confidence was so necessary. From that moment sacrifice began .   .   . The war in Europe created more or less money pressure abroad, and capitalists there were less liberal in their investments here, at a time when their assistance would have been most acceptable." The wheat crop was small and the cotton production lessened by the pressure of cholera. " A worse panic began in the interior, and especially in the West and North-west. In Ohio, Indiana, Illinois, Michigan, Wisconsin, Iowa, and Missouri, and, to some extent, in the States on the south of the Ohio, a large circulation of bank-notes, mostly of the free banks, had been obtained through expenditures for railroad purposes, and the general expansion of business. When the contraction began, this circulation came in rapidly, and found the banks wholly unprepared to meet it. . . . All the banks which held balances at the East drew for them, and borrowed to the extent of their credit besides, while between twenty and thirty, perhaps more, of institutions which were really solvent were compelled to suspend payment. A large number of private bankers were carried down in the crash, and the distress became general. . . . During all this severe pressure in the money market, and general disturbance of public confidence, it is a cause for congratulations, that the mercantile community have stood the trial so nobly. . . . The reason of this may be found in the increased supply of metallic currency remaining in the country. Over one hundred millions in gold coin have been added to the circulation of the United States since the discovery of gold in California. Thus, although the rates of interest have been high for nearly eighteen months, there has been no such *scarcity* of money as has been felt in former periods of commercial embarrassment, . . . The banks have been severely tried, but those in our largest cities (with the exceptions before noticed) have mostly stood the shock unmoved." *

CRISIS OF 1857.

In 1856 railroad building once more extended to 3,642 miles, nearly all in the Western States. The spring of 1857 being very late, and the prospect for the crops bad, many prophecies of trouble were published, but, as the season turned out well, the fears were dispelled, and scarcely any one seems to have apprehended the coming trouble. A fall in stocks, however, took place in the summer, to the great embarrassment of the large number of persons who held call loans for which they had given stock collat-

* Merch. Mag. : December, 1854.

eral. The first actual shock was the failure, on the 24th of August, of the Ohio Life and Trust Co., which had borrowed largely on call in New York, and loaned the funds where they were not immediately available. The liabilities were about seven millions. The credit of this institution had been very high, and its failure was followed by a general desire to test the foundations of credit. Such an attempt could not do otherwise than produce a general downfall.

	1855–6.		1856–7.	
	Per ct. specie to cir.	Per ct. specie to cir. and deposits.	Per ct. specie to cir.	Per ct. specie to cir. and deposits.
Eastern States........	14.	8.4	13.4	8.18
Middle States........	37.35	11.79	37.2	11.5
Western States........	21.5	15.8	18.3	13.2
Southern States......	50.4	28.7	41.6	24.2
South-western States.	27.4	15.4	21.7	13.2
Average.	30.13	16.01	26.44	14.056

At this period no rule seems to have governed issues save to keep one-third of the circulation in specie, and in some States even this dwindled down to one tenth or one-twelfth. Such a rule, however, is entirely fallacious, as any other arbitrary rule of reserve must be, and it proved in the time of trial that there was no strength to endure any shock.

The New York banks expanded and contracted in 1857 as follows:

	LOANS.	SPECIE.	CIRCULATION.	DEPOSITS.
Jan. 3, 1857.	109,100,000	11,100,000	8,600,000	95,800,000
Apr. 4, 1857.	114,800,000	11,500,000	8,800,coo	97,300,000
July 3, 1857.	115,0c0,000	12,800 000	8,900,000	98,800,000
Aug. 8, 1857.	122,000,000	11,700,000	8,900,000	94,400,000
Aug. 29, 1857.	116,500,000	9,200,000	8,600,000	84,800,000
Oct. 17, 1857.	97,200,000	7,800,000	8,000,000	52,800,000
Nov. 28, 1857.	94,900,000	24,300,000	6,500,000	79,500,000
Dec. 12, 1857.	96,500,000	26,000,000	6,300,000	75,300,000

The loss of the steamship "Central America" with over a million of treasure enhanced the stringency.

A large number of failures of banks and firms, especially brokers, produce dealers, and persons depending on Western collections, took place in September. Bills on the seaboard were hardly obtainable in the interior at 10 and 15 per cent. premium. On the 12th and 13th of September the banks of Philadelphia, Washington, Baltimore, and many interior towns suspended. Stocks fell 40 or 50 per cent., and 20,000 persons were thrown out of work in New York City within a fortnight. The universal demand of the banks was for relief by expansion, but the contrary course was pursued with the utmost vigor. There was indeed no room for expansion. The utmost resources had been employed in good times, and there was no reserve strength. The hoarding of currency which takes place at all such times still further enhanced the trouble.

The "panic" immediately followed, but, as was said often at the time, it broke out first inside the banks. When it was seen that no help was to be expected, and that the banks of New York and Boston were likely to suspend, there began a run on the deposits. On the 13th of October the New York banks (with one exception) suspended. They were followed in a few days by the Boston banks, and by the others who had hitherto held out, with only a few exceptions.

Exchange now fell to 100 and even to 90, and bills were not saleable. Exports almost ceased, and gold began to move this way. The increase in the stock in bank appears in the above table. The New York banks agreed to take country bills at par, interest to be charged after December 1st. The country issues, thus encouraged, formed remittances, which were redeemed by drafts against the produce which they caused to be forwarded.

The state of things was better in New Orleans than elsewhere. The banks there had been stronger than anywhere else. Of nine banks, only four suspended at all, and they only for a few days.

The Pennsylvania legislature authorized the suspension until May. In New York the Constitution forbade the legislature to authorize suspension of specie payments either directly or indirectly. The judges of the Supreme Court, however, met and agreed not to grant any injunction unless the bank was insolvent or guilty of fraud. Thus even a constitutional provision proved as ineffectual as any law had ever been—- I will not say to prevent a suspension, for the suspension was inevitable, but to enforce a

system of banking which would not lead to suspension, and the plan of securing circulation by
pledge of stocks proved unavailing to allay a
panic.

The Secretary of the Treasury interfered
again in this case by purchasing bonds.

In the inquiries which were made as to the
causes of the crisis, the state of the currency was
generally recognized as the root of the trouble.
The over-trading, over-importation, stock speculation, extravagance, etc., were generally ascribed
to this, but there were some who found other
causes for the crisis. One writer, after enumerat-
ing these secondary incidents as causes, gave
another, as the immediate occasion, and that was
—the telegraph. He thought nothing could
cure the trouble permanently but a protective
tariff. Others ascribed it almost entirely to the
payment of interest on deposits, and some States
passed laws forbidding this. The payment of
interest on deposits is like every other business
risk,—the man who undertakes it must measure
his own ability to do it, and the lender or depositor must judge whether the person or institu-

tion to whom he lends can do what is undertaken.

The newspapers were also filled with homilies
on extravagance and exhortations to "confidence," but the matter is, in a panic, that the confidence, so long entertained, is now recognized
as unfounded. It is the force of the truth which
makes the trouble, and how can it avail to try to
make men still delude themselves? In general,
however, the fact was recognized, that the great
means of keeping the business of the country
sound, so far as any thing can control haste for
riches, is to keep the currency sound, and that the
only way to keep the currency sound is to have
it actively and actually converted into coin.
Convertibility is not enough, if it is only nominal,
and if no one tests its reality because public
opinion frowns on such an act, or bank displeas-
ure follows it.

The pressure passed away in the course of the
winter. The liquidation was rapid, and by
spring business was again in motion. The New
York banks resumed on the 12th of December,
and others followed gradually and informally. In

the spring money was very easy, and United States Treasury notes were sold at an average of 4½ per cent. interest.

In the meantime the surplus revenue had been applied to the reduction of the public debt, which, in 1853, was 67,000,000, and in 1857 (July 1st), 29,000,000. In March, 1857, the tariff was reduced to an average of 20 per cent. on dutiable imports.

ALTERATION OF THE COINAGE.

The law of 1834, having underrated silver in the coinage, had the effects described above (page 110). In March, 1853, a law was passed,* similar to the English law of 1816, to obviate the difficulty of throwing either one or the other metal out of circulation. On this plan, silver is purposely overrated in the coinage so that it is worth more as coin than as metal. There is, therefore, a loss in exporting or melting it. The silver dollar was not altered, but it had disappeared and ceased to be a coin of the country. The fractional coins were made to weigh: 50 cts.,

* See p. 292.

192 grains standard (nine-tenths fine) ; 25 cts., 96 grains. At the rate of 15.625 to 1 for silver to gold, two half dollars are worth .9533 of a gold dollar. This fractional silver was coined by the government out of purchased metal, and not upon demand of holders of bullion. These coins were therefore made legal tender only for sums less than five dollars. It is evident that this was no depreciation of the coinage.

The reaction from the crisis of 1857 was so rapid and complete that its lesson was only partially learned. Things went on until the war very much in the old way. The state of the currency is sufficiently shown by the following table :

ABOUT	CIRC.	DEPOSITS.	LOANS.	SPECIE.
Jan. 1, 1857	214,700,000	230,300,000	684,400,000	58,300,000
1858	155,200,000	185,900,000	583,100,000	74,400,000
1859	193,300,000	259,500,000	657,100,000	104,500,000
1860	207,100,000	253,800,000	691,900,000	83,500,000
1861	202,000,000	257,200,000	696,700,000	87,600,000
1862	183,700,000	296,300,000	646,300,000	102,100,000
1863	238,600,000	393,600,000	648,600,000	101,200,000

In March, 1858, Mr. Balfour, of Boston, classified the note issues of the country as follows :

Notes for	$1	to the amount of		7,000,000
"	2	"	"	4,000,000
"	3	"	"	3,000,000
"	5	"	"	15,000,000
"	10	"	"	5,000,000
"	20	"	"	13,000,000
"	50	"	"	12,000,000
"	100	"	"	·8,000,000
"	500	"	"	35,000,000
"	1,000	"	"	30,000,000
"	5,000	"	"	2,000,000
Total........................				134,000,000

THE CURRENCY AT THE OUTBREAK OF THE WAR.

No year in American history has been more prosperous than was the year 1860. The cotton crop of that year was unprecedented, reaching 4,600,000 bales. The grain crops, although not so extraordinary, were very good. After the election in November the attitude of the Southern States created great anxiety in commercial circles. Business was contracted, imports declined, and finances were arranged in anticipation of a coming storm. Foreign exchanges fell, and gold began to be imported, prices being low and imports suspended.

During the winter, the Southern members of Congress took their departure, and, after the inauguration of President Lincoln, increased revenues being required, the tariff was revised. The opposition to protection being withdrawn, this tariff revision, undertaken for revenue, was carried out in the interest of protection, and in a manner hostile to revenue, thus weakening the country at the very moment when it needed its utmost strength. This result being at once experienced, an effort was made at the extra session of Congress to secure a modification of the protective features, but without success. The country was once more embarked on the protective policy, which received an extension in the following years unexampled save by the most unenlightened nations on earth.

The opinion being circulated that the war was to be short, and that the people would not submit to taxation, the financial measures of the session were confined to the provision for 50,000,-000 of demand notes, 250,000,000 of $7\frac{3}{10}$ Treasury notes to run three years, and a six per cent. loan of 250,000,000 to fund the Treasury notes.

A property tax was apportioned amongst the States, but part of it was repealed as impracticable, part was paid by charges for sums expended in fitting out troops, and it produced no active revenue to the general government. Its nett result was to establish the machinery which was afterwards used in collecting internal revenue.

The people were in the meantime contracting their expenses, closing up their engagements, practising economy, and in general adjusting their affairs to war circumstances in the manner which common-sense dictated. The banks were in a conservative position, and the weak ones were strengthening themselves to the utmost of their ability. The imports were small and the exports large, for, although cotton was no longer an available export, the grain crop was large and sold at good prices. The exports of merchandise exceeded the imports by 67,000,000, and the imports of specie exceeded the exports by 16,000,-000. This movement began in November, 1860, and lasted until December, 1861. Evidently the natural laws which bring to every financial situation its own cure were here in full operation. In the fall of 1861 the government borrowed 100,-000,000 in gold of the banks, in two instalments, and 50,000,000 more in its own paper.

Such was the situation when Congress met in December, 1861. Never did any man have such an opportunity to win immortality as a financier as was now offered to Mr. Chase. The situation had at this moment few difficulties. The people were less sanguine that the war would be short than they had been in the previous summer. They had contracted their expenses to the lowest point, and production was reduced to the necessary supply for consumption. They held their disengaged capital ready to the demand of the government, if it should act with promptness and decision, and support its own credit. Nor was it the capital of the country alone which was available. War taxes must and always do trench upon income. It was the active productive power of the nation, which might be turned to war making, which was the great resource. The nation was not only willing to be taxed, but itself understood generally that only when it was being taxed could it give full credit to its own paper promises. The Congress, moreover, was ready to give to the Secretary all he asked. If he had been the minister of the Czar he could not have disposed more absolutely of the national resources. All that was needed was a firm, clear, bold policy, showing that he understood himself and the situation.

The Treasury report presented no such policy. It did not take the lead at all. It discussed government paper disparagingly, suggested a national banking system tentatively. It only showed that the nation was drifting into financial embarrassments for want of a policy. The real financial question of the day was: whether we should carry on the war on specie currency, low prices, and small imports, or on paper issues, high prices, and heavy imports. The alternative was not understood because no one distinctly comtemplated the latter course, but it was sure to be the result of drifting under no policy.

The complications with England about the Trent case came upon the reaction of disappointment at the message and report, and in December gold began to be exported. On the 17th of that month the New York banks stoutly resolved that suspension was unnecessary, but the drain upon their gold went on as follows:

December	7	....	42,300,000
"	14	....	39,400,000
"	21	....	36,800,000
"	28	....	29,300,000
January	4	....	23,900,000

From this time it began to increase again, and was 30,000,000 on March 8.

SUSPENSION.

In the last days of December, 1861, all the banks suspended. This they did without any earnest attempts to avoid it, and certainly without any necessity. Instead of regarding a suspension as a calamity to be submitted to only after years of war, when the national resources should be actually exhausted (as the suspension of the Bank of England proved that it is), many looked upon it as the natural preparation for war.

This suspension greatly complicated the situation. Gold rose to a premium of one or two per cent., at which it remained until April. The 202,000,000 of bank paper, or rather the 150,-000,000 in the Northern States, proved the stumbling block in the way of all sound financial measures. The influx of the precious metals in the previous year together with the supply from California, and the amount previously existing, gave 200 or 250 millions of gold in the Northern States on the 1st of December, 1861, together with 150,000,000 of bank paper, an amount amply sufficient to float government loans, or to allow 200,000,000 of government notes to be issued, if the bank-notes had been withdrawn. This specie, however, could not stay in the country, if the bank-notes remained, filling the channels of circulation, and not subject to re-demption, so soon as the government made any additions.

The specie borrowed by the government from the banks, and expended, would have found its way back to the banks if unimpeded in its cir-culation, that is, if it had been the only currency; but, with irredeemable notes afloat and gold at a premium, this gold was withdrawn and hoarded, and only appeared again to be sold at the high premium two or three years after.

The government could not borrow more gold, of the banks, having exhausted their stock, and, if it borrowed further, must take irredeemable notes which might be multiplied to any amount. This was made the great argument for the Legal Tender Act, and was another way in which the bank-notes clogged the movements of the government.

The economy of convertible paper issues is assumed and repeated by many persons who have never taken the pains to analyze that economy to see wherein it consists, and how great it is. I am not prepared to take "total abstinence" ground against paper issues, because I believe that they may be made useful and economical, though we have not yet learned how to do it, but whenever the account is made up of the advantage and cost to the American *public* of their bank issues, there will be a heavy charge on account of the loss and mischief they caused at the outbreak of the war, to say nothing of the previous losses from panics and commercial crises which they helped to bring about.

It would be tedious and unnecessary to follow here the various financial manœuvres of the winter of 1861 and 1862. It is a simple record of temporary makeshifts alternating with one another, frittering away the credit of the government, disregarding its true resource in the patriotism of the people, and offering large profits to those who handled the government loans. Of the banks, those which clung to the old-fashioned principles of finance, disapproved of the course things were taking, and refused to participate, found themselves losing. Those which fell in with the new order of things made enormous profits.

THE LEGAL TENDER ACT.

The embarrassments of the government becoming greater and greater, the bill for an issue of legal tender notes was hastily prepared and offered in the House. Mr. E. G. Spaulding, of Buffalo,* claims to have been the author of this

* Financial History of the War.

act, and no counter-claimant has ever arisen. The act was earnestly opposed by some of the oldest and best members of both houses, but it was pressed as " necessary," and forced through with the energy and decision which, earlier in the session, so much needed to be exerted in another direction. So far as I know, Mr. Owen Lovejoy is the only man who is on record as having put his finger on the irredeemable bank-notes as the greatest evil in the situation. The bill was signed on the 25th February, 1862.

This act was passed, as the debate shows, as a temporary war measure. On the part of its advocates, Mr. Thaddeus Stevens at the head, it was urged and probably believed, that the legal tender clause would prevent depreciation and give credit to the notes.

Pelatiah Webster wrote in 1791: " The fatal error, that the credit and currency of the continental money could be kept up and supported by acts of compulsion, entered so deep into the minds of Congress, and of all departments of administration through the States, that no considerations of justice, religion, or policy, or even experience of its utter inefficacy, could eradicate it. It seemed to be a kind of obstinate delirium, totally deaf to every argument drawn from justice and right, from its natural tendency and mischief, from common sense, and even common safety. This ruinous principle was continued in practice for five successive years, and appeared in all shapes and forms, *i. e.* in tender acts, in limitations of prices, in awful and threatening declarations, in penal laws with dreadful and ruinous punishments, and in every other way that could be devised, and all executed with a relentless severity, by the highest authorities then in being, viz., by Congress, by assemblies and conventions of the States, by committees of inspection (whose powers in those days were nearly sovereign), and even by military force ; and, though men of all descriptions stood trembling before this monster of force, without daring to lift a hand against it, during all this period, yet its unrestrained energy proved ever ineffectual to its purposes, but in every instance increased the evils it was designed to remedy, and destroyed the benefits it was intended to promote. At best its utmost effect was like that of water sprinkled on a blacksmith's forge, which indeed deadens the flame for a moment, but never fails to increase the heat and force of the internal fire. Many thousand families of full and easy fortune were ruined by these fatal measures, and lie in ruins to this day, without the least benefit to the country, or to the great and noble cause in which we were then engaged.

"I do not mention these things from any pleasure I have in opening the wounds of my country, or exposing its errors, but with a hope that our fatal mistakes may be a caution and warning to future financiers, who may live and act in any country which may happen to be in circumstances similar to ours at that time."

Here was a warning from our own history of what must be the tendency of any legal tender law, whether more or less stringent. So far from sustaining, it could only injure the credit of the paper.

The precedent of the English Bank Restriction was frequently and erroneously referred to, and inferences were drawn which were simply

ignorant. The spirit of the debate was that of
panic. The finances had been allowed to drift
into a serious condition, and then, instead of applying cool and calm reason to find out and correct mistakes, recourse was taken to the last
and most desperate resources. The financial interests of a great nation for an indefinite future
were staked upon a desperate resource, to tide
over a temporary exigency. When the lessons
of history were quoted they were answered by
the flag and the eagle. When caution was
urged in view of possible future exigencies, it
was answered by prophecies of military success and denunciations of rebels. When the
need of deliberation was urged, it was answered
by clamor in regard to the necessities of the
government. When it was said that irredeemable
paper had always wrought ruin, it was answered
that our resources were unlimited, and that these
precedents did not make a rule for us. When it
was prophesied that the paper would depreciate,
and that we should not be able to retrace our
steps, the prophets of evil were indignantly
pointed to the "pledged faith" of the United

States, and asked if they thought that would be violated. The inference that the notes must be made legal tender, because the government needed money, was never analyzed, and its fal-lacy never shown. The question whether it is necessary to issue legal tender notes is a question not of law, but of political economy, and political economy emphatically declares that it never can be necessary. The proposition involves an absurdity. Whatever strength a nation has is weakened by issuing legal tender notes.* One might as well say that it is necessary to open the veins of a weak man who has a heavy physical task to perform. All history shows that paper money with a forced circulation is not a temporary resource. It cannot be taken up and laid down as we choose. It is a mischief easily done but most difficult to cure.†

* See the extracts from the debate of 1819, especially Lord Grenville's speech, p. 296.

† See Chapter III.

EFFECTS OF LEGAL TENDER ISSUES.

The notes were first issued in April, 1862. Gold began to rise and to be exported. The following table from the "Merchants' Magazine," for July, 1862, shows how immediate and direct was the effect.

(Five figures omitted.)

	GOV. PAYT'S.	BANK DEPOSITS.	SPECIE.	EXPORT SP CIE.	GOLD. PREMIUM.	EXCH. ON LONDON.
April 12	4.6	93.7	34.5	1.5	1¾	111¾
" 19	12.5	95.1	34.6	.6	1¾	112
" 26	24.7	101.8	35 2	1.1	1½	112½
May 3	22.7	109.6	35.1	.7	2¾	113¼
" 10	17.1	115.5	32.2	1.5	3¼	.114
" 17	9.8	120.0	30.2	1.0	3¾	114
" 24	10.4	122.6	30.6	.9	3¼	115
" 31	6.8	125.4	34.3	.8	3⅝	114¾
June 7	6.5	125.5	31.2	1.6	4¼	115
" 14	9.8	125.6	31.1	2.0	6⅞	118
" 23	8.4	126.6	31.0	3.1	7	121

High gold and exchange stimulated exports, for high nominal prices were realized, but, as home prices advanced, and the foreign prices of export were governed by foreign circumstances, these large returns proved fallacious, and the heavy pressure on the Western agricultural interest began, which led to an outburst, in 1873, of loud and ill-directed complaints. Heavy imports followed upon heavy exports of merchandise and gold, and the paper inflation and fictitious prosperity enabled people to pay heavy duties, large gold premium, and high exchange for the imported articles. The mills, forges, and factories were active in working for the government, while the men who ate the grain and wore the clothing were active in destroying, and not in creating capital. This, to be sure, was war. It is what war means, but it cannot bring prosperity.

One immediate effect of the Legal Tender Act was to destroy our credit abroad.. Stocks were sent home for sale, and, as Bagehot shows, * Lombard Street was closed to a nation which had adopted legal tender paper money. No sales of bonds could be made in England until the war closed, and the amount of legal tender to be issued was finally fixed by facts. The loans at home were scarcely more successful. Much was said in Congress about the disgrace of "shinning" through Wall Street to borrow money for national use, and a foolish pride of seeing the bonds quoted at par, led to such restrictions on

* Preface to the last edition of the "English Constitution."

the Secretary that he was obliged to resort to the most disadvantageous transactions with lenders, and to continue paper issues until a six per cent. bond sold at par indeed, but for a currency worth from 60 to 70 cents on the dollar. The notes he paid out to government creditors were accumulated in banks, and then deposited again in the United States Treasury at five per cent.

By August all specie had disappeared from circulation, and postage-stamps and private note-issues took its place. In July a bill was passed for issuing stamps as fractional currency, but in March, 1863, another act was passed providing for an issue of 50,000,000 in notes for fractional parts of a dollar—not legal tender. For many years the actual issue was only 30,000,000, the amount of silver fractional coins in circulation in the North, east of the Rocky Mountains, when the war broke out. In 1872 this issue was forced up to between 40 and 50,000,000, producing a redundancy and enhancing retail prices.

The Legal Tender Act provided for funding the notes in six per cent. 5-20 bonds. Very few were so funded even with money at four per cent., an instructive fact for those who now hope to fund the outstanding notes by simply allowing it to be done. However, this fixed the price of a six-per-cent. bond at par in paper, and, as the Secretary might not sell below the market price, he could not negotiate with bankers on terms which allowed them a profit. This clause was, therefore, repealed.

The interest on the bonds was payable in gold, duties being payable in gold, but the 50,000,000 of notes issued in August, 1861, and 10,000,000 in February, 1862, were receivable for all dues. They were at a premium just less than gold, for the payment of duties, and very little gold came in until these notes had all been paid in. During 1862, the government bought gold to pay interest. It was not until 1863 that the popular sales of bonds afforded a steady resource of means of payment, and the duties produced a gold income for paying interest. The advance of prices, however, had vastly increased the expenditure of the government, and the sum total of the debt is increased to an amount, which it would be idle to try to estimate, by the paper inflation.

On the 25th of February, 1863, the National Bank Act was passed, but it did not go into operation, and did not affect the situation, until two or three years afterwards.

On the 23d of March, 1863, Congress passed the 900,000,000 Loan Act, allowing the Secretary to borrow that sum in ten-forty bonds at *not more* than six per cent., *or* 400,000,000 of it in Treasury notes at not over six per cent., legal tender, redeemable in paper in three years, *or* 150,000,000 of it by issuing legal tender notes. All the old notes which were fundable in six per cent. bonds were called in, and exchanged for new notes not so fundable, and the Secretary was allowed to sell bonds below the market price.

Gold being at 140–150, that is, the paper dollar worth 65 or 70 cts., 75,000,000 ten-forties were taken at about par at six per cent. The Secretary was now led to try the ten-forties at 5 per cent., but the currency was not sufficiently depreciated to float them at or near par, and they were not taken. He then used his alternatives, issuing 175 millions one and two year Treasury notes. Gold rose to 200–220 or above, making the paper worth 45 or 50 cts., at which point the 5 per cent. ten-forties floated. The amount sold up to October 31st, 1865, was $172,770,100. Mr. Spaulding reckons up the paper issues which acted more or less as currency, on January 30th, 1864, at $1,125,877,034. 812,000,000 bore no interest. He disapproves of the 900,000,000 Loan Act on account of the discretion it allowed to the Secretary, and the inflation to which it led; but a policy like that of the Legal Tender Act collects errors as it advances, and those who inaugurate it should know that they can never control it, nor throw off responsibility for its ultimate consequences.

June 17th, 1864, Congress forbade time rates for gold. The effect was to enhance the premium, and, on July 2d, the law was repealed. The Legislature of New York had previously attempted to stop speculation in gold by forbidding banks to loan on bills of foreign exchange, one of the most legitimate operations in banking.

By an act of June 30, 1864, the amount of greenbacks is fixed at 400,000,000, and " such additional sum, not exceeding 50,000,000, as may be temporarily required for the redemption of temporary loans."

THE TARIFF.

By successive amendments during the years 1861–1866, the tariff had been extended to cover over 1,500 different articles, and had been adjusted and readjusted, by those who had the manipulation of it, until it had established an iron-bound system of protection. The duties collected in 1865 were 54 per cent. of the dutiable imports. Such a rate was hostile to revenue. It produced 84.9 millions.*

The internal taxes had also been multiplied on what Mr. Wells aptly described as the Donnybrook Fair principle—wherever you see an article, tax it. In 1866 the receipts from internal taxes were 309.2 millions, and from customs 179,000,000.

The patriotism and devotion with which the American people recognized the necessity of taxation and submitted to it, are not surpassed in

* Finance Report, 1872.

history; but their sacrifices were abused on the one hand by interested parties, so that the taxes were paid without accomplishing the object, and, on the other hand, their sacrifices were wasted by unscientific taxation.

The increase of internal taxation was made a pretext for increase of duties, but when, under Mr. Wells' recommendations, internal taxes were gradually abolished, no reduction of duties followed. After 1870 some reductions were made, but now, in 1874, with a threatened deficit of revenue, the great need of the country is for some man to introduce thorough and comprehensive reforms in the interest of revenue—to perform the rôle of Sir Robert Peel in the early forties.

The people of the United States have a patriotic attachment to the "greenback," because they think that it "saved the country." A gallant Senator, who is an advocate of inflation, recently grew indignant at the opponents of paper money for reflecting on the "blood-stained greenback." Under the contagion of the poetry, one might reply that the fear now is, lest, if the Senator has his way, the greenback may not yet also be stained with tears.

On the 31st of October, 1865, the total debt was, \$2,808,549,437.50; the greenbacks issued, \$428,160,569; the National Bank notes, 185,-000,000; State Bank notes, 65,000,000; fractional currency, \$26,057,469.20*; total currency, \$704,-000,000.

CONTRACTION OR INFLATION?

The war being ended, the financial question took this form: Shall we withdraw the paper, recover specie, reduce prices, lessen imports, and live economically until we have made up the waste and loss of war, or shall we keep the paper as money, export all our specie which has hitherto been held in anticipation of resumption, buy foreign goods with it, and go on as if nothing had happened?

Mr. McCulloch, who was now Secretary of the Treasury, proposed to contract the inflated paper, and pursue the former alternative. On the 18th of December, 1865, the House voted,

---

* Spaulding.

144 to 6, to authorise a contraction of 10,000,000 in the next six months, and of 4,000,000 per month after that. This operation went on until January, 1868, but, in the meantime, the National banks were going into operation, being allowed 300,000,000 of circulation, 150,000,000 apportioned by population, and 150,000,000 by banking capital, and their notes more than compensated for the greenbacks withdrawn. During the year 1867, also, war fears being laid aside, speculation had sprung up and begun to absorb the redundant paper. The turning point at which the greenback contraction met the bank-note expansion was January, 1868. On January 1, 1866, the banks stood as follows :

CIRCULATION.	DEPOSITS.	LOANS.
213,200,000.	513,600,000.	498,800,000.

During the whole year 1866, there was a superabundance of currency at New York, and money ruled at 5 to 7 per cent. for the best 60 day two name paper.

January 1st, 1867, the banks stood :

CIRCULATION.	DEPOSITS.	LOANS.
291,000,000.	555,100,000,	608,400,000.

In January there was a crisis in stocks, and the rate was 8 to 10 for the same paper as above. For the next six months the money market was dull and easy. In July many dry-goods firms failed, and rates were 8 to 10. August and September were easy, but in October the rate was again 10.

On the first day of January, 1868, the banks stood:

CIRCULATION.	DEPOSITS.	LOANS.
294,300,000.	531,800,000.	616,600,000.

At this juncture outcries were raised against contraction by those who were engaged in the movement of expansion, though, in regular business, credit was still kept in the narrow bounds to which it had been reduced during the war, and the people at large, understanding that the Legal-Tender Act was a war measure, and expecting in good faith that resumption must follow peace, had made their arrangements accordingly. Congress forbade any further contraction, and we turned to the second of the above alternatives, which we have since consistently followed.

PAPER MONEY WITH A FIXED LIMIT.

The era of paper money on which we then entered has one peculiar feature, unprecedented, so far as I have been able to learn, in the history of paper money. *Our paper money is redundant, but fixed in amount.* The greenbacks stood, when Mr. McCulloch's contraction was arrested, at 356,000,000. The bank-notes were fixed at 300,000,000, but subsequently, July, 1870, 54,000,-000 more were authorized. The fractional currency was fixed at 50,000,000. The bank-notes have never quite reached 350,000,000, and the fractional has never reached its limit. The withdrawal of the three-per-cent. compound interest notes, which had been held as bank reserves, operated as a contraction, but the allowance to the country banks to keep ⅜ of their reserves in the redemption cities operated as expansion. Allowing for these variations, the limit of legal currency was fixed, until the Fall of 1873, at 750,000,000. Nearly every nation which has ever used paper money has fixed its amount, and set limits which it has solemnly promised again and again not to pass, but such promises are vain. The intention, when they are made, is honest, but it is impossible to keep them. A man might as well jump off a precipice intending to stop half way down. It remains to be seen whether we too, when the redundancy is absorbed by high prices and excessive credit, will break over the limit, as every other nation has done, under the inevitable constraint which it then imposes,—but the phenomena thus far, are those of a redundant paper with a fixed limit.

COURSE OF THE MARKET.

To trace out its operation would require a history of the money market for the last six years. The inflation of credit which went on all over the country so soon as it was understood that specie payments were indefinitely postponed, is only imperfectly presented in the following table showing the state of the National Banks at different dates.

		Circulation.	Deposits.	Loans.	Per ct. Resrv.		* Ag. Clearings at N. Y. per annum.
					Red. Cities.	States.	
		Millions.	Millions.	Millions.			
1868	Jan. 1 ..	294.3	531.8	616 6	33.3	23.9	28.4 thous. millions.
	July 1...	294.9	575.8	655.7	32.5	24.0	
1869	Jan. 1...	294.4	563.5	644.9	32.7	22 9	37.4
	July 1...	292.7	574.3	636.3	29.5	21.6	
1870	Jan. 1...	292.8	546.2	688.8	34.8	23.4	27.8
	July 1...	291 1	542.1	719 3	32.7	22.7	
1871	Jan. 1...	302.2	561.9	768.3	29.7	22.6	29.3
	July 1...	307 7	602.1	789 4	31.3	22 9	
1872,	Oct 1....	333.4	625.7	872.5	25.3	19.3	32.6
1873	Apr. 10	336.2	663.9	903 8	25.8	20.5	33.9
	Sept. 12.	339.0	622.6	940.2	24.5	20.7	

In 1868 the market was easy, save in March and April, when the rate varied from 8 to 12, and in October, November, and December, there being a lock-up in November, and the Western demand making itself felt. In 1869, the market was stringent throughout the year. It was declared in October, to be " worse than for eight years." Stock speculation was active, and it was remarked that it was continually absorbing more and more currency. The redundant paper in

* The annual aggregate clearings from 1853 to 1862 averaged 5,000,-000,000. In 1863 they were 14,000,000,000 and rose steadily. This is introduced only as a general indication of the increase of transactions

New York was absorbed, and the state of things was realized which was to come three years later for the country at large.

The high rates of 1869 drew funds to New York for loan on stock security. The year 1870 was marked by great ease. Money flowed into New York in abundance. Rates on call were from 4 to 6, and on best paper 6 to 7½ throughout the year. The only excitement was in July and August, at the breaking out of the war in Europe.

In 1871, the demand of funds for railroad building became very marked. The market was easy until September, when it was quoted stringent, though rates were not high. This lasted during the autumn, and was ascribed to the "movement of the crops."

In 1872, there was nothing remarkable until the crop movement began again, when the rates advanced sharply, and commercial paper could not be quoted. The Secretary of the Treasury issued 5,000,000 of the 44,000,coo withdrawn by Mr. McCulloch. His efforts to withdraw these again kept the market stringent, and rates excessive, throughout the winter.

During these years large quantities of American securities were negotiated in Europe. These were very moderately estimated—for the first three-quarters of 1873—at 100,000,000.

In 1873, the farmers' movement against the railroads impaired confidence in railroad bonds as an investment. When the crop movement began again the demand of the country banks led to a demand from the city banks upon the brokers, and precipitated a panic on the stock exchange. The failure of several large banking houses engaged in the sale of railroad bonds increased the excitement. The closing of the stock exchange, and suspension of the city banks, obliged the country banks to contract their loans, and brought the industry of the country to a standstill. There was little or no "panic" outside of New York, but it is evident that a crisis in the operation of the paper money had been reached, and that crisis involved a reduction of prices and business. As the stock exchange was the place at which the redundent currency was employed, the crisis was first developed there, by the demand for the return of the surplus. The shock, however, was transferred to the regular industries of the country. The expansion by the issue of a part of the 44,000,000 gradually restored the prices of stocks, but production was restrained, and the effect which lasts yet, and promises to last longest, is the reduction of wages.

During the crisis greenbacks were hoarded, which was thought to prove "how good they were." If the currency consisted of clam-shells, and a crisis should come, in which it was to be feared that clam-shells might be scarce, clam-shells would be hoarded; much more if there was fear that the next currency might be pebbles.

Studying these facts in the light of the previous history, we perceive that the annual pressure in the autumn, increasing in force from year to year, was a premonition of the effect which must be apprehended whenever the expansion of credit and prices should have absorbed the entire redundancy of the currency. We have seen in the history of the Massachusests colony that each new issue was followed in a few years by a new crisis, and an outcry about hard times and scarce money. The law which governs this is apparent. The rise of prices and multiplication of credit operations will go on to absorb any amount of currency whatever. If then, the amount be fixed, the expansion must come up to and press against this fixed barrier. This pressure will become apparent first at that season of the year at which the normal requirement is greatest. At that time there will be great distress occasioned by the need of withdrawing currency from the use in which it is engaged. As it cannot be imported, and the law forbids its increase, there is no relief. It must be withdrawn, and the consequences must be endured. Then it is said that the currency is not elastic, and schemes are invented for making it so ; but no device whatever can make it elastic. An elastic body is one which will both expand and contract, but a paper currency never contracts itself. Any device which has elasticity for its object will have expansion for its effect.

In its more general effects, the paper currency with a fixed limit produces a steady advance in the rate of interest, and also a reduction of prices.

These effects are both traceable in the history of the last five years. The whole story which precedes goes to show that the value of a paper currency depends on its *amount*. At the time of issue, or during a war in which the issuer is engaged, it depends in some degree on his credit; but when it settles down in peace as the normal medium of exchange, its value comes to depend almost purely on its amount. This amount, of course, is relative to the requirements of the country for the purpose of performing its exchanges. What the requirement is, however, no man can tell. There is no rule for finding it. It does not depend on population, or wealth, or the amount of the exchanges. It bears no fixed relation to any known or ascertainable quantity. An agricultural country wants more, for the same population and wealth, than a manufacturing country. A sparsely populated country wants more, other things being equal, than a densely populated one. A country in which the means of communication are poor wants more, other things being equal, than a country with good means of communication. It is idle to attempt to compute it at so much per head, or so much per thousand of wealth. Currency is economized also by banking arrangements and clearing-house processes; the requirement is reduced by railroad extension, and all facilities of communication.

How far these conflicting influences have affected the actual requirement of the United States for circulating medium on a specie basis no one can even guess. It is properly an empirical question. We can only try. If we had a currency of specie value, we should get just as much as we need, and then we should know how much that is, but then, too, we should no longer care. Statisticians would be interested in it, but the finance and business of the country would not hang upon it.

If, then, we assume that, on the whole, this country does require more than it had in 1861, this increase of the normal requirement goes on inside of and under the paper expansion. It produces a pressure on the inflated speculative prices from within, at the same time that they are restrained without by the fixed limit of the paper. The effect must be a reduction of prices; and such a reduction having occurred within the last five years is the best proof that the currency requirement is greater than it was.*

In view of all this, the notion of " growing up " to the fixed volume of the currency receives its just depreciation. The London "Economist" unfortunately seemed to lend some countenance to this notion during the month of October, 1873, and it was taken up on this side of the water by some who enjoyed considerable influence as conservative authorities.

If we suppose the requirement of currency to increase from the growth of wealth and population faster than it decreases from improved communication and banking facilities, then a certain growing may be admitted, but, as it goes on, it exerts a slow, gradual, and pitiless contraction on prices, broken only, in Spring and Fall, by a succession of commercial crises. If then, there was backbone enough in the nation to endure this without having recourse to expansion, the growth might go on for ten or twenty years, by

* See the Diagram at the end of this Chapter.

which time perhaps 750,000,000 of currency might be the specie requirement. No historical precedents exist to guide us in judging whether this process would indeed go on under such circumstances. As a matter of speculation, I am inclined to believe that the actual course of things would be that after every crisis wages would fall, industry would be checked, and the country would be slowly and gradually arrested in its entire industrial life. The nearest analogies are in the history of Massachusetts,* and in the history of England from 1812 to 1819.† Evidently, before any such state of things came about we should break out of the restraints in some way, but then there would be an end of the growing up. According to present appearance, the first shock is to push us into inflation, and so the hypothesis falls to the ground.

However, to pursue the supposition, granting everything, when we grow up to 750,000,000, we cannot resume. At that point there may be no premium on gold, and prices may be at specie level, but there would still be no specie in the

* See p. 23.   † See p. 280.

country. To carry on specie payments would require at least 250,000,000 of gold. We must either buy this, and cancel an equal amount of paper to make room for it, or wait to grow up 250,000,000 more.

No notion which has been propounded in regard to our situation is more plausible, or involves more practical impossibilities than this of resumption by " growing up."

———

If, now, any one is disposed to believe that there are any circumstances in this country, which are so different from those of other countries that inferences from the history of the latter are of no value for the former, here is the history of the currency of this country, briefly and cursorily presented, but sufficiently to show how, from the very outset, our industrial development has been crippled by bad arrangements in this respect. English writers have lately given up the discussion of currency questions, and have taken the tone of passing by people who bother their heads about this subject as " possessed." The same tone has

been borrowed here by a certain school which imports its *tone* even more than its ideas.   No one
knows what a sick and weary subject paper money
is unless he has made it a specialty.   I have
stated, below,* in its more proper connection, the
distinction which is here to be observed; when
the currency is sound it takes care of itself, and
other considerations of far higher scientific character come in to require attention: when the currency is redundant, irredeemable paper, it floats
everything, and becomes a prime consideration.
The English are fortunate in having experience
only of a sound currency, and being able to make
light of evils they do not know, although they
must yet again take up the subject, for, that the
Bank Act of 1844 is not a scientific settlement of
the currency question, is proved by the fact that
it could not be imitated by any other nation.

For us, the currency question is of the first importance, and we cannot solve it, nor escape it, by
ignoring it.   We have got to face it and work
through it, and the best way to begin is, not by
wrangling about speculative opinions as to untried

* Page 253.

schemes, but to go back to history, and try to get hold of some firmly established principles, from which we can proceed with some confidence and a certain unanimity.

We often boast of the resources of our country, but we did not make the country. What ground is there for boasting here? The question for us is: What have we made of it? No one can justly appreciate the natural resources of this country until, by studying the deleterious effects of bad currency and bad taxation, he has formed some conception of how much, since the first settlers came here, has been wasted and lost.

EXPLANATION OF THE DIAGRAM.

The heavy line being taken as zero point, or equality of exports and imports, the ⊥⊥⊥⊥⊥ line shows the excess of exports or imports of merchandise, by its variations above or below that line, exports being reckoned downwards, and imports upwards. The line ——— marks the excess of imports or exports of specie in the same manner. The dotted line . . . . . . denotes the amount of bank or other paper per capita. The light dotted line between the years 1848 and the end shows the production of gold in California.

The line of prices at the top of the diagram is made by adding the lower annual averages given in the Finance Report of 1863 down to that year. From 1848–1873 the line is formed by adding the January quotations from the table given in the Finance Report for 1873. Over eighty articles are included in each, but they are not the same articles. Therefore the scale is rewritten to bring the starting point in 1864 even with the ending point in 1863, and the two parts should only be compared for relative fluctuations. In the last-mentioned table a hundred-weight of iron and of hemp was taken, instead of a ton of each, as given, and railroad bars were struck out because not given in 1864. Evidently the relation between the prices of 1863 and 1864 do not appear at all.

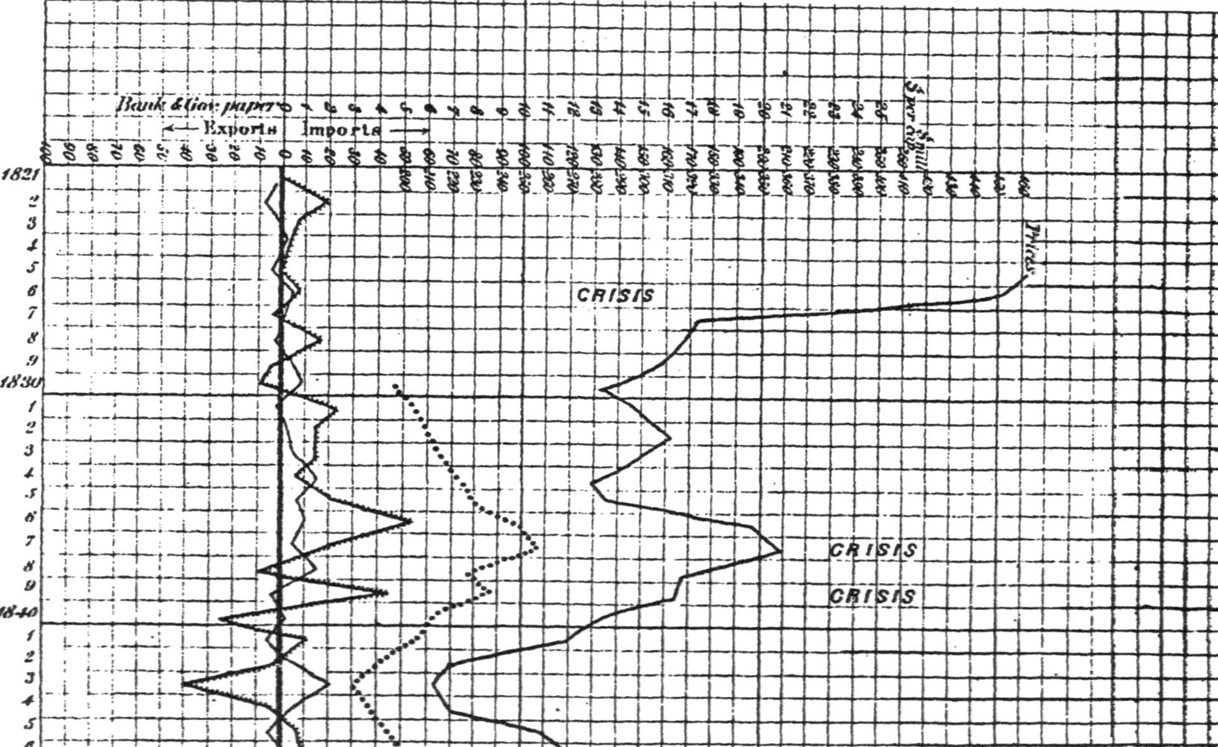

Bank & Com: paper
Exports
Imports
per cent
per million
Prices
CRISIS
CRISIS
CRISIS
1821
1830
1840

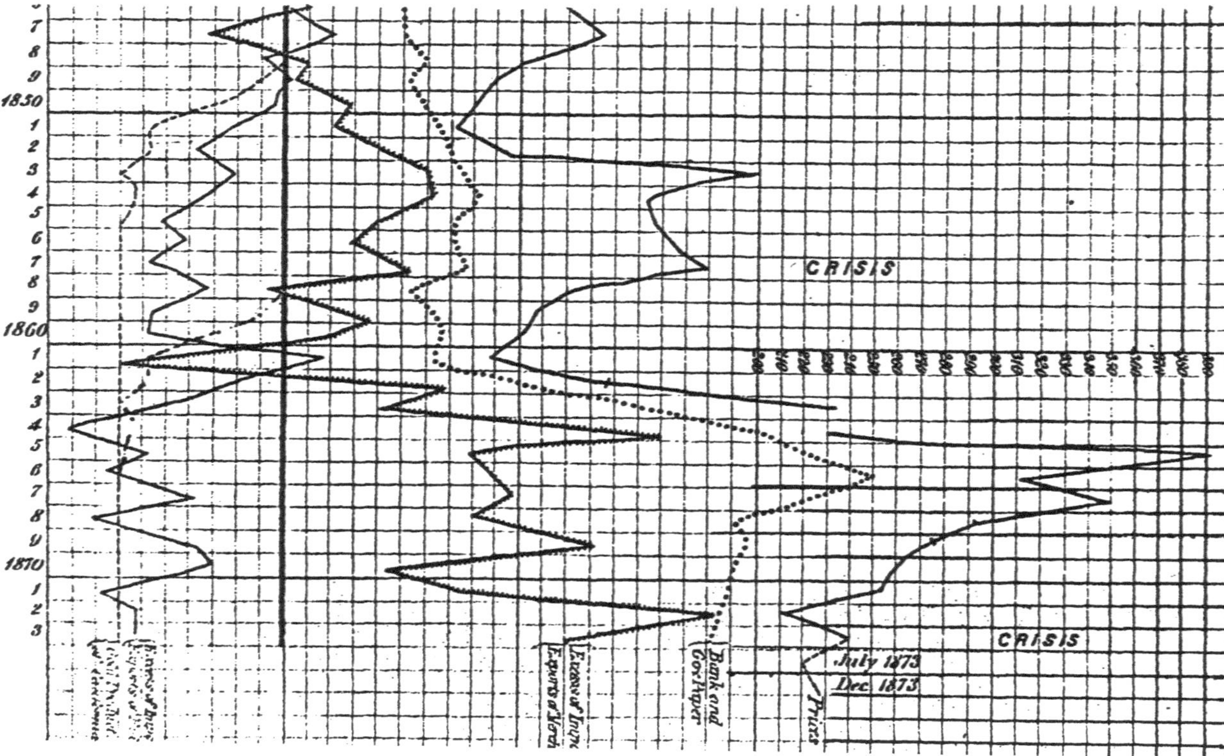

1850
1860
1870
CRISIS
CRISIS
July 1873
Dec. 1873
Prices
Bank and
Gov't Payer
Excess of Imp'ts
Exports of York
Excess of Imp'ts
Exports of York
Excess of Imp'ts over Exports
in Merchandise

CHAPTER II.

THE ENGLISH BANK RESTRICTION.

IN the year 1795, the currency of the British Islands consisted of the notes of the Bank of England, the English country banks, the Scotch banks, the Bank of Ireland, and the Irish country banks, and of coin. By the monopoly clause of the charter of the Bank of England, no banking firm consisting of more than six partners could issue demand notes in England. Strong joint stock banks were therefore illegal, but tradesmen of every grade set up as " bankers," and issued notes. These were the " country banks." They were not chartered banks, but private bankers who issued notes. The Scotch system was a perfectly free one. There were three great chartered banks. The others were joint stock companies and free partnerships, and they conducted their business solely on business responsibilities. After some unlucky experiments in fancy banking, during the last century, they settled down to solid, conservative methods of operation. They meet with encomiums on every hand, and they deserve them, but the reason why they deserve them is lost sight of by those who fix their attention on the *system*. The system is the best conceivable; but it involves one indispensable condition of success. It requires vigilance, sagacity, science, and moderation on the part of the bankers. The freer any system is, the more it requires these characteristics. The Scotch banks have succeeded because their managers have possessed these qualities. The same system, on a " paper basis," or managed by unreasoning and ignorant avarice, is a short road to ruin. The Bank of Ireland and the Irish country banks were very similar in their organization and relations to the English banks.

The circulation of the Bank of England, in February, 1795, was £14,017,510; its specie, £6,127,720. The circulation of the English country banks at this time is not known, no statistics having been collected. It was estimated in the parliamentary debate of 1811 to have been from four to six millions. The amount of specie in circulation in 1795 was estimated in the same debates at from twenty-five to forty millions. The Lords' Committee, in 1819, gave this estimate for the circulation before the Restriction:

Coin.... ....£25,000,000
Bank of England notes......... 10,500,000
Country notes and Scotch notes... 7,000,000

Total for England and Scotland.. £42,500,000

Lord Liverpool estimated the coin, in 1797, at thirty millions; Mr. Rose, at forty millions; Tooke, after reviewing the evidence, thinks it was at most twenty-two and a half millions.

CAUSE OF THE RESTRICTION.

In 1796, the great powers being allied against France, and England assisting chiefly by subsidies, Pitt began to draw upon the Bank for the necessary supplies. Originally the Bank was forbidden to lend to government, except by permission of Parliament, but Pitt took advantage of an act of indemnity which was asked for in

1793 to cover previous cases in which the Bank had done this, to make the act so read as to repeal the prohibition entirely. His drafts becoming more and more exhaustive to the specie of the Bank, it proceeded to contract its notes. To the alarm thus occasioned, came, in addition, a rumor of intended invasion. A run on the country banks followed, which precipitated a demand on the Bank of England. In February, 1797, the specie reserve was but little over one million. The Bank was meanwhile contracting its circulation with all its energy, and had reduced it in February, 1797, to nine millions. The directors declared to the Bullion Committee, in 1810, that they thought this had been a grave error and had greatly enhanced the crisis. The necessities of the government, in the meantime, were greater than ever.

Under these circumstances an Order in Council was issued forbidding the Bank to pay specie until the will of Parliament could be known. This order was issued on the 27th of February, and was extended to the Bank of Ireland on the 2d of March, 1797. Tooke ("Prices," I. 204), says that the suspension might have been avoided by one or two days' more perseverance, and that the run on the Bank of Ireland was over before the order to suspend was received. The directors of the Bank of Ireland did not want to suspend. On the 3d of May, Parliament passed an act suspending payments in England and Scotland until the 24th of June. Notes under £5 were at the same time allowed to be issued. From the manner in which this suspension came about, by an injunction of the government, it is known as the Bank Restriction.

ACTS CONTINUING THE RESTRICTION.

On the 22d of June, 1797, the Restriction was continued until one month after the next meeting of Parliament. On the 30th of November, 1797, it was continued until six months after the war should close. On the 3d of Jan., 1799, the Bank, having over seven millions of bullion, declared itself ready to pay sums under £5 in coin, and to redeem its notes dated before January 1st, 1798. Its notes had increased from eleven to sixteen millions. April 30th, 1802, the

Peace of Amiens having been concluded, the Restriction was extended until March 1st, 1803, although the Bank was ready to resume. February 28th, 1803, it was extended until six weeks after the next meeting of Parliament. On the 13th of December, 1803, war having been declared, the Bank Restriction was extended until six months after the ratification of a definitive treaty of peace. On the 18th of July, 1814, Napoleon having abdicated, and peace being anticipated, the Restriction was extended until March 25th, 1815. March 2d, 1815, it was continued until July 5th, 1816. March 21st, 1816, it was continued until July 5th, 1818, in order, as the preamble to the act stated, to give the Bank time to prepare for resumption. May 28th, 1818, this preamble was repeated before another act which extended the Restriction until July 5th, 1819. The Bank took no measures of preparation for resumption until after the act of 1819, to be mentioned below.

BANK-NOTES NOT LEGAL TENDER.

The bank-notes were never made legal tender. The question whether they were to be
such was put to Mr. Pitt in the House when
the Restriction was ratified. He replied that
they were to be so from the Bank to the public
When pressed on this point, especially by Mr
Nicholls, who asked, " whether it was his inten
tion that the notes of the Bank of England
should be a legal tender from the Bank to the
public creditor," and declared that, if so, it was
an act of insolvency, the minister evaded a reply.

In 1801, Mr. Grigby demanded of Oakes &
Co., country bankers, gold for a five-guinea note
issued by them. They offered a £5 Bank of
England note and five shillings. He refused the
note, and demanded gold, and as he could not
get it, he sued. He gained the suit at the as-
sizes, and the question of law being reserved for
the four judges of Common Pleas, they all
agreed that the plaintiff was in his rights, and
that notes were not legal tender between man
and man.

In 1810, a Jew named De Yonge, and a stage-driver, James King, were prosecuted for selling and buying guineas at a premium in paper. The cases were brought under an act of Edward VI. against trading in gold or silver at other than rates fixed by law. The men were convicted, the penalty being a year's imprisonment and fine, but they were admitted to bail, and sentence reserved. After long delay, the twelve judges in the Exchequer Chamber decided that their cases did not come under the statute cited.

In 1811, Lord King demanded his rents in specie or paper equivalent. No one denied his right to make this demand, but " he was vehemently abused for incivism." In the same year, and with reference to this act of Lord King, Lord Stanhope introduced an act, which was passed, making it a misdemeanor to buy or sell guineas at more than their denominational equivalent in paper. If a debtor offered notes he was to be free from distraint, but the creditor retained all other remedies. How near this came to a legal-tender law it would be hard to define. The courts never passed upon it. By the force of public opinion,

and a general disposition to make the best of circumstances, the notes were used universally.

EFFECTS OF THE RESTRICTION IN ITS FIRST STAGE.

The harvest of 1800 was almost a failure. In the summer of that year the exchanges became unfavorable, and gold, which might be legally ex-ported (*i. e.*, that obtained by melting foreign coin), rose to a premium. The mint law provided that bullion should be coined for any one who presented it. One ounce of gold was coined into £3 17s. 10½d. of the coinage, without charge to the individual who offered it. He therefore re-ceived again just what he gave, only in a manu-factured form. The only loss or expense to him consisted in the interest lost while he was wait-ing. The market cash price for gold was, on account of this loss, £3 17s. 6d. per ounce. At the time mentioned, June, 1800, exportable gold rose to £4 5s. per ounce in notes, and in January, 1801, it was at £4 6s.

The premium on gold which might be "sworn off" for exportation ranged generally during this period three or four shillings per ounce higher than non-exportable gold. Tables showing the gold premium differ, some of them quoting domestic and some of them exportable gold.

When the question of the Restriction came up at the Peace, in 1802, it was argued that resumption was impossible because the exchanges were adverse. Lord King and Mr. Fox argued that to resume was the way to make them favorable. Their doctrine was that the redundancy of the paper was the cause of the premium on gold and the adverse exchange, but they found no hearers. The bank-notes in February, 1802, were fifteen millions, the specie in bank seven millions.

In 1804, the exchanges with Dublin became adverse to that place, and a parliamentary committee was appointed to investigate the cause.

They ascribed the outflow of gold from Ireland to England to the redundancy and depreciation of the Irish paper. The doctrines they laid down were the same which were afterwards embodied in the Bullion Report, but this Irish report never attracted much attention.

COMMERCIAL AFFAIRS.

In 1806, Napoleon declared, by his Berlin decree, the coast of England under blockade, and forbade all trade with her. England retaliated by the Orders in Council blockading all ports of France and her allies. The Americans, who, as the chief neutral carriers, were the greatest sufferers, retaliated in the following year by the embargo, forbidding their ships to trade with either belligerent.

In 1806, the French invaded Spain. In 1807, Russia entered into an alliance with France. In the same year the English made an attack on Buenos Ayres and effected a lodgment there.

These political and military events had important effects on trade.

As the Baltic and Spain were closed, active speculations in timber and wool, of which the supplies were thus cut off, sprang up. The new opening in South America was also eagerly seized upon for speculative trade. At the same time great public works (bridges over the Thames, etc.,) were in progress, and a joint stock company mania broke out. The years 1808, 1809, and 1810 were marked by the progress of these speculative movements.

The Bank in the meantime was extending its issues. Following the February quotations still, we find that the note circulation in 1806 was 17 millions; in 1807, 16.9 millions; in 1808, 18.1 millions; in 1809, 18.5 millions; in 1810, 21 millions.

This increase, however, is, in itself, a matter of very small moment. It is upon other incidental political and financial circumstances, which acted and reacted upon one another in the most complicated manner, and in regard to which our information is very meagre and unsatisfactory, that the results to be noticed depended. No one has ever made a thorough and comprehensive analysis of all the forces which were here in action, and divergent opinions have naturally arisen where men looked at the facts only in a certain point of view, or took account of only a certain limited range of facts. The present object is only to trace the broadest features of the situation, and deduce incontroverted inferences.

The country bank circulation is of the first importance amongst the factors which we have here to take into account, but unfortunately it is impossible to ascertain what it was. Its expansion, however, is certain, from the fact that the number of these banks, which had been 270 in 1797, was 600 in 1808, and 721 in 1810. Their circulation was estimated at 25 or 30 millions. That these issues were feeding the speculation is evident. It appears also that some very small notes were in circulation. Cobbett gives a representation of a seven-shilling note issued at Tunbridge Wells. (Vol. xviii. 172.)

The premium on gold was also steadily advancing during these years. In 1810, McCulloch puts the price of bullion at £4 10s. per oz., or 15 per cent. depreciation of the notes. The Bullion Committee put the depreciation at 15½ per cent. It makes a difference, as stated above, whether exportable or non-exportable gold is quoted.

THE BULLION REPORT.

The state of things above described attracted public attention, and in January, 1810, Mr. Horner moved for a committee "to inquire into the high

price of gold bullion and to take into consideration the state of the circulating medium, and of
the exchanges between Great Britain and foreign
parts." The report of this committee was published in August, 1810, but did not come up for
discussion in the House until May, 1811.

THE QUESTIONS AT ISSUE.

As soon as the witnesses began to be examined,
it appeared that there was a widespread belief
that it was not the paper which had depreciated,
but the gold which had advanced—a notion which
has been advanced in other periods of paper
money. The witnesses were bankers, merchants,
and bullion brokers, and included the Governor
and Deputy-Governor of the Bank of England.
The first question to which the committee addressed itself was, therefore, this : Is the bank-
note depreciated in value ? Is that the cause of
the premium on gold, or is there some other ? To
us such a question may seem idle, but it certainly
was not so when the Governor and Deputy-Governor of the Bank of England, and the Chancellor of the Exchequer, took the negative. As

there was no public quotation of bullion, transactions being illegal, and men handled "guineas" and "shillings" in paper in ordinary trade, it is not so surprising that such a notion might at any rate be popular. It was assisted further by the great dislike to admitting that Bank of England notes were "depreciated" like the paper money on the continent.

There were facts also tending to show that disturbances in the value of the precious metals were taking place. Gold was growing dearer from obstructions in the supply, from hoarding, and from demand for war expenditures.*

Tooke ("Prices," I. 130) infers that "there must have been a greatly increased demand for the precious metals and a consequently increased value of them during the war, *more than sufficient* to compensate for the utmost quantity spared from circulation as coin in this country, or even for the utmost rate of annual increase from

* The eager demand for bullion in England is shown by an incident mentioned by Chevalier. The French Treasury, by transactions with its agents in 1806, came into possession of drafts of the Spanish Government on bullion in Mexico, but since the battle of Trafalgar England controlled the sea, and France could not bring over the metal. A Dutch bank negotiated a transaction between the belligerents by which the French Treasury realized its drafts, and an English frigate brought the treasure to England,

the mines," that is, that the enhancement of the value of gold equalled the depreciation of paper. J. S. Mill thinks that this is proved, but Chevalier (*Ec. Pol. III.* 454) puts the matter in the right light. If gold had risen there ought to have been less of it, and prices should have been lower. The bank paper, therefore, even if not absolutely increased, was in excess relatively to what it ought to have been and would have been under specie payments. Prices, if not below old specie figures, were relatively inflated.

I abstain from pursuing this suggestion, but regard it as the key to a correct solution of the contradictions in which many of the best authorities on this subject have been involved.

The second question which the committee had to consider, was: Why are the exchanges 18 or 20 per cent. against England?

The importance of this inquiry for us may not be at once apparent. We have very wisely separated the quotations of exchange from those of gold. We quote exchange in gold, and thus the fluctuations of the two are kept separate and presented independently. But when there was no quotation of gold, evidently the exchange rates were the indicator on which the variations between paper and bullion were marked.

But this is not all. The witnesses, almost without exception (and the exceptions were not clear and precise in their opinions), maintained that the adverse exchange was due to an adverse balance of trade or of payments. The question involved was, therefore, this: Is an adverse balance of trade the explanation of an outflow of gold?—or: Is a favorable balance of trade the force to which we must look to bring an influx of gold? There is no question in finance which now demands our study so imperatively as this one. The false notions of the balance of trade infest almost every discussion of our present circumstances which one reads or hears. It is assumed that the movement of the precious metals from country to country is caused by the balance of trade one way or the other, and, as the movement of the metals is a phenomenon of the first importance in any question of resumption, the reasoning which starts with this doctrine is all fallacious. The balance of trade was exploded by Quesnay and his followers a century ago, and was gibbeted in the Bullion Report, but it stalks the money market and the national treasury to-day, an uneasy ghost, which it seems impossible to lay.

It is a vexatious task, and one which always makes a scientific man feel ridiculous, to set vigorously to work to demolish an old error which no well-informed man any longer holds, but, in our present situation, and under our political system, popular errors are of the utmost importance, and no pains should be spared in patiently exposing them. The fallacy here is in the word "balance." If it means *equilibrium*, it may be used correctly to denote the equality of exports and imports, but then it regulates itself, and no power can control it. If it means *remainder*, and suggests analogies of book-keeping, it is a mere myth to which no fact corresponds, and is to be entirely rejected. This question will be noticed further when we come to speak of the debate on the report.

The third question which the committee had to consider was offered by the conduct of the

Bank. It is to be noticed that the English inconvertible paper was a bank issue of no fixed amount, while our present paper money was issued to an arbitrary limit at which it was established. The question, therefore, was: How shall the Bank know when it has given the country just the amount which it requires, and when it passes the limit so that its issues become excessive? Under a convertible system they found out, of course, by a demand on them for gold for exportation (clandestine or open, as the case might be). They could not, generally speaking, press notes on the public beyond the requirement, though with a usury law and a law against export this would be possible to some extent.

They therefore went on during the specie times, to discount all good bills, at short date, for real transactions, at five per cent. and never troubled themselves about gold or the exchanges. They pursued the same course under the Restriction, and the question before the committee was: Whether these conditions were sufficient, in the absence of convertibility, to guard against inflation, or whether the Bank might inflate while observing this rule?

This question has the highest importance for us, if we are to have "free banking" on paper.

The report of this committee is perhaps the most important document in financial literature. Its doctrines have been tested both ways, by disbelief and by belief, by experiment of their opposites and by experiment of themselves. They are no longer disputable. They are not matter of opinion or theory, but of demonstration. They are ratified and established as the basis of finance. They may be denied, as the roundness of the earth was denied even five years ago, and as Newton's theory of the solar system was denied until within twenty-five years, but they have passed the stage where the scientific financier is bound to discuss them.*

* On account of the interest attaching to this document and its historical and scientific importance, it is given in full in the Appendix. In the notes on the report the subordinate points in which it is regarded as erroneous or questionable are noticed.

SUMMARY.

The doctrines of this report may be summed up thus :

1. The value of an inconvertible currency depends on its *amount* relatively to the needs of the country for circulating medium (only to a very subordinate degree on the security on which it is based or the credit of the issuer).

2. If gold is at a premium in paper the paper is redundant and depreciated. The premium measures the depreciation.

3. The limit of possible fluctuations in the exchanges is the expense of transmitting bullion from the one country to the other. If it costs 2 per cent. to transmit bullion, the fluctuations of the exchange due to the ratio of imports and exports never can exceed two per cent. above or below par. Par of exchange is the par of the metals, weight for weight, in the two coinages.

4. If there is a drain of the precious metals, it is due, aside from exportations to purchase food or pay armies, etc., to the presence of an inferior currency of some sort in the country it leaves.

5. If the inferior currency be removed, the exchanges will be turned, the outflow will stop, and, if any vacuum is created, gold will flow in to supply it.

Gold will not flow in while the inferior currency fills the channels of circulation.

6. In the presence of a panic the duty of the Bank is to discount freely for all solvent parties.

The still more fundamental laws involved are these :

1. The amount of gold in the world will suffice to perform the exchanges of the world. If there be more or less, it will only affect the average level of prices the world over.

2. Every nation will have that portion of the stock of gold in the world which is proportioned to its trade. Each nation will have just as much as it needs.

3. A better and a worse currency cannot circulate together. The worse will drive out the better.

The committee also incidentally condemn the usury law and the law forbidding the exportation of the precious metals.

The discussion of these doctrines in the House and by the public will be noticed below. The reader will have a more correct impression of the attitude in which the doctrines of the report came up for discussion, if we present the events in their chronological order.

THE CRISIS OF 1810.

The Report of the Bullion Committee was ordered printed in June, 1810, and was before the public in August of the same year. Meantime, in July, 1810, the bubble burst. The accounts of the Bank were not published at this time and the amount of the discounts was not known. A motion of Mr. Huskisson on April 5th, 1811, to call on the Bank for such a return, was negatived. The Bullion Committee had called for a statement of discounts, and had received a paper under promise of secrecy. It leaked out in some way, and a set of figures were circulated, but their correctness seems always to have been in doubt. Macleod stated that the discounts in 1795 were £2,946,500; in 1809, £15,475,700; and in 1810, £20,070,600.

A report was made in 1832 of the state of the Bank from 1778 to 1831. It is given in Tooke's "Prices," vol. II. There is a similar table (Feb. reports) in McCulloch's Adam Smith, p. 508, and Dict. of Commerce, art. "Banks." The two are combined in the diagram opposite p. 310, which presents the movements of the note circulation and bullion for each six months during the period 1790 to 1830.

Mr. Baring, in his evidence before the Bullion Committee, and Mr. Huskisson in his speech on the motion above referred to, bear ample testimony to the repetition of the old phenonemon of speculation under inflated paper issues. The enterprises undertaken were indeed of the most extravagant kind. For instance, speculations in South America took ludicrous shapes, being in no way adapted to the circumstances of that country. A company was formed to send out Scotch milkmaids to make butter in Buenos Ayres. But when the milkmaids saw the beasts they had to deal with they shrank from the encounter. A corps of laborers was required to secure the animals at milking time, and when the butter was made it was found that the people preferred oil.

The question of prices during this period leads to difficult and controverted questions which lie beyond the limits set for the present undertaking. The standard work on the subject is Tooke's "Prices," in which a certain view is very ably defended. Mr. Tooke combated the popular notion, which seeks the explanation of all price fluctuations in the fluctuations of the amount of currency. It is permitted to doubt, however, especially in view of American experience, whether he made sufficient allowance for the radical differences between a convertible and an inconvertible currency, when he discussed the period of the Restriction on the same principles which he applied with so much justice to the convertible system. The popular metaphor of "floating," although it is not well analyzed, is very apt. On a system of even nominal convertibility the motives of speculation and of price fluctuations lie outside of the currency in industrial and commercial circumstances. Speculation in the widest and best sense controls the amount

of the currency. On an inconvertible system
the amount of the currency controls speculation.
If it is not redundant its effect is slight; if it is
very excessive, it "floats" everything, and becomes the controlling consideration. No one
believes that an inconvertible currency suspends
the operation of any of the economic laws which
govern prices, but, if it is redundant, it decides
whether the fluctuations in price of a unit of
a given commodity shall be above and below $1
or above and below $2. Every contraction or
expansion alters this general level.

It is certainly erroneous to believe that redundant inconvertible paper increases all prices
equally. It is one of its hardships that it increases prices of merchandise more than wages; of
luxuries and comforts more than of staple articles ;
that is, it lessens the command of laborer, artisan,
and farmer over comforts. The articles taken into
account by Tooke are all staple articles, and he
shows that these had not increased in price up to
1810. As a test of his argument, which cannot be
regarded as conclusive, since it only shows in
general that there were ordinary economic

causes to account for the direction up or down of every fluctuation of each article, but never measures the exact force of such causes, I have combined the prices given by him in his tables at periods corresponding to those for which the state of the currency is given in the diagram, (opposite p. 310) and inserted a line of prices. This balances off incidental causes, and ought to show whether the average of prices underwent any influence from the amount of the currency or not. There is no accord with the amount of the Bank of England circulation, but there is an unknown factor of country-bank circulation of which we have no estimate, save for the years 1810–1818. (See p. 284) The uppermost line in the diagram represents the total circulation during these years. The parallelism of the price line with it is evident. Also the general parallelism of the price line with the " price of gold " line is apparent, and, if the latter may be taken to indicate the fluctuation of the total amount of paper, then an influence of the amount of paper on the general average of prices seems undeniable. It is to be remembered that the English paper was never recklessly inflated, and that, up to 1810, it was managed very conservatively; secondly, that the control of the amount of currency over prices is more immediate and complete the more redundant it is (it seems that, up to 1810, at least, there had been no such inflation as to float prices); and thirdly, that political and military events were at this time exerting great and sudden effects on prices. The fluctuation of five hundred shillings on the price line in the first six months of 1817, was due to one article—oil. In the next six months, hops advanced two hundred shillings. The downfall in 1818 was due to the crisis.

The warehouse system had been introduced during the last four or five years, and large stocks of colonial produce were being carried by means of the expanded discounts above indicated. Manufactured goods found no market save as they could be smuggled to the continent. The raw materials on which speculation had fastened consequently fell in price. Commerce was almost at a stand-still. The goods exported to South America found no market, for the South

Americans had nothing with which to buy, and the foolish enterprises in that direction could, of course, bring in nothing but shame and loss. British goods in the Baltic towns were confiscated, and the climax was reached when a period of fine weather restored hopes of the harvest, and ruined those who had been led by the bad weather early in the season to speculate for high prices in grain. "The crash began in July with the failure of some great commercial houses. In August a London bank stopped; and several country banks were brought down by its fall. Wild fluctuations in prices followed, and in November, the number of bankruptcies in England, which had usually been under one hundred, had risen to two hundred and seventy-three, 'besides stoppages and compositions,' as the Commercial Report declared, 'equal in number to half the traders in the kingdom.' Manufacturers no longer trusted the merchants nor employed the operatives. In Manchester, 'houses were stopping not only every day but every hour.'

"The commissions of bankruptcy for the year now amounted to two thousand three hundred and fourteen, of which twenty-six were against bankers. The hunger of the operative classes, and the outcry against machinery as the main cause, prepared the events of the succeeding dark years." *

PUBLIC DISCUSSION OF THE BULLION REPORT.

The Bullion Report falling in the midst of this period attracted universal attention. It was hotly discussed in all assemblages of merchants and bankers, and called forth a swarm of pamphlets. It was evident that the witnesses before the committee had fairly represented the opinions which were almost universal in the business community, and they were all contrary to those of the report. It was insisted that the paper had not depreciated; that paper was the best money; that to use gold and silver was barbarous and behind the age; that "guineas were an incumbrance" (although De Yonge was prosecuted for selling this incumbrance for export—a point

---

* Harriet Martineau's Hist. of Eng. I. 294.

which Cobbett was fond of reiterating); that a pound sterling was an " ideal unit;" that a pound sterling was the interest on £33 6s. 8d., at three per cent., which would be £1; that paper money supplied capital, made money plenty, and caused prosperity; that the country had grown up to the increased currency; that the war could not be carried on without paper; that the balance of trade " of course " drew off the gold; that it was impossible to resume while the exchanges were adverse; that Great Britain was in the debtor relation, and could not resume while she was so. In short, there is no possible fallacy now preached in the United States about paper money which was not then and there brought forward, with the single exception of the " elasticity " notion.* As their paper was not fixed in amount, that notion had no place. It seems that there can be no new fallacy to be discovered in regard to paper money. The field is exhausted.

* The reader who is curious to pursue this analogy is referred to Cobbett's Register, vols. 18 and 19. Cobbett's Paper *vs.* Gold goes over the whole subject of paper money in detail. The quotations from contemporaneous literature, the letters from persons who dissented from his views, and the allusions to current events, combine to form a picture of the times which is in striking analogy with all which we now see and experience.

THE PARLIAMENTARY COMMITTEE ON THE COMMERCIAL CRISIS.

On the 7th March, 1811, a committee of the House on Commercial Credit reported. They attributed the crisis to overtrading, failure of South American speculations, and also to the warehousing system. A meeting of merchants in London passed resolutions to the effect that the crisis was mainly due to storing a large stock of goods in bond which the warehousing system had encouraged. The wealth and credit of England thus seemed to them to have caused its calamity. It was proposed in Parliament to issue six millions of Exchequer bills in loans to merchants and manufacturers, to enable them to tide over the crisis. Those who favored this plan adopted the above explanation of the crisis, though nobody explained how the colonial producers had forced Englishmen to carry their stocks for them while the continent was closed. The opponents urged that the currency was really redundant and was the favoring circumstance of the speculation, and that the issue of Exchequer bills would cause further expansion and enhance the difficulty. The bill was passed, but only two millions were ever taken up.

THE DEBATE IN THE HOUSE.

Mr. Horner opened the debate on his Report on the 6th May, 1811, in a very able speech, giving an elucidation of the principles of the report. He had entered upon the investigation with no prejudices and no special knowledge of the subject, but he brought to bear upon it the resources of a well-trained mind, and a single determination to accept such results as might appear upon a full and careful investigation.

The propositions he advocated had, therefore, the character of scientific results, and the man who could so undertake an important inquiry in the face of popular clamor and prejudice, gave promise of the highest statesmanship. "He died," in 1817, "at the age of thirty-eight, possessed of greater public influence than any other private man."

I know of no more instructive documents for the student of finance than the debates of 1811

and 1819. They do not cover the more abstruse
questions in regard to the regulation of a convertible currency, questions which yet require
attentive study and a definite solution, but they
avail to establish those fundamental propositions
in regard to the meaning and function of money,
which, if a man once thoroughly grasps them,
guarantee him against the most flagrant fallacies
which obscure the subject of currency, and enable him to perceive these fallacies whenever
they recur in the thousand and one "schemes"
which are now daily set afloat.

Of the three questions involved in the report,
as stated above : Is the paper depreciated? Why
are the exchanges adverse? How ought the
bank to regulate its issues?—the first and third
have no great importance for us. No one denies
that our paper is depreciated, unless it be those
who think that we have "grown up" to the currency, though that notion seems to have gone out
of fashion again. The question of regulating an
inconvertible bank paper is not our question, because our paper is fixed in amount. But the
second question of the Bullion Committee has

great importance. It is the one in regard to which doctrines opposed to those of the Bullion Report are most frequently affirmed and most profoundly believed amongst us, and there is no hope of any exit from our circumstances until we get to understand the laws which govern the distribution of the precious metals and those laws of currency which are connected therewith. It will be remembered, as stated above, that the question about the exchanges is really this question: If the exchanges are adverse to such a degree as to produce a serious and prolonged outflow of the precious metals, where must we look for the cause? Is it due to the balance of payments or to some deterioration of the currency? Or, to put the same question in another form: If we desire to produce an influx of gold, to what force must we look to cause it? Must we look to the " balance of trade," or can we do anything in the matter save sit still and wait for the balance of trade to turn? Can we bring it about by correcting some error in the currency?

The answer to these questions given in the report and by those who supported it is, that the balance of imports and exports never can move the exchanges either above or below par more than just enough to start a movement of bullion. On a specie system, any outflow of bullion would bring down prices and immediately make a remittance of goods more profitable than one of bullion, and, if the exportation of bullion was artificially continued (as, for instance, to pay the expenses of a foreign war), it would reduce prices until a counter-current would set in and restore the former relative distribution all the world over. If all nations used specie, or even paper and specie, in only due proportion, it would be as impossible for one nation to be drained of specie as for New York harbor to be drained of water by the tide, and, on the same supposition, it would be as absurd for the Secretary of the Treasury or a committee of Congress to regulate the currency as for the same powers to see to it that New York harbor gets its fair share of water on every tide. If a country produces gold, its surplus product goes out as a commodity, without an unfavorable exchange, and does not here come into account. If, therefore, there is an outflow of gold, serious and long-continued, accompanied by an unfavorable exchange, it is a sign that there is an inferior currency behind the gold, which is displacing it. The surplus of imports of goods above the exports of goods is nothing but the return payment for this export of gold, and is not a cause, but a consequence. If, finally, we want to turn this tide and produce an influx, there is only one way to do it, and that is simply to remove the inferior currency. As for waiting for the balance of trade to turn and bring gold into a country which has a depreciated paper currency, one might as well take his stand at the foot of a hill and wait for it to change into a declivity before climbing it.

The authorities of the Bank strenuously denied that their issues, so long as they were made at 5 per cent. on bills representing real transactions, at three months' date, could become excessive, or that the bank issues could affect the exchanges. The committee and their supporters held that this rule would not be a guarantee against inflation, but that, if the exchanges were adverse and bullion was being exported, it was a sign that the paper was excessive, and that the Bank should check its issues. The Bank maintained that it had nothing to do with the exchanges, and could not govern its issues by any reference to them. The bullionists maintained that while the paper was inconvertible, the adverse exchange and the premium on gold were the only signs by which the Bank could judge when its issues were excessive. Thus the real issue was, whether, in case of a drain of specie, we must look at the ratio of imports to exports, or at the ratio of paper currency to requirement, for the explanation of it, and the means of checking it.

In reviewing the debate briefly, I confine attention mainly to those parts which bear on this question of the exchange.

Mr. Horner offered sixteen resolutions, of which the most important may be condensed as follows:

1. That the legal tender in England is gold and silver only.

2. That a shilling is $\frac{1}{62}$ of a troy pound of silver, $\frac{925}{1000}$ fine.

3. That a "guinea" is $\frac{2}{80}$ of a troy pound of gold, $\frac{11}{12}$ fine.

4. That Bank of England notes promise to pay pounds sterling, a pound being $\frac{20}{21}$ of a guinea as above.

5. That Bank of England notes are depreciated—are not worth what they stipulate to pay.

6. That the reason of this is an excessive issue.

7. That the exchanges have been greatly depressed (or, as we should say, very high*), for a long time, partly owing to heavy payments abroad, but chiefly to the depreciation of the notes.

8. That the Bank ought to regulate its issues by the price of bullion and the exchanges.

9. That the remedy is to return to convertibility.

10. That the law extending the Restriction be amended so as to resume in two years.

---

* The English quote exchanges by the amount of the foreign currency which £1 will pay. This is not without exception, any more than our own custom of quoting dollars and cents required to pay a unit of the foreign currency, but it is the prevailing usage. High and low are therefore used in an inverted application in the two countries. Low exchange in this usage tends to an exportation of bullion.

Mr. Rose criticised the report paragraph by paragraph, showing that it was contradictory to the evidence offered to the committee. This was perfectly true; the committee took the facts of their witnesses, but interpreted them in the sense diametrically opposed.

Mr. Thornton (member of the committee) cited the experience of the Bank of Paris. In 1805 it advanced indirectly on government anticipations. " The consequence of this transaction was an augmentation of the paper of the Bank of Paris. A drain of their cash followed; the diligences were found to be carrying off silver into the departments, which the bank, with a view to its own safety, had continually to bring back, with much expense and trouble. The circulating medium of the metropolis had now become evidently excessive. Greater facilities were afforded for borrowing in that quarter than in other places, and the country wished to partake in those opportunities of extending purchases which the metropolis enjoyed. But the paper of the bank would not circulate in the departments. It was therefore necessary first to exchange it for coin, and the coin being then carried away from Paris, the plenty of circulating medium would equalize itself through the French territory. . . . There arose a premium on silver at Paris, and an unfavorable exchange between Paris and the departments of France, and this was proportionate to the expense and trouble of bringing back the silver from the departments. . . . The Bank of Paris at length stopped payment. The government was consulted. The bank was directed to reduce its paper, and in the course of three months, having pursued this principle, it opened without difficulty. The discount on its paper, or, in other words, the premium on coin, had varied from 1 to 10 or 12 per cent., but after the reduction of paper it ceased. The exchanges of France with foreign countries had also turned about 10 per cent against that country."

Mr. Vansittart opposed the resolutions. He argued that the committee ought to have recommended the repeal of the restriction on the exportation of the metals, in order to carry out their own principles. This was true; but he argued that it was illegal to export, therefore the committee were in the position of recommending by implication what was illegal. He denied that there was any "standard" in England, or ever had been, consisting of any weight of metal of a certain fineness, but asserted that it was the pre-rogative of the Crown to regulate the value of money. The proof of this was that silver was legal tender by sale up to £25, but everybody knew that the current shillings were worn below weight; therefore, because a man might put off smooth shillings on his creditor for a debt under £25, there was no standard of what a shilling ought to be in England. Also the law allowed guineas to be legal tender until worn 1 grain and a fraction below weight, therefore there was no fixed weight from and below which this grain and a fraction was to be reckoned.

He also made a great point of demanding to know whether "depreciation" meant depreciation relatively to bullion or to commodities, or refer-red to the credit of the issuer. No one took the trouble to reply that it made no difference with the fact.

He became the hero of the occasion by proposing counter-resolutions, that *the pound sterling has no relation to any weight of metal of a given fineness*, and that *bank-notes* " *have hitherto been, and are at this time, held in public estimation to be equivalent to the legal coin of the realm, and generally accepted as such, in all pecuniary transactions to which such coin is lawfully applicable.*" Guineas were at the time at 15 or 20 per cent. premium, and members of both houses testified in the debate that, although specie had disappeared, and all prices were set in paper, yet there were two prices everywhere, when metal was offered.

This gentleman afterwards became Chancellor of the Exchequer and champion of the Sinking Fund, which was kept up by borrowing at a higher rate than it yielded. He ended life as Lord Bexley.

Mr. Huskisson (one of the committee) pointed to the fact that Spanish dollars, which had been imported for use as " change," and which were worth 4s. 6d. in English coinage, had been rated at 5s., and then, as the depreciation went on, that it had been necessary to rate them at 5s. 6d. to keep them in circulation. He asked whether

the believers in " abstract currency" ever heard of
an abstract payment or an abstract dinner. Ad-
verting to the notion that £1 was 3 per cent. of
£33 6s. 8d., he asked, pertinently enough,
whether this would not fit any conceivable depreciation. The conception of £1 was necessary to
define £33 6s. 8d., which again was necessary to
the definition of £1.

Mr. Morris stated a case which occurred in
1801, in which a creditor had refused tender of
notes, and the court unanimously sustained him
in his position that gold only was legal tender.

Mr. Parnell (one of the committee) took more
clear and decided ground in some respects than
any one else. All parties generally agreed in
sparing the Bank. He refused to join them.
" If, instead of one bank having been established with so immense a capital, and such great
exclusive powers, the trade of banking had been
left free, and several banks had been allowed to
grow up with the improving wealth of the country, the public would have derived equal accomo-
dation, without any of the risk or any of the evils
to which it has been exposed by the enormous

power that has been given to this one establish-ment." He declared that the paper was in an unsound state before 1797. He stated the fundamental doctrine that "a country will always have as much coin as it wants, provided no impolitic act of legislation interferes to force it out of circulation." He attacked the small notes, declaring that the notes under £5 displaced coin equal to their amount.

Mr. Manning, who spoke for the Bank, declared himself "one of those old-fashioned, practical men who thought the balance of payments an article of great importance in the regulation of the exchanges." Showing that the foreign remittances had been £26,000,000 the last year, he argued that the price of gold must have advanced.

Mr. A. Baring, who had been on the committee, and enjoyed high authority, gave more weight to the balance of payments than the committee, but joined them to a certain extent in attributing the unfavorable exchange to the paper. He thought the true cause for anxiety was the debt and not the paper issue.

Mr. Sharp (of the committee) showed that

12*

at Hamburg and Amsterdam, where there was no suspension, but where military oppression was at its harshest, the exchanges were favorable, and that at Paris, the only other place on the continent where inconvertible paper had not been issued, but where war expenditures were highest, exchanges were favorable and there was no drain of the metals.

The *Chancellor of the Exchequer, Mr. Perceval*, did not enter very deeply into the question. His point was, that no excess of circulation had been *proved*. He said that gold was not the standard, nor silver, but gold *and* silver bound down by law to a certain relation to each other. Unfortunately for this notion, no law can possibly bind them together.

Mr. Canning made by far the most eloquent speech on the subject. He advocated the resolutions of Mr. Horner, but thought it inexpedient to resume at that time. He wanted the resolutions passed, except the one for resuming in two years, in order to place the House on the record for sound financial ideas. Referring to the Chancellor's assertion that the excess had not been *proved*, he said that it was impossible to prove any such thing. No relation exists between the aggregate transactions and the requirements for currency, nor, if there did, would it be possible to ascertain the aggregate transactions. The rise in prices is a symptom, but only a symptom. There is no excess unless there is depreciation, and if there is depreciation there is excess. The only pertinent question is, therefore, whether there is depreciation.

"The noble lord (Castlereagh) has indeed devised a singular definition of this measure [of value]. He defines it to be a 'sense of value in reference to currency as compared with commodities.' . . . 'A sense of value!' but whose sense? With whom is it to originate? and how is it to be communicated to others? Who is to promulgate, who is to acknowledge, or who is to enforce it? How is it to be defined? and how is it to be regulated? What ingenuity shall calculate, or what authority control its fluctuations? Is the sense of to-day the same as that of yesterday, and will it be unchanged to-morrow? It does fill me with aston-

ishment that any man of an accurate and reasoning mind should not perceive that this wild
and dangerous principle (if principle it may be
called) would throw loose all the transactions of
private life, all contracts and pecuniary bar-
gains, by leaving them to be measured from day
to day, and from hour to hour, by no other rule
than that of the fancies and interests of each individual, conflicting with the fancies and interests
of his neighbor."

" No dream, it must be owned, could be more
extravagant than the visions of those practical men who have undertaken to refine away
the standard of the currency of the realm into a
pure abstraction. There is indeed something
perfectly ludicrous in the inconsistency and injustice with which they impute a love of abstraction
to their opponents, while they are themselves
indulging in the most wanton departures from
substance and reality. ' Beware of abstractions,'
say they to the Bullion Committee when they
find fact and law laid down as the foundation of
its report. ' Beware of abstractions,' say they,
to the honorable and learned chairman of the

committee, when they find in his first seven resolutions nothing like theory or imagination, but a clear, concise,—a dry and faithful recapitulation of those rules which the statutes of the country have established for the weight and fineness of its coin. . . . And this admonition comes from whom?—from the inventors and champions of ' abstract currency '—from those who, after exhausting in vain every attempt to find an earthly substitute for the legal and ancient standard of our money, have divested the pound sterling of all the properties of matter, and pursued it, under the name of the ' ideal unit,' into the regions of nonentity and nonsense ! "

" In addition to the motives of policy, there are, as I have heard this night, not without astonishment and dismay, considerations of justice which preclude any systematic reduction of the amount of our paper currency. Such a reduction, it is argued, would change the value of existing contracts and throw into confusion every species of pecuniary transactions, from the rent of the great landed proprietor down to the wages of the peasant and the artisan. Good

God! what is this but to say that the system of irredeemable paper currency must continue forever! What is it but to say that the debts incurred, and the contracts entered into, under the old established legal standard of the currency, including the debts and contracts of the state itself, are now to be lopped and squared to a new measure, set up originally as a temporary expedient?"

Referring to Mr. Vansittart's resolution about paper and gold being equal, he said:

"Speaking impartially, I must say that if I had seen this proposition anywhere but where it is, fairly printed and numbered in the right honorable gentleman's series, I should have thought it an invention of his antagonists, calculated to place the fallacy of his doctrine in the most glaring and ridiculous point of view, but carrying the license of exaggeration beyond pardonable limits, and defeating its purpose by the grossness of the caricature."

"Suppose, for instance, ten millions sufficient to carry on all the transactions of the country: fabricate fifteen millions of paper instead of ten, the whole fifteen will circulate. The only consequence will be that the commodities for which it is exchanged will rise fifty per cent. in their nominal price. Make those fifteen millions twenty—the addition will, in like manner, be absorbed into the enhanced prices of commodities. Excess of currency cannot be proved to the conviction of those who will not admit depreciation to be the proof of it."

Mr. Horner's resolutions were defeated by a vote, on the first, of 151 to 75, and the one for resumption in two years by 180 to 45.

Mr. Vansittart's counter-resolutions were passed on the fifteenth of May, the one declaring gold and paper equal by 151 to 75; and so the House put upon its records that a guinea was equal to a one-pound note and a shilling, when £100 paper would buy only £86 in gold.

In this debate the "theorists" and the "practical" men found themselves in sharp contrast. The Bullion Committee took the evidence of their witnesses as to fact but gave their own explanation of the facts. They carried the best thinkers in the House with them, but found the practical bankers and city men, and the great mass who did not understand the matter, and who had an invincible dislike to admitting that bank-notes were depreciated, against them. In this case, as always, theory and practice are inseparable. The city men had a theory of their facts. It was really one theory against another; the one drawn from a narrow routine: the other a philosophical and scientific generalization from a broad range of facts. The theorists were beaten, and the nation went on for eight years' further experiment of the paper. We have now to pursue the verdict of history and experience as between the two parties.

COMMERCIAL EVENTS FROM 1810 TO 1819.

"Nothing had been seen since the beginning of the century to compare with the distress of 1811 and 1812. . . . Our manufacturers were set fast, and could not pay wages on which their workmen could live; and workmen could not live on low wages when the average price of wheat was 112s. [the quarter, of 8 bushels], and that of meat 8d. or 9d. per pound. The ordinary course of manufacture, particularly of the hardware manufacture, was broken up. The factor * stepped in between the employer and the operative, and made his market of the necessities of both, leaving them discontented with each other. The employer sold off his stock at a loss, and the workmen made inferior wares by means of advances from the factor for materials."†

Nature seemed to make common cause with war and bad finance. The winter of 1812 was extraordinarily severe, and the accidents by flood and fire were numerous. Crimes began to multiply in that accord between physical distress and moral decay so often noticed. Wages were down at starvation point. Spinners had 7s. 6d. per week in a time of high prices for the necessaries of life. The recent introduction of machinery and the extension of the factory system would have caused an inevitable period of pressure on hand-workers. Now these causes fell in with others to enhance the distress. The artisans, in striking analogy with our own farmers

---

* The appearance of the "middle-man" ought to be noticed.

† Martineau's History of England, I. 329.

at the present time, sought their foe in the nearest and most palpable shape in which the bad circumstances of the time pressed upon them. They attacked the machines, burned the factories, and united in riotous disturbances. The corn laws were in full force, and prevented the relief which might have come from other countries in time of scarcity, while manufacturers were entangled in a mesh of restrictions of every description, more ruinous even than Napoleon's Decrees or the Orders in Council. "The war and famine price [of grain] of 1812 was reached again in the latter part of 1816, 1817, and 1818. The golden days of the deity that is found in no mythology—the anti-Ceres—were returned. But the people were starving. Misery and insurrection filled the land." The harvest of 1815 was abundant, and to prevent importations, all such were prohibited when wheat was under 80s. In 1816, in spite of this law, the agriculturists were once more "in distress." The years when they were not so, down to the repeal of the corn laws in 1846, were the few years when nature refused her bountiful returns.

In 1814 peace was restored, and it was believed that commerce must at once revive. Anticipating this, enormous exportations were made to the continent and to the United States " The shippers found to their cost, when it was too late, that the effective demand on the continent for colonial produce and British manufactures had been greatly overrated, for, whatever might be the desire of the foreign consumers to possess articles so long out of their reach, they were limited in their means of purchase, and accordingly the bulk of the commodities exported brought very inadequate returns."

They found that it is impossible to "inundate" a country with foreign commodities, or to "drain off its bullion" by foreign trade, if it does not want to be drained. As for a true exchange of goods, the laws hampered it by all sorts of restrictions and prohibitions.

Thus, in 1816, after the long endurance of the war, and the dragging misery of 1812, '13, and '14, broken only by fitful gleams of prosperity, this " overtrading" prostrated commerce and manufactures together, and agriculture was no better off.

Turning now to the currency to observe its movements contemporaneously with these expansions of speculation, we find a great difficulty in the impossibility of estimating the country bank circulation. The best information we have is given in the report of the Lords' Committee of 1819. They gave two estimates as follows. The rate of gold per oz. is added from McCulloch's Adam Smith.

(Five figures omitted.)

	Bank of England.	Country Banks. 1st Est.	Total.	Country Banks. 2d Est.	Total.	Gold per ounce.		
						£.	s.	d.
1810	22.5	21.3	43.9	21.8	44.3	4	10	0
1811	23.2	20.9	44.2	21.5	44.8	4	4	6
1812	23.2	20.0	43.'	19.9	43.1	4	15	6
1813	24.0	22.3	46.3	22.5	46.6	5	1	0
1814	26.9	21.6	48.5	22.7	48.6	5	4	0
1815	26.8	20.3	47.2	19.0	45.8	4	13	6
1816	26.5	15.5	42.0	15.0	41.6	4	13	6
1817	28.2	15.8	44.1	15.8	44.1	4	0	0
1818	27.2	20.0	47.2	20.5	47.7	4	0	0

The steady expansion until 1816 is at once apparent, and its effect on prices is distinctly shown by the gold premium, which advances with the expansion of the paper. In 1816, when the revulsion came, the country banks failed in great numbers. The contraction of their issues was so great that, though the Bank of England *increased* its issues in 1817, the gold premium fell, and the paper was within a few pence of par. Resumption at this time would scarcely have cost a struggle. However, no effort of this kind was made. On the contrary, no sooner was the immediate crisis over, than a new expansion commenced. (See the diagram at the end . of this chapter.)

The harvest failing in 1817, the price of wheat rose above 80s., and the ports were opened; speculation in grain was active during that year. 1818 presented the same phenomena, but now were added speculations in silk, wool, cotton, and other raw materials. Imports were double or treble what they had been in 1816.

In 1817, the Bank voluntarily undertook to redeem its notes dated before Jan. 1st, 1817, but, adhering to the doctrine that the issues could not affect the exchanges, it continued to expand the circulation, while paying out gold. The laws against exportation having fallen into neglect, a run upon the Bank began, and a rapid exportation to France took place. The government ordered the Bank to cease paying specie. According to the doctrines of the Bullion Report, to expand the circulation with gold at a premium and the exchanges adverse, and then pay on demand, was as certain to produce exportation as it would be, if a tub full of water should be lifted on one side, that the water would run out. The fact seemed to fall in with this doctrine.

Another incident which co-operated in the financial situation of 1818 was the reduction of interest on the Exchequer bills. This, coming just at a time when several foreign nations were anxious to negotiate loans, led to a great exportation of coin for investment in such loans, the rate of interest offered being higher than the new rate for Exchequer bills. On a specie basis, and with no usury law, such a movement could have no perils; but in the existing circumstances, the Bank was led to make more advances on government securities and augment the inflation. It paid off by contract with government those who refused to hold the securities at the lower rate.

The most powerful cause, however, which was at work, and the one of which the last-mentioned was only a secondary form, was the reduction of paper issues on the continent. The loans were contracted to accomplish this. If it had not been that these issues had produced abnormal relations throughout Europe and America, which, as soon as they were rectified and the normal state of things restored, must produce a redistribution of the metals, the loans would have had no importance. The force of this cause it is impossible to estimate, but it lay at the bottom of the fluctuations of bullion at the Bank during the years 1816 to 1819.

The crash came in the fall of 1818, and numerous failures occurred during the winter. By February the Bank of England circulation had fallen to 25.1 millions. The subject of cash payments was now once more forced on public attention.

THE COMMITTEES OF 1819.

Both Houses of Parliament appointed committees on the Resumption. Each committee rendered two reports consecutively. These reports were not in themselves very able documents, but it appeared from the reports, and from the evidence of the persons examined, that the public conviction in regard to the questions discussed in 1811 had entirely changed.   It was now admitted by all but very few that the currency was depreciated, and that the adverse exchanges and outflow of gold were consequences of the presence of depreciated paper, and must last so long as the paper remained—consequently, that, to resume specie payments, the whole problem was to get rid of the paper.   These doctrines were disputed by no one save, strangely enough, the directors of the Bank of England.   They passed a resolution that they could see no good ground for the opinion that the Bank had " only to reduce its issues to obtain a favorable turn in the exchanges, and a consequent influx of the precious metals."

There was, however, a strong party of city men who opposed resumption, and petitioned against it on account of the ruin which contraction would bring upon the country.   The Bank of England also offered a " Representation " opposed to any legislation fixing a time for resumption. The difficulties involved in contraction no one denied.

It was agreed on all sides that the movement must be gradual and careful, if made at all. Thus the question was narrowed down to this: Is it expedient, in view of the effects of the suspension which we have experienced, and in view of the benefits of a sound currency, to set to work manfully to endure the distress for the sake of the good? On that issue the city men took the negative, the statesmen the affirmative.

The plan proposed for resumption, was founded on Ricardo's theory of currency, more familiarly known as the Hamburg currency.

On this plan, metal may be deposited in the Bank, being weighed and assayed, and its value in a set denomination is put to the credit of the depositor. No coin is used, but generally business is done by transfers on the Bank's books of credits thus made. When payments out of Bank are demanded, they are made in ingots, weighed, assayed, and stamped. It was proposed that the Bank should redeem its notes in ingots of sixty ounces weight after February 1st, 1820, and until the 1st of October, 1820, at £4 1s. per ounce; from October 1st, 1820, to May 1st, 1821, at £3 19s. 6d.; from May 1st, 1821, to May 1st, 1823, at £3 17s. 10½d.; and after May 1st, 1823, in coin on demand. This was amended so that it should pay in ingots at £3 17s. 10½d. after May 1st, 1822, instead of May 1st, 1821.

THE DEBATE OF 1819.

Mr. Peel opened the debate. He said: "He was ready to avow, without shame or remorse, that he went into the committee with a very different opinion from that which he at present entertained, for his views of the subject were most materially different when he voted against the resolutions brought forward in 1811, by Mr. Horner, as the chairman of the Bullion Committee. Having gone into the inquiry determined to dismiss all former impressions which he might have received, . . . he had resolved . . . to adopt every inference which authentic information or mature reflection should offer to his mind. . . . He conceived them [the principles of the Bullion

Report], to represent the true nature and laws of our monetary system."

" All the witnesses examined before the committee strongly recommended the establishment of this [metal] standard, one witness alone excepted, who was an advocate for the indefinite suspension of cash payments. But when this witness was asked whether the indefinite suspension of cash payments was to exist without any standard of value, he answered: 'No—the pound should be the standard.' He was required to define what he meant by the pound. His answer was, 'I find it difficult to explain it, but every gentleman in England knows it.' The committee repeated the question and Mr. Smith answered, 'It is something which has existed in this country for eight hundred years—three hundred years before the introduction of gold.'"

"Sir Isaac Newton . . . entered on the examination of this subject, but that great man came back to the old, the vulgar doctrine, as it was called by some, that the true standard of value consisted in a definite quantity of gold bullion. Every sound writer on the subject came to the

same conclusion—that a certain weight of gold
bullion, with an impression on it denoting it to be
of that certain weight and of a certain fineness,
constituted the only true, intelligible, and adequate standard of value, and to that standard
the country must return, or the difficulties of our
situation would be aggravated as we proceeded."

" That the excess of commercial speculation
which led to such evils was the consequence of
an over-issue of paper currency was a fact not to
be disputed."

" If the continuance [of this system] should be
sanctioned by the House, let it not be imagined
that they ought to measure its future evils by its
past."

Silver had been demonetized in 1816, and the
shillings since that time pass current at six per
cent. above their value as metal. Gold is the
only legal tender for sums above £2. The
object of this law is to avoid the effect of fluctuations in the value of the two metals as compared
with each other. The United States passed a
similar law in 1853. (See p. 187.)

It was believed by many that this law would

prove fatal to resumption in gold, and that only silver would circulate. The provision that silver should be legal tender only for 40s. precluded any such danger.

Mr. Tierney objected to the proposed scheme for resumption. He wanted to have the Bank thrown on its own responsibility to resume on a set day, the government repaying, as was proposed, £10,000,000 of the advances of the bank before the day of resumption. He was a very able man, with a reputation for pugnacity. For instance: " The House did not withdraw its confidence from the Bank from any doubt of its wealth or integrity, but from a conviction of its total ignorance of the principles of political economy."

Alderman Heygate denied inflation and depreciation.

Sir H. Parnell said that any one who still denied this would pay little heed to any further elucidation. He said: " There was another subject so connected with the question before the House that he thought it peculiarly entitled to the consideration of Parliament. He meant the usury laws, for it was evident that if those laws remained in their present state they must operate very injuriously with regard to the supply of capital for the purposes of trade, by diminishing the means of obtaining discounts."

Mr. Gurney (banker) opposed resumption. He dreaded the effects of contraction, and wanted the standard lowered so that 1 oz. of gold should be £4 os. 6d.

Mr. Canning closed the debate, saying that it was "the unanimous determination of Parliament that the country should return, as speedily as possible, to the ancient standard of value in the establishment of a metallic currency." [Loud and universal cries of "Hear! hear!"]

In the House of Lords, the *Marquis of Lansdowne* said: "He hoped the country would never again hear of the theories founded on the abstract idea of a pound sterling as a unit, or a bank-note and a shilling being in public estimation equal to a guinea; on the tendency of gold to fly to other countries where it was dearer, without producing any change of value, and other absurdities of that kind. These theories, which had been so ruinous to the country, deserved to be stigmatized as they were by the bill before their lordships, every enactment of which declared their falsehood. By acting on them the country had been overwhelmed by an oppressive mass of debt and grinding system of taxation, all the evils of which were augmented by the fluctuation of values."

Lord Liverpool thought that the restriction had enabled the country to go through the war. Also, that the opposition to the plan proposed really raised the question, not of resuming sooner or later, but whether to resume at all.

Lord Lauderdale thought that the demonetization of silver had done great mischief, turned the exchanges, and driven out gold in 1817; that the paper was not really depreciated, but at par with silver coinage ; that it was quackery to say the Clearing House economized currency ; and that the plan proposed, together with the mint law, would bring ruin.

Lord King said that if no day was fixed,

the Bank would not get ready, as it had not since the Peace.

Lord Grenville said that, " having considered this restriction as one of the greatest calamities under which this suffering country had labored; having frequently had occasion to lament and deplore the part which he had himself taken on its original proposition in prolonging it for the term of the then existing war . . . he could not help expressing his joy and satisfaction that the country was at last arrived at that period in which it could look forward with certainty to the repeal of this injudicious and unfortunate measure." He declared that an irredeemable paper currency was, under any circumstances, a greater evil than good; that "he hoped it would be recorded of him as his decided conviction, that in proportion to the danger under which the country labored, he would almost say, in proportion to the extent of that danger, was the impolicy and desperate madness of such a measure as they were now considering how to rescind. . . . He could show how the miseries of 1816 followed on the issues of the preceding year; he could show how the excessive issues of country paper, which could not maintain itself like bank paper by legislative enactment, led to a fearful depreciation, and without any fault of individuals, by the mere force of the system, involved the whole kingdom in one general desolation. Not only its trade and commerce, but its agriculture, its landed interest, even classes the most remote from connection with, or even knowledge of, the paper system, found themselves suddenly consigned to total and inexplicable ruin. If their lordships could see at their bar, not merely the victims of commercial failure, but those numerous persons of all ages, sexes, and classes, who had unconsciously suffered without even understanding how or whence the evil fell upon them, such a spectacle would fill their lordships with horror; and he sincerely believed that not only would no voice be raised for the maintenance of such a system in commerce, but not even in war.'

He also urged strongly the necessity of making the Bank independent of government.

The bill was passed, and the government having repaid £10,000,000 of the advances of the Bank, which was recognized as an indispensable condition of resumption, the act went into operation. At the same time the law forbidding the exportation of the precious metals was repealed.

OPERATION OF PEEL'S ACT OF 1819.

A great fall of prices took place in 1819 as a sequel to the operations of 1818. Tooke denies strenuously that the operation of the act caused this fall. There was no run upon the Bank for gold, partly because the people did not care for it, partly because the plan of ingot redemption did not tempt them to do so, but chiefly because the fall in prices turned the exchanges and there was no profit on exportation. The Bank steadily contracted its issues, and the country banks were forced to do the same. The issues and the price of gold were as follows:

		Bank of England notes.	Bullion in Bank of England.	Price of gold per ounce.		
				£.	s.	d.
Feb.	1819	25.1	4.1	4	1	6
"	1820	23.4	4.1	3	19	11
"	1821	23.8	11.8	3	17	10½
"	1822	18.6	11.0			
"	1823	18.5	10.3			

The Bank resumed payment, by its own wish and the permission of Parliament, on May 1, 1821.

Peel's act would, under any circumstances of trade, have enforced contraction and accomplished resumption, but under the series of events of the following years, it is certain that it had no direct effect whatever. The revulsion and fall of prices, and shock to credit of 1819 repeated the opportunity of 1817. The exchanges became favorable, more currency was needed, as always in a time of crisis, and the Bank contraction which did not begin until late in 1819 (the circulation was higher in August than in February) took place easily, as confidence was restored and notes, becoming abundant, flowed to the Bank, without exerting any pressure on the market, unless it might be the negative one of restraining speculation. Peel's act had only the indirect effect of setting a time for resumption which was understood to be in earnest, whereas former dates fixed had been practically indefinite adjournments. England is the only country which, after falling into the use of inconvertible depreciated paper, has returned to specie payments save through bankruptcy. It did so by taking advantage of the revulsion following a commercial crisis to reduce the amount of the paper.

On issuing from the era of redundant and depreciated paper, it is necessary to turn to *prices* as the test and indication of economic circumstances. (See p. 253.) The inquiry into prices, however, is the most difficult and delicate which the economist is called upon to undertake, and one of the most perilous, whenever undertaken piecemeal, or without skill, or to support a theory.

Tooke investigated prices during this period with a skill which is universally acknowledged, and proved conclusively that the fall which took place was not due to contraction. Gold was continually coming into circulation and filling up any vacuum caused by the contraction.

The years 1819–1822 were years of abundant

harvests and low prices for grain, and the agricultural interest was accordingly in distress. There were, however, additional causes for this distress. During the war, the high prices had led the farmers to increase their expenditures and raise their style of living. Poor lands had also been hired at high prices and brought under cultivation. These injudicious ventures could not be sustained in times of peace and plenty, and those who had embarked in them found themselves ruined. In 1822 Mr. Western led an assault upon Peel's bill as the cause of the distress, and the resumption then went through its last and severest peril. It is true that the proposition of Mr. Western for a committtee of inquiry into the action of the bill was negatived by a heavy vote, but it appeared that there were some active and influential men who wanted to return to paper, and others who thought a great mistake had been made in not accepting the depreciation and reducing the standard, and they were supported by a clamorous party suffering under distress. They did at last secure the concession that the notes under £5 were allowed to circulate until 1832, instead of being withdrawn in 1824 as the law then pro-vided.

Meanwhile manufactures were steadily recovering, and wages were advancing in purchasing power by the fall of grain and imported commodities.

CRISIS OF 1825, AND ABOLITION OF SMALL NOTES.

In the year 1824 the interest on the government five per cent. stock was reduced to 4 per cent. the Bank engaging to pay off the dissentients. One result of this was to lead to large investments in foreign loans. The prosperity of manufactures led to large importations of cotton and other raw materials. Joint stock companies were organized to engage in all sorts of enterprises, some of them fanciful and absurd, and a great speculation in South American mines began. The state of the Bank was:

		Notes.	Bullion.
Feb.	1823	18.5	10.3
"	1824	19.7	13.8
"	1825	20.7	8.7
"	1826	25.4	2.4
"	1827	21.8	10.1

In 1823-4 the Bank, being strong in bullion, extended its discounts, thus sustaining the advancing movement by the usual mode under the convertible system. But at the end of 1824 the exchanges became adverse, and an outflow of bullion began. The Bank, nevertheless, continued to extend its issues. In May, 1825, prices suddenly fell. The speculation came to a crisis; country banks failed in large numbers; one of the large London banking houses failed, and all had to undergo severe runs. It was not until some months later that the mercantile community sustained the shock, but it fell upon them with terrible force. The bank-note now came in to fulfil its office at such a period. During the rise of the speculation, the issues had been only gradually and slowly increased, but, in the breakdown of credit, notes were required in large numbers. The question was whether the Bank should extend its issues, and run the risk of ruining itself, or contract, and ruin the public. It adopted the former course, discounting freely at 5 per cent. for all solvent borrowers. The lucky discovery of a box of £1 notes which had been withdrawn, stored away, and forgotten, enabled them to pursue this policy to the utmost. It appeared, however, that very few of these last notes were needed. There are two elements in every commercial crisis, one the *crisis* of a false or exaggerated mercantile movement of some sort, and second, the *panic* of those who fear everything, but they do not know what. The plan here described is a specific remedy for the panic element. It was prescribed by the Bullion Report, and thus another of its doctrines was ratified.

The Bank found itself with only £2,459,510 in bullion in February, 1826. To the parliamentary Committee appointed to investigate the crisis, Mr. Horsley Palmer testified that the drain of gold was chiefly due to the £1 notes, these being in the hands of holders most liable to panic. Small notes were at this time subject to a stamp, and the government took the step of prohibiting any more stamps to be issued.

When Parliament met this step was blamed as unconstitutional, but the ministers declared that they had taken the step because, if any day had been fixed beyond which no stamps should be issued, or if the subject of small notes had come up for discussion, there would have been a rush for stamps. They proposed to allow the small notes already stamped to run until April 5, 1829, and then to allow no more notes under £5 in England. The debate on this proposition was long, and on the part of the opposition unclear and not to the point.

The proposition was advocated by *Mr. Huskisson*, who said that "a permanent state of cash payments and a circulation of one and two pound notes could not co-exist." He urged that specie was the poor man's currency, and that, while there were no small notes, commercial crises might sweep over the mercantile community, but could not affect the laboring classes.

Mr. Grant said, that "in every wise system of currency it was a primary element that paper should be convertible at pleasure into a metallic currency, and that all small payments and the great bulk of the circulation should be in gold."

Alderman Heygate said, that the country bankers would be forced to withdraw their small notes within three years, which would bring ruin. He said that the act of 1819 was intended to bring back the old standard, but that it had raised that standard. The proof was that the coins were exported on account of their "fineness and beauty."

Mr. Attwood propounded a new law of the distribution of the precious metals: "The share of the precious metals which any country, rich or poor, could maintain, if there was any truth in experience, would be in the proportion of about half an ounce of gold against a quarter [8 bushels] of wheat, which gave 40s. or 50s. a quarter of this money, and no more."

Thus the opposition ran over the whole history of the Restriction and the whole theory of money, but the question was, whether, having a convertible currency, they should have in it notes under £5.

Mr. Canning said: "If on the present occasion I am for withdrawing, within a limited time, the one-pound note from circulation, it is not from the mere love of theory, but because I have seen it practically proved in the experience of

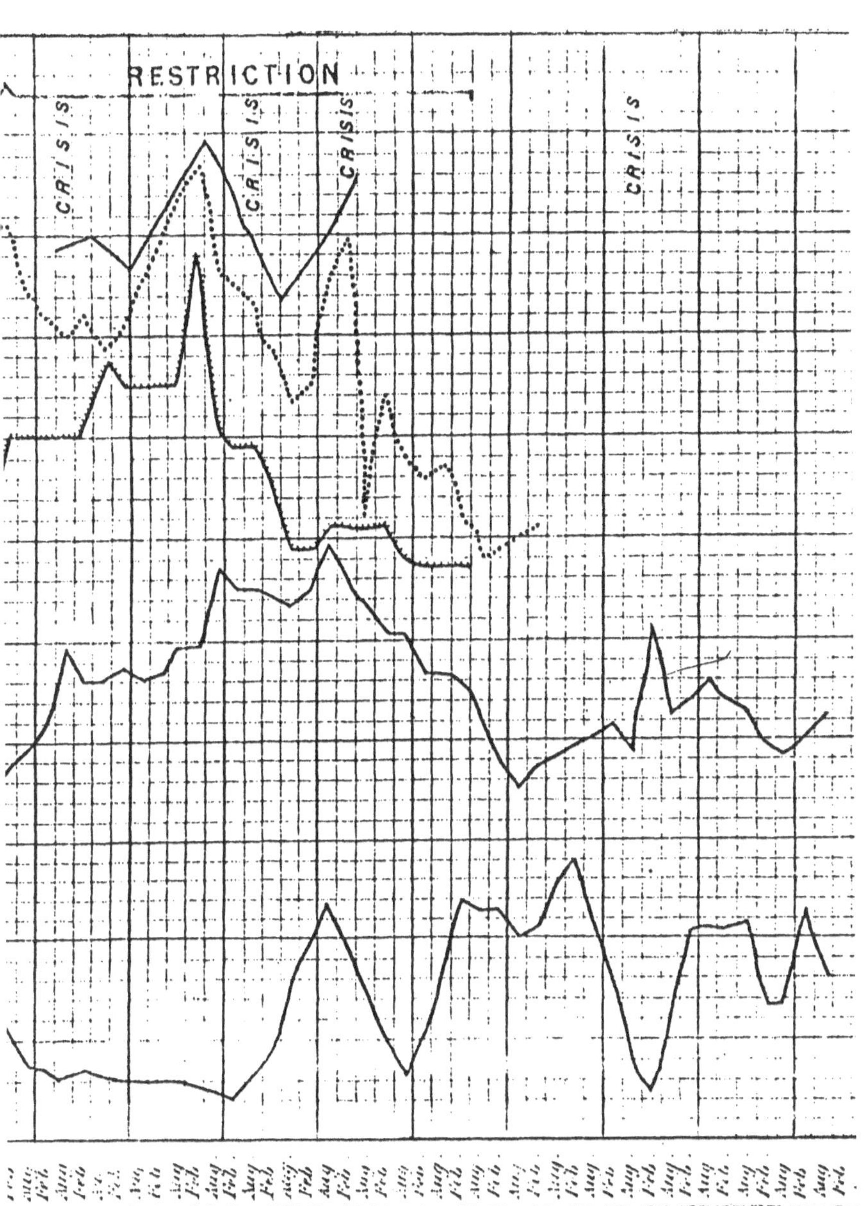

RESTRICTION
CRISIS
CRISIS
CRISIS
CRISIS

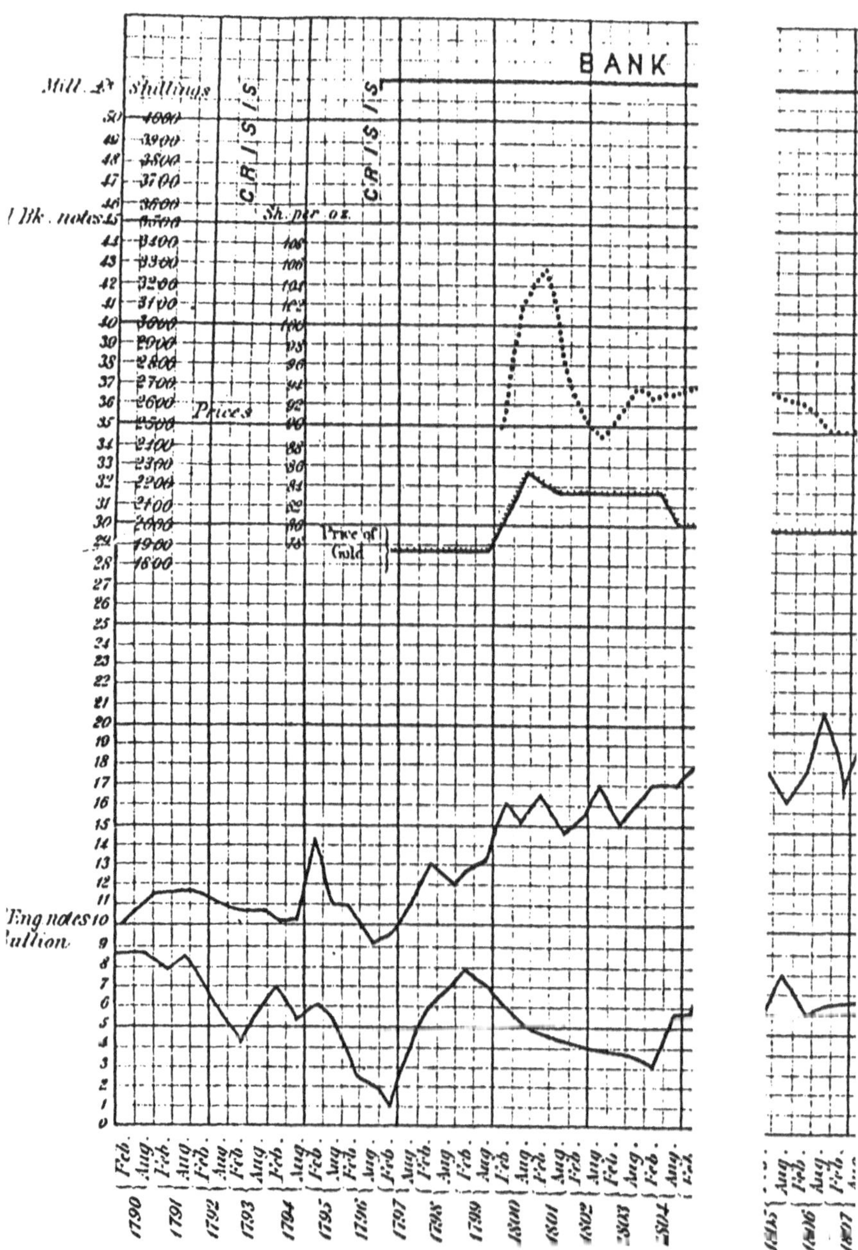

BANK
Mill.£
Shillings
CRISIS
CRISIS
Sh. per oz.
Bk. notes
Prices
Price of Gold
Eng. notes
Bullion
1790 Feb. Aug.
1791 Feb. Aug.
1792 Feb. Aug.
1793 Feb. Aug.
1794 Feb. Aug.
1795 Feb. Aug.
1796 Feb. Aug.
1797 Feb. Aug.
1798 Feb. Aug.
1799 Feb. Aug.
1800 Feb. Aug.
1801 Feb. Aug.
1802 Feb. Aug.
1803 Feb. Aug.
1804 Feb. Aug.
1805 Feb. Aug.
1806 Feb. Aug.
1807 Feb. Aug.

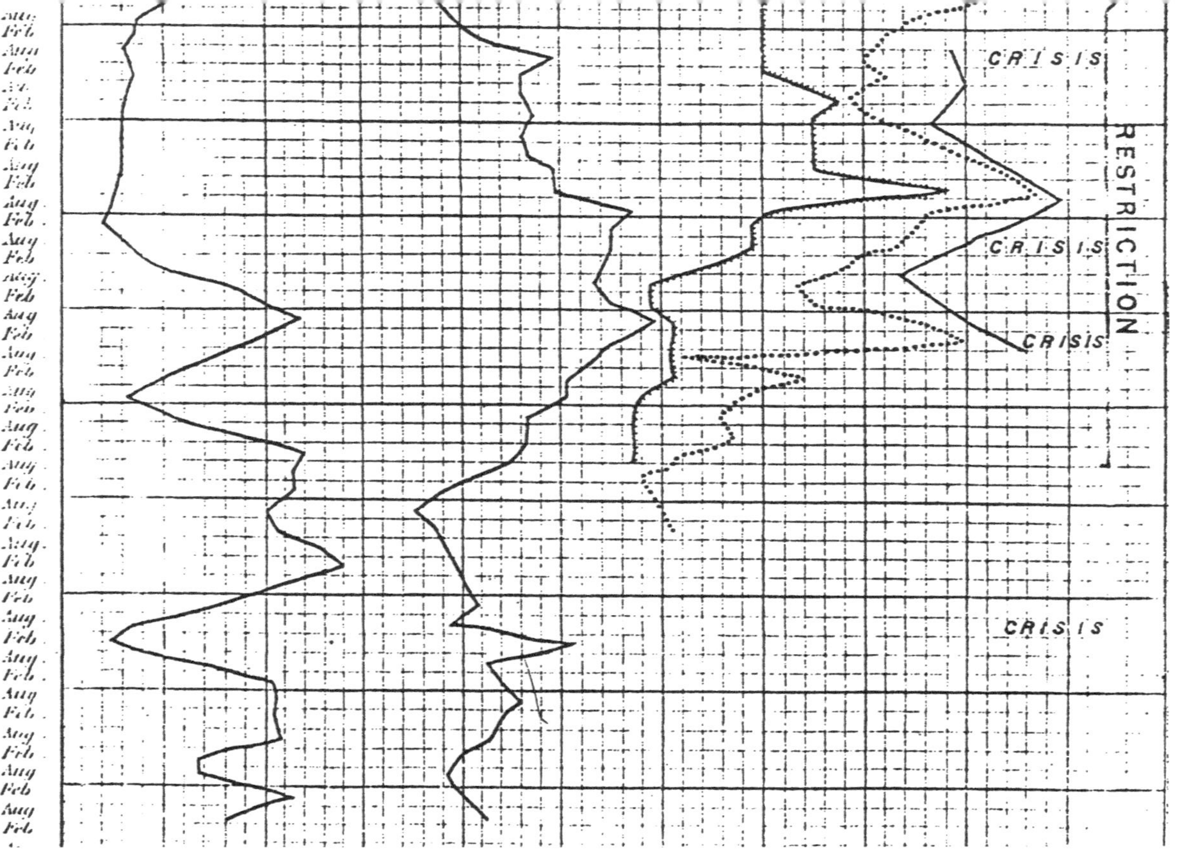

1809
1810
1811
1812
1813
1814
1815
1816
1817
1818
1819
1820
1821
1822
1823
1824
1825
1826
1827
1828
1829
1830
1831
Aug
Feb
RESTRICTION
CRISIS
CRISIS
CRISIS
CRISIS

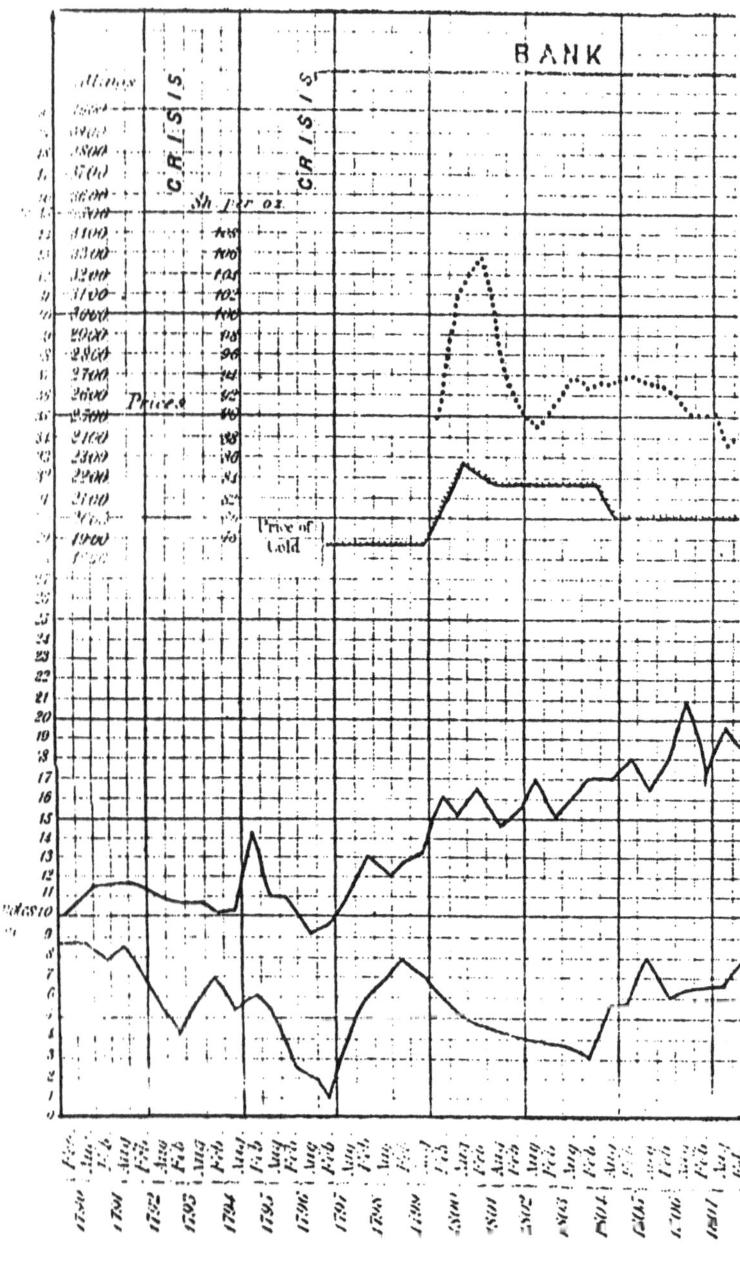

BANK
CRISIS
CRISIS
Sh. per oz.
Price
Price of Gold

years which have elapsed since the Bullion Com
mittee sat, that the circulation of the small notes
cannot co-exist with a metallic currency."

" It is vain to think of introducing gold amidst
the overwhelming spread of small paper circulation. The small paper chokes up all the ordinary
channels of circulation, so that the gold, though
issued from the Bank, cannot flow into them, but
is returned to the source from which it came."

A test-vote, not directly on the question,
showed two hundred and twenty-two in favor,
and thirty-nine against. The small notes were
withdrawn in 1829.

There have been fluctuations enough since
then, and events which have illustrated and
proved some weighty principles of currency, but
they lie beyond the scope of the present undertaking.

Specie payments could not be regarded as
fixed on a solid basis until the small notes were
withdrawn. In the year 1827, the Bank of England directors gave in their adhesion to the doctrines of the Bullion Report, and those doctrines,
together with the exclusion of the small notes,

have been the foundation of the English convertible currency ever since.

The question how to *regulate* a convertible currency is still hotly disputed, and is far from a solution. It seems that art can help nature here as well as elsewhere, but we may be very sure that it can so help here only *as* it does elsewhere, —by following and assisting, not by supplanting and coercing.

A convertible currency is, like steel, not a natural product, but an artificial development, and in many respects superior, but it is as if we had not yet discovered the law by which to make the artificial product so that it should be neither too brittle nor too elastic, too hard nor too soft. One thing is very certain—that our blundering experiments have hitherto cost us far more than we have gained or saved.

So much, however, in regard to the laws which govern paper issues, as was laid down in the Bullion Report, is established beyond dispute. Its doctrines are the alphabet of modern finance.

The assertion has been many times made, in the United States, within the last year, that the period of the Restriction, in England, was a period of prosperity and financial success. A diligent reading of the appropriate documents, historical and legislative, has failed to bring to light any evidence at all to support this notion, or to lead to acquaintance with any English authority, contemporaneous or subsequent, who looks upon this period as anything else than a time of distress and humiliation.

EXPLANATION OF THE DIAGRAM.

In the following diagram, some of the movements of the period of the Bank Restriction are presented in a manner more distinct than any statistics can attain. The Bank of England circulation advanced steadily during the Restriction, under the rule adopted by the directors (p. 265). So soon as the crisis of 1818 brought a reduction, and Peel's act of 1819 enforced resumption, the Bank was forced to act upon the principles of the Bullion Report, though it still rejected them in theory, and retain its notes as they came back. So soon as the reduction of the issues began, everything conspired to assist it, and it went on until August, 1822, although specie payments were nominally resumed in May, 1821. The line at the top of the diagram, between 1810 and 1819, represents the total circulation of Bank of England and country-bank notes for the only period for which we have any estimate of them (see pp. 255 and 284). It shows the nett reduction in 1816, though the Bank of England kept up and increased its notes, and the increase in bullion (lowest line in the diagram) meets it exactly in accordance with the doctrine enunciated by the bullionists. When the total notes increased again in 1817, the bullion declined. When the Bank of England contracted, in 1819 and 1820, the country banks were forced to do the same, and the bullion increased. In 1824, under new inflation, it declined. The sudden increase and decrease of Bank of England notes in 1825, was in obedience to the doctrine of the Report in regard to the method of dealing with a panic (pp. 250, 304).

On the price line, see p. 252. The articles whose prices are summed up each six months are: 1 cwt. ashes; 1 cwt. bristles; 1 cwt. coffee; 1 lb. cochineal; 1 cwt. copper; 100 lbs. cotton; 1 ton flax; 1 ton hemp; 1 cwt. hops; 10½ cwt. lead; 1 lb. indigo; 1 ton iron; 252 gals. oil; 1 cwt. butter; 304 lbs. mess beef; 1 cwt. rice; 1 cwt. saltpetre; 1 lb. raw silk; 1 lb. cinnamon; 100 lbs. pepper; 1 gal. rum; 1 cwt. sugar; 1 cwt. tallow; 1 barrel tar; 1 lb. tea; 1 load timber; 1 cwt. tin; 100 lbs. tobacco; 1 lb. wool; 8 bu. wheat.   I have varied somewhat from the units of quantity in Tooke's tables in order that the fluctuations of each article might have an equal effect on the aggregate.

The price of gold is taken from the table in Tooke's " Prices," Vol. II.

CHAPTER III.

AUSTRIAN PAPER MONEY.[*]

THE First Austrian National Bank was founded about the year 1700, but was transferred to the authorities of the city of Vienna very soon after. This bank issued notes in moderate amounts, which bore interest and commanded a premium. In 1762, this apparently rich source of wealth was seized upon as a resource for the distress of the government, and from that time to this Austria has been under the dominion of paper; from that time on, for more than a century, every year has seen a deficit in the Austrian finances.

The new notes bore no interest, and were for sums from five to one hundred gulden. They "were to be taken everywhere in payment." It was forbidden to export coin, and base coins of small denominations were issued. The latter,

* Republished from the "Financier" of October 25th, 1873.

nevertheless, went to a premium in paper as the notes increased. This increase was at the same time persistently represented by the government as a temporary necessity, the Bank having been allowed to issue notes in return for its advances to the government. "In 1802, the country was flooded with counterfeit seven-kreutzer pieces." They nevertheless were at a premium in paper. In 1807, copper coins were issued so base as to be on a level with the paper. Meanwhile the issues had been increasing; the government had found that there was no returning on the course on which it had entered. The wars with Napoleon demanded supplies, and there were no resources. The prohibitive system had crushed the indigenous industry of the country, made smuggling the most profitable of all forms of business, and created a few weak, exotic industries. Prices had risen so high that the nominal sums required for army supplies, etc., were enormous. The note issue in 1796 was 47,000,000; in 1800, it was 200,000,000; in 1806, it was 449,000,000. There were, besides, counterfeits in immense quantities. The laws against counterfeiting or

being possessed of counterfeits were so severe,
and the difficulty of detecting them so great, that
people feared to take notes at all, and this of
course enhanced the premium.

The succeeding years saw new "patents" in
regard to the finances issued every few months;
each project was more desperate or more tyran-
nical than the last. Trust funds were required
to be invested in public securities or bank-notes,
and deposited with the Bank; then these were
taken by the State, which became responsible to
the owners. All silver plate was ordered to be
brought to the public offices to be assayed at a
heavy charge. It would be tedious to enumerate
these desperate and revolting financial measures;
each was brought forward with pleas of necessity,
loud protestations of desire for the national
welfare, confessions of past faults, and promises
that each measure should be final. All of them,
however, proved unavailing.

In 1810, the next stage was reached, a stage
which the student of paper money meets so regularly in its history, that he anticipates it sooner
or later, in one form or another, in every new in-

stance. A new class of notes was issued called "redemption-notes," to represent coin, and to exchange for paper at the rate of one for three. By using these, the government prevented its expenditures from running up such enormous figures. This plan, and others intended to support it, failed to attract even the popular attention; all confidence in the promises of the government was lost. The misery was wide and deep, reaching even the well-to-do classes. Persons on salaries found themselves in the pecuniary position of day laborers; the peasants and country people who tilled the soil had its products for food, but trade was brought to a stand-still. Says Springer, whose history we follow and quote here and below:

The pecuniary corruptibility of the Austrian civil officers, and the opinion cherished by all classes, even by the Emperor, that the civil servants did not serve the state honestly, but would at any time sacrifice its interests to their own, took its origin in this period. The civil officers carried on afterwards as a habit what they had learned in a period of necessity.

The wretchedly paid custom officers connived at and shared in the smuggling. In 1810 the bank-notes fell to 500 for 100, then to 800, and finally to 1,095.

This state of things came to a crisis in 1811. On the 20th of February of that year a patent was issued, whose appearance and character the historian thus describes:

The secret document which was to decide the weal or woe of millions had been sent out sealed to the government authorities. They were to break the seals at five o'clock in the morning on the 15th of March, and to post up the document an hour later. Long before daybreak, crowds were collected in the streets of all the cities waiting for the fateful moment, and betraying as much excitement as if the report of a decisive battle were expected. With eager haste they drank in every word of the document . . . which sowed the seeds of hate, and made distrust of the monarch a universal feeling. Some few could rejoice: they had unexpectedly become rich. Others, and by far the most, cursed and lamented. The fate of the beggar had befallen them in a night.

The bank-notes, of which there were over a thousand million gulden in circulation, were reduced by the proclamation to one-fifth of their nominal value, and were to be exchanged for redemption-notes, called the Viennese legal-tender. These latter became, and remain, the Austrian legal-tender currency. The government promised to issue of these only enough to convert the outstanding bank-notes, viz.: 212

million gulden. Taxes were to be paid in the new currency; government pensions and salaries in the same. The debased 30 and 15 kreutzer coins were to be rated at 6 and 3 kreutzers, and the interest on the national debt was to be reduced one-half. The smallest redemption notes were for 25 gulden, so that the poorest people who held 1, 2 and 5 gulden notes could not exchange them. On the other hand, it was believed that certain persons, who hastily adjusted their affairs just before the patent was issued, in a manner to avoid loss, had received secret information of its contents.

In the following May the redemption-issues were at 216, and in June at 338; the bank-notes were at 1,690 to the 100 silver. The only recourse, in the midst of new necessities, seemed to be to issue more paper. The solemn promise of the Emperor in the patent from whose effects the country was still smarting, and on which the virulence of popular hate and the sharpness of popular wit had been expended, stood in the way of any such issue. The difficulty was obviated by giving the new notes a new name—"anticipation-notes." In the decree for issuing them it was anxiously explained that they were only exchequer bills for anticipating the revenue. At first, 45 millions were issued, but the issues were secretly increased to 426 millions. In 1816 the amount of paper money was over 638 millions, and, says the historian :

Austria offered the strange spectacle of a State buried in the stillness of death—a grotesque conglomerate of States of different sizes, some of which did not dare, others of which did not know how, to breathe independently and freely. . . . Undeniably, the paper money exercised the worst influence on the *morale* of the people. Frugality and diligence were lost virtues. Vulgar pleasure-seeking and wild extravagance became habitual even in the lowest classes. Of what use to care for the future ? Why not enjoy to-day all the pleasures of the senses? How could any one hesitate to pay 200 gulden for admission to a ball ? In fact the "money" had no value, and, if one stood reflecting, he might lose ball and money both. The very fact of speaking continually of large sums, which, however, in truth amounted to but very small value, stimulated to frivolity and folly. So the ground was prepared for developing the celebrated " Viennese" disposition ; and the loafer-life, in which the hot-spiced pleasures of the palate seemed the highest good, became indigenous to "the unique city of the Emperor."

In 1816, the Austrian National Bank was founded. It was intended to draw in the paper money, both as subscription to capital, and through the agency of the Bank in the conversion of treasury notes. Its relation to the government, which deposited 50 millions in silver to begin the operation, robbed it of confidence at the outset. It bought the notes at more than the current rate, so that there was a profit in buying them on the Bourse and taking them to the Bank. A run ensued which forced almost immediate suspension. Loans were then raised for redeeming the notes, and the mass of them was reduced to 181 millions.

In 1817, the Bank shares were once more offered, and with better success. The Bank went into operation and still remains, but government guarantees were given which were burdensome to the Treasury and robbed the Bank of independence. Its operations were mainly transactions with the government; its means could not be employed in furthering the industry of the country; and to this day a large part of its assets consist of government obligations, and until these are paid its usefulness is crippled. The " anticipation-notes " were reduced in number; their value improved, and their fluctuations were narrower. In 1827, these notes were reduced to ninety-nine millions, and in 1840 to ten millions. The period of peace was employed in this effort, and with a sound industrial system and no deficit, an equal amount of energy might have conquered the evil. As it was, however, the notes were redeemed by loans, the deficit was met by loans, and after 1830 Austria entered on a ruinous policy of armed peace. The relations with Hungary were bitterly hostile, and the policy of repression proved exceedingly expensive. New loans were continually required; the energy of reform died out; the power to decide on a policy was wanting; the dread of confession and of self-denial was deep-seated; the habit of putting off and of seeking temporary makeshifts was established.

In 1848, a run on the Bank, at the outbreak of the revolution, reduced the coin reserve from eighty-five to thirty-five millions. Forced circulation was given to the bank notes, and the events of that and the following years had the good result of rousing the nation from its stupor. Baron Von Czoernig, chief of bureau in the department of commerce and industry, details fully the measures taken to regenerate the nation. Austria was in the position in 1850 in which Colbert found France. Efforts were made to reform the tax system, and important changes were made in the right direction, The currency also received attention, but the history consists of little more than a record of changes from one form of paper to another. The deficit still continued; the expensive repression in Hungary seemed more necessary than ever, and the Crimean war forced Austria once more to heavy military expenses. The war of 1859 in Italy, and of 1866 with Prussia, produced new emissions of paper, and Professor Bergius, of Berlin, quotes the Austrian finance minister as saying, in 1868, that if new complications should arise in Europe it would be necessary to issue more paper.

After 1866, however, the repressive policy

in Hungary was abandoned, and a freer industrial system was adopted. The panic of
the summer of 1873 is the latest incident in this
miserable story. The *Journal des Econo-
mistes* for June last gave the following account and explanation of it:

The financial crisis at Vienna was not simply a stock exchange crisis, but a general one, an effect of extravagance in
new undertakings, and of a fever of speculation which took
possession of all classes of the population.

After the war of 1866, a large emission of paper money took
place, both on the part of the State and on the part
of the Bank, all legal tender.. The abundance of paper
led to a belief in the abundance of capital, and prompted to
undertakings of all kinds. These influences were assisted by
the abundance of the harvests of 1867 and 1868. Urged on
by the opposition, the State encouraged by guarantees of dividends the construction of railroads which had been neglected
during the war. Speculation also seized upon credit institutions of various kinds, which were multiplied in all the great
centres, on industrial establishments, on constructions in the
cities, and on land. Hence ensued a great quantity of bonds
and securities, good and bad, which there was not time to class-
ify, and which produced a glut. They led to all the financial
expedients usual in such cases, advertisements, reports, emissions of paper, loans of all forms, tempting the prudence of
buyers and provoking the distrust of the Bank of Vienna and
of other credit establishments. The great speculators, finding
their means surpassed, suspended. The smaller ones imitated
them. Strong houses were shaken, and the panic followed.
It was necessary to close the Bourse for a day to prevent violence amongst the speculators. There were great calamities
and some suicides.

After the crisis measures were taken to find a remedy. The Chamber of Commerce, the directors of the great financial establishments, the municipality of Vienna, etc., called on the government, which, of course, could do nothing, By permitting the Bank to raise its emissions to 500 millions it put the same in a position to discount and to make advances on national securities. Fusions and combinations and guarantees are being planned. The most important relief, however, is given by the purchases of good securities, which the low prices induce. As for bad securities, they disappear in the general clearing up. Thus end all crises—offspring of delusion.

An able writer in the same journal for September gives as the circulation on the 30th of June, 1873, 380 millions of treasury notes and 340 millions of bank-notes. The Bank holds 144 millions in specie, " enough to bring its notes to par if it were not for the treasury notes and the debt of the State to the Bank, part of which cannot be realized." In commenting on the character of the city of Vienna, outwardly grandiose and pretentious, but badly drained and otherwise provided, and upon the light and frivolous character of the people, the same writer refers these phenomena to the financial disorder and paper money as chief causes.

No one can deny that the above is a most instructive study in political and financial disease.

The popular mind rests on instances like the French assignats, or our continental money, as showing the error of paper money where it absolutely perishes. It is thought that, short of this, only alarmists see danger. The story of Austria shows that an irredeemable paper currency is a national calamity of the first magnitude, of which one may indeed find greater or less examples, but of which the least is a peremptory warning to statesmen and financiers. It is like a disease in the blood, undermining the constitution and spreading decay through all the arteries of business. A young and vigorous nation, with a sound political system, may stand it far better than an old one, with feudal traditions; but in its measure and according to circumstances it is pernicious, if not fatal. It is not like an acute disease; it is like an invalid state with occasional fever.

We may also infer from Austrian experience what the " London Economist " recently inferred from ours, that the interference of government with banking is as mischievous as its interference with any other trade. The Emperor of Austria was not intentionally a liar. When he said he would issue so much and no more, he meant it. He only did not know that he was releasing a power which he could not curb again. He was promising to perform a financial miracle. His broken promises, however, cost him and his government all credit with his people, and it is now frequent subject of remark in Austria that the more solemn the asseverations of the government the more ludicrous they appear to the people. A government which interferes with banking exposes itself to great danger of error, and such errors cost it popular confidence sooner than any others.

CONCLUSION.

IF these chapters of history have been narrated with any success, they carry their own lesson with them. There are many who sneer at history and foreign experience as inapplicable to our circumstances, and toss off the lessons of history with impatient contempt, but these very persons never talk on financial topics for five minutes without referring to what " the Bank of England does," or what " England did " during the Bank Restriction. The only remarkable fact about their references is that the facts are often incorrectly stated, and the inferences illogically and unscientifically drawn. From this it appears that they object, not to the force of historical arguments, but to the trouble of correctly informing themselves about historical facts.

There are very many, however, who are willing to learn from history and science, and are led astray by the sweeping assertions, incorrect references, and dogmatism of those they are obliged to trust. It is for these that these chapters have been written.

It will be observed, then, that there is nothing new to be discovered about the operation of paper money. There is no new invention possible for making it "as good as gold," no new device conceivable for making it elastic, no difficulty connected with it which has not been experienced, no phenomenon of its development for which we have not abundant analogies. If any qualification of these assertions is necessary, it is only this, that no scheme of intro-convertible bonds for giving elasticity to a currency of fixed amount has ever been tried, or, so far as I know, proposed. This scheme is the only one which fully illustrates what is derisively called "theory," for it stands on no facts, appeals to no experience, is deduced from no observation, but is purely imaginary and speculative. It has a certain plausibility, but all the observed phenomena of paper money go to show that it would make the paper elastic only in one direction.

For a nation which has fallen into this mistake, there are only three courses of action which are even logically conceivable: to go on, to turn back, to stand still. The last is the "growing up" idea, and may be ruled out at once as impracticable. To try to stand still will inevitably end in drifting onwards into inflation. It will be much gained, therefore, if we come to face the situation as a grim alternative, for such is its actual character.

To go on to further inflation, whether by free banking, intro-convertible bonds, or direct issues, means simply bankruptcy and repudiation. Each new issue will produce, only for a time, ease and apparent prosperity, to be followed in a few years by a new crisis and new distress, then a new issue, and so on over again. Reform will then be no longer possible, and we must run the course to its end, in which the paper disappears as ignominiously as the continental notes.

If we choose the other alternative, it is useless to try to deceive ourselves at all in regard to what it involves. To talk of resumption and of issuing the 44 millions, or of establishing free banking on 5–20's, in the same breath, is a contradiction. If we want specie payments, we must have specie, and, if we want specie, the entire history before us repeats to weariness that we must get the paper out of the way. This is the first condition, and, until we are willing to face it, it is useless to discuss resumption at all. The doctrines drawn from the previous chapters are not doctrines of financial science so much as stumbling-blocks which lie at the door of that science. We have seen by abundant evidence, that the movement of the precious metals from country to country is not governed by the balance of trade, as is assumed in nearly all discussions of this subject. An economist of to-day who makes an assault on the "balance of trade" feels as if he were taking a sledge-hammer to break through an open door; but this doctrine is made the starting-point of discussing our finances in public documents, in speeches in Congress, and in most of the pamphlets and newspaper articles one meets with. We have seen, however, that the transaction is not one to which the term balance properly applies. Whenever a nation has complained that an adverse balance of trade was drawing off its specie, we have seen that an inferior currency of some kind was displacing the better one, and that the increased imports of merchandise were only the return payments for the gold or silver which had been dispensed with by employing a cheaper medium. We have seen also that prices alone govern the flow of the precious metal, or, more strictly stated, that the movement of the metals and the prices of commodities in different countries act and react upon one another in such a way as to keep up the exact natural relation of prices between different countries, and give to each country in the world's market its full relative advantage in production. If, therefore, a nation had a specie currency, a drain upon it by an adverse balance of trade, a foreign payment, or any other similar cause, would immediately produce a lowering of prices and a return current of specie until the natural level was once more restored. We have also seen that it is an error to say that there is not enough gold and silver in the world to perform the exchanges. Whatever gold there is, is enough. The only difference would be whether one grain of gold would buy one thousand grains of wheat or one hundred thousand.

We have also seen that the metals will distribute themselves amongst the nations in exact proportion to their requirements, if there is no interference in the shape of inferior currency. If a vacuum is left by the destruction of paper, specie comes in to take its place, as occurred here after the revolutionary war and after the bank crash of 1839. It may have to be bought back, however, very dear; that is, by giving many goods for it, or what is the same thing, goods at low prices. If the requirement rises above the supply, specie flows in to fill the gap, as we see after every commercial crisis.

These principles govern the question of resumption. If we want the specie, we here see how we must go to work to get it. It is not possible, save by withdrawing a portion of the paper. When we suspended, we overissued. The consequence was a rise of prices, increase of speculation, and export of specie. Large importations of merchandise followed, and exportation was loaded with disadvantages. The course of resumption is the opposite in every particular. When the paper is withdrawn, prices fall, speculation is restrained, specie flows in. Importations are discouraged, exportations increase and go to pay for, the gold. It may be added that, as the former process was smooth and agreeable, so the latter is hard and distressing. When the specie is given up, large quantities of it, comparatively, are given for little merchandise; when it is sought again, it must be bought at a disadvantage.

No nation has ever had the courage to pursue this course except England, and she only entered upon it after two or three commerical revulsions had destroyed a large part of the paper, never immoderately redundant; she entered upon the effort under the guidance of a high order of statesmanship; she took advantage of the fall in prices and business stagnation following a crisis; and her resumption was not complete until after the withdrawal of the small notes in 1829. Other nations, like Austria and Russia, have gone on for generations, sinking deeper and deeper, crippled in their military and industrial strength by this inheritance, not knowing how to endure it or how to get rid of it, or, like France and our own colonies, have gone through bankruptcy and repudiation. These are the alternatives, and it has been well likened to the choice of a man in a house on fire who jumps out of the second story rather than wait to be driven up to the third or fourth or the roof.

If the withdrawal of the paper should be resolved upon, the best way to accomplish it is the one which is simplest and most straightforward; that is, to raise a surplus revenue and with it cancel the government issues, It is not consistent with the present purpose to criticise the various schemes which have been proposed. They all involve some kind of conversion of one sort of paper into another, and every such change complicates a system already far too intricate, and every such change involves chances of unforeseen events, or of unexpected effects, for they consist of experiments on totally untried ground. Some of these schemes involve no actual reduction of the outstanding paper, and can lead to nothing but expense and injury to the public credit. Others do involve a diminution of the paper and seek to accomplish it without the distress which it must occasion. It is certainly most desirable that any possible application of science to this end should be invented, but all such plans involve the danger of political events during the next five or six years, which cannot now be foreseen, and they assume also that the scheme will be faithfully carried out whenever it begins to press hard, as at some time it certainly must. Past experience leads us to doubt whether this latter assumption would be justified by the event. Our object here, however, is simply to establish by history and science, what are the indispensable *conditions* of resumption, and to place the problem in such light that it may be perceived how it must be attacked, if it is to be solved at all.

APPENDIX.

REPORT FROM THE SELECT COMMITTEE ON THE HIGH PRICE OF GOLD BULLION.

Ordered, by the House of Commons, to be printed, 8 *June,* 1810.

THE SELECT COMMITTEE appointed to enquire into the cause of the High Price of Gold Bullion, and to take into consideration the state of the Circulating Medium, and of the Exchanges between Great Britain and Foreign Parts;—and to report the same, with their Observations thereupon, from time to time, to the House;—Have, pursuant to the Orders of the House, examined the matters to them referred; and have agreed to the following REPORT:

Your Committee proceeded, in the first instance, to ascertain what the price of gold bullion had been, as well as the rates of the foreign exchanges, for some time past; particularly during the last year.

Your Committee have found that the price of gold bullion, which, by the regulations of his Majesty's Mint, is 3*l.* 17*s.* 10½*d.* per ounce of standard fineness, was, during the years 1806, 1807, and 1808, as high as 4*l.* in the market. Towards the end of 1808 it began to advance very rapidly, and continued very high during the whole year 1809; the market price of standard gold in bars fluctuating from 4*l.* 9*s.* to 4*l.* 12*s.* per oz. The market price at 4*l.* 10*s.* is about 15½ per cent. above the Mint price.

Your Committee have found, that during the three first months of the present year, the price of standard gold in bars remained nearly at the same price as during last year; viz., from 4*l.* 10*s.* to 4*l.* 12*s.* per oz. In the course of the months of March and April, the price of standard gold is quoted but once in Wettenhall's tables; viz., on the 6th of April last, at 4*l.* 6*s.* which is rather more than 10 per cent. above the Mint price. The last quotations of the price of gold, which have been given in those tables, are upon the 18th and 22d of May, when Portugal gold in coin is quoted at 4*l.* 11*s.* per oz. : Portugal gold coin is about the same fineness as our standard. It is stated in the same tables, that in the month of March last, the price of new doubloons rose from 4*l.* 7*s.* to 4*l.* 9*s.* per oz. Spanish gold is from

4½ to 4¾ grains better than standard, making about 4*s*. per oz. difference in value.

It appears by the evidence, that the price of foreign gold coin is generally higher than that of bar gold, on account of the former finding a more ready vent in foreign markets. The difference between Spanish and Portugal gold in coin and gold in bars, has of late been about 2*s*. per ounce. Your Committee have also to state, that there is said to be at present a difference of between 3*s*. and 4*s*. per ounce between the price of bar gold which may be sworn off for exportation as being foreign gold, and the price of such bar gold as the dealer will not venture to swear off: while the former was about 4*l*. 10*s*. in the market, the latter is said to have been about 4*l*. 6*s*. On account of these extrinsic differences, occasioned either by the expense of coinage, or by the obstructions of law, the price of standard gold in bars, such as may be exported, is that which it is most material to keep generally in view through the present inquiry.

It appeared to your Committee, that it might be of use, in judging of the cause of this high price of gold bullion, to be informed also of the prices of silver during the same period. The price of standard silver in his Majesty's Mint is 5*s*. 2*d*. per ounce ; at this standard price, the value of a Spanish dollar is 4*s*. 4*d*. or, which comes to the same thing, Spanish dollars are, at that standard price, worth 4*s*. 11½*d*. per ounce. It is stated in Wettenhall's tables that throughout the year 1809, the price of new dollars fluctuated from 5*s*. 5*d*. to 5*s*. 7*d*. per ounce, or from 10 to 13 per cent. above the Mint price of standard silver. In the course of the last month, new dollars have been quoted as high as 5*s*. 8*d*. per ounce, or more than 15 per cent. above the Mint price.

Your Committee have likewise found, that towards the end of the year 1808, the Exchanges with the continent became very unfavourable to this country, and continued still more unfavourable through the whole of 1809, and the three first months of the present year.

Hamburgh, Amsterdam, and Paris, are the principal places with which the Exchanges are established at present. During the last six months of 1809, and the first three months of the present year, the Exchanges on Hamburgh and Amsterdam were depressed as low as from 16 to 20 per cent. below par ; and that on Paris still lower. The exchanges with Portugal have corresponded with the others ; but they are complicated by some circumstances which shall be explained separately.

Your Committee find, that in the course of the month of March last, that is, from the 2d of March to the 3d of April, the exchanges with the three places above mentioned received a gradual improvement. The exchange with Hamburgh rose gradually from 29. 4. to 31. ; that with Amsterdam from 31. 8. to 33. 5. ; that with Paris from 19. 16. to 21. 11. Since the 3d April last to the present time, they have remained nearly stationary at those rates, the exchange with Hamburgh, as stated in the tables printed for the use of the merchants, appearing as much against this country as 9*l.* per cent. below par ; that with Amsterdam appearing to be more than 7*l.* per cent. below par ; and that with Paris more than 14*l.* per cent. below par.

So extraordinary a rise in the market price of gold in this country, coupled with so remarkable a depression of our exchanges with the continent, very early, in the judgment of your Committee, pointed to something in the state of our own domestic currency as the cause of both appearances. But before they adopted that conclusion, which seemed agreeable to all former reasonings and experience, they thought it proper to enquire more particularly into the circumstances connected with each of those two facts ; and to hear, from persons of commercial practice and detail, what explanations they had to offer of so unusual a state of things.

With this view, your Committee called before them several merchants of extensive dealings and intelligence, and desired to have their opinions, with respect to the cause of the high price of gold and the low rates of exchange.*

I.

It will be found by the evidence, that the high price of gold is ascribed, by most of the witnesses, entirely to an alleged scarcity of that article, arising out of an unusual demand for it upon the continent of Europe. This unusual demand for gold upon the continent is described by some of them as being chiefly for the use of the French armies, though increased also by that state of alarm, and failure of confidence, which leads to the practice of hoarding.

Your Committee are of opinion, that, in the sound and natural state of the British currency, the foundation of which is gold, no increased demand for gold from other parts of the

*See note on page 267.

world, however great, or from whatever causes arising, can have
the effect of producing here, for a considerable period of time,
a material rise in the market price of gold. But before they
proceed to explain the grounds of that general opinion, they
wish to state some other reasons which alone would have led
them to doubt whether in point of fact, such a demand for gold,
as is alleged, has operated in the manner supposed.

If there were an unusual demand for gold upon the continent, such as could influence its market price in this country,
it would of course influence also, and indeed in the first instance,
its price in the continental markets ; and it was to be expected
that those who ascribed the high price here to a great demand
abroad, would have been prepared to state that there was a
corresponding high price abroad. Your Committee did not
find that they grounded their inference upon any such information ; and so far as your Committee have been enabled to ascertain, it does not appear that during the period when the
price of gold bullion was rising here, as valued in our paper,
there was any corresponding rise in the price of gold bullion in
the market of the continent, as valued in their respective currencies. Mr. Whitmore, indeed, the late governor of the bank,
stated, that in his opinion it was the high price abroad which
had carried our gold coin out of this country ; but he did not
offer to your Committee any proof of this high price. Mr.
Greffulhe, a continental merchant, who appeared to be remarkably well informed in the details of trade, being asked by the
Committee, if he could state whether any change had taken
place in the price of gold in any of the foreign markets within
the last year? answered, "No very material change that I am
aware of." Upon a subsequent day, having had time to refer
to the actual prices, he again stated to the Committee, "I beg
leave to observe, that there has been no alteration of late in
the Mint price of gold in foreign places, nor have the market
prices experienced an advance at all relative to the rise that has
taken place in England ; one of the papers I have delivered
shews the foreign prices reduced into sterling money at the
present low rates of exchange, and the excess above our market price may be considered as about equal to the charges
of conveyance." The paper he refers to will be found in the
Appendix ; and this statement made by Mr. Greffulhe throws
great light upon this part of the subject; as it shews, that the
actual prices of gold in the foreign markets are just so much
lower than its market price here, as the difference of exchange
amounts to. Mr. Greffulhe's paper is confirmed by another,

which has been laid before your Committee. Mr. Abraham Goldsmid has also stated to your Committee, that during that part of last year when the market price of gold here rose so high, its price at Hamburgh did not fluctuate more than from 3 to 4 per cent.

Here your Committee must observe, that both at Hamburgh and Amsterdam, where the measure of value is not gold as in this country, but silver, an unusual demand for gold would affect its money price, that is, its price in silver; and that as it does not appear that there has been any considerable rise in the price of gold, as valued in silver, at those places in the last year, the inference is, that there was not any considerable increase in the demand for gold. That permanent rise in the market price of gold above its Mint price, which appears by Mr. Greffulhe's paper to have taken place for several years both at Hamburgh and Amsterdam, may in some degree be ascribed, as your Committee conceive, to an alteration which has taken place in the relative value of the two precious metals all over the world ; concerning which, much curious and satisfactory evidence will be found in the Appendix, particularly in the documents laid before your Committee by Mr. Allen. From the same cause, a fall in the relative price of silver appears to have taken place in this country for some time before the increase of our paper currency began to operate. Silver having fallen in relative value to gold throughout the world, gold has appeared to rise in price in those markets where silver is the fixed measure, and silver has appeared to fall in those where gold is the fixed measure.

With respect to the alleged demand for gold upon the continent for the supply of the French armies, your Committee must further observe, that, if the wants of the military chest have been latterly much increased, the general supply of Europe with gold has been augmented by all that quantity which this great commercial country has spared in consequence of the substitution of another medium of circulation. And your Committee cannot omit remarking, that though the circumstances which might occasion such an increased demand may recently have existed in greater force than at former periods, yet in the former wars and convulsions of the continent, they must have existed in such a degree as to produce some effect. Sir Francis Baring has very justly referred to the seven years' war and to the American war, and remarks, that no want of bullion was then felt in this country. And upon referring for a course of years to the tables which are published for the use of

the merchants, such as Lloyd's lists and Wettenhall's Course of
Exchange, your Committee have found that from the middle of
the year 1773, when the reformation of the gold coin took
place, till about the middle of the year 1799, two years after
the suspension of the cash payments of the Bank, the market-
price of standard gold in bars remained steadily uniform at the
price of 3*l.* 17*s.* 6*d.* [being, with the small allowance for loss by
detention at the Mint, equal to the Mint price of 3*l.* 17*s.* 10½*d.*]
with the exception of one year, from May, 1783, to May, 1784,
when it was occasionally 3*l.* 18*s.* During the same period it is
to be noticed, the price of Portugal gold coin was occasionally
as high as 4*l.* 2*s.*; and your Committee also observe, that it was
stated to the Lords' Committee in 1797 by Mr. Abraham New-
land, that the bank had been frequently obliged to buy gold
higher than the Mint price, and upon one particular occasion
gave as much for a small quantity, which their agent procured
from Portugal, as 4*l.* 8*s.* But your Committee find, that the
price of standard gold in bars was never for any length of time
materially above the Mint price, during the whole period of 24
years which elapsed from the reformation of the gold coin to
the suspension of the cash payments of the Bank. The two
most remarkable periods prior to the present, when the market
price of gold in this country has exceeded our Mint price, were
in the reign of King William, when the silver coin was very
much worn below its standard, and in the early part of his
present Majesty's reign, when the gold coin was very much
worn below its standard. In both those periods, the excess of
the market price of gold above its Mint price was found to be
owing to the bad state of the currency; and in both instances,
the reformation of the currency effectually lowered the market
price of gold to the level of the Mint price. During the whole
of the years 1796 and 1797, in which there was such a scarcity
of gold, occasioned by the great demands of the country bankers in order to increase their deposits, the market price of gold
never rose above the Mint price.

Your Committee have still further to remark upon this point,
that the evidence laid before them has led them to entertain
much doubt of the alleged fact, that a scarcity of gold bullion
has been recently experienced in this country. That guineas
have disappeared from the circulation, there can be no question; but that does not prove a scarcity of bullion, any more
than the high price proves that scarcity. If gold is rendered
dear by any other cause than scarcity, those who cannot purchase it without paying the high price, will be very apt to con-

clude that it is scarce. A very extensive home dealer who was examined, and who spoke very much of the scarcity of gold, acknowledged, that he found no difficulty in getting any quantity he wanted, if he was willing to pay the price for it. And it appears to your Committee, that, though in the course of the last year there have been large exportations of gold to the continent, there have been also very considerable importations of it into this country from South America, chiefly through the West Indies. The changes which have affected Spain and Portugal, combined with our maritime and commercial advantages, would seem to have rendered this country a channel through which the produce of the mines of New Spain and the Brazils pass to the rest of the world. In such a situation, the imports of bullion and coin give us the opportunity of first supplying ourselves ; and must render this the last of the great markets in which a scarcity of that article will be felt. This is remarkably illustrated by the fact, that Portugal gold coin is now sent regularly from this country to the cotton settlements in the Brazils, Pernambuco, and Maranham, while dollars are remitted in considerable quantities to this country from Rio Janeiro.

It is important also to observe, that the rise in the market price of silver in this country, which has nearly corresponded to that of the market price of gold, cannot in any degree be ascribed to a scarcity of silver. The importations of silver have of late years been unusually large, while the usual drain for India and China has been stopped.

For all these reasons, your Committee would be inclined to think, that those who ascribe the high price of gold to an unusual demand for that article, and a consequent scarcity, assume facts as certain of which there is no evidence. But even if these assumptions were proved, to ascribe the high price of gold in this country to its scarcity, seems to your Committee to involve a misconception, which they think it important to explain.

In this country, gold is itself the measure of all exchangeable value, the scale to which all money prices are referred. It is so, not only by the usage and commercial habits of the country, but likewise by operation of law, ever since the act of the 14th of his present Majesty [finally rendered perpetual by an act of the 39th year of the reign] disallowed a legal tender in silver coin beyond the sum of 25*l.* Gold being thus our measure of prices, a commodity is said to be dear or cheap according as more or less gold is given in exchange for a given quantity of that commodity ; but a given quantity of gold itself will never be exchanged for a greater or a less quantity of

gold of the same standard fineness. At particular times it may
be convenient in exchange for gold in a particular coin, to give
more than an equal quantity of other gold ; but this difference
can never exceed a certain small limit : and thus it has happened
that the Bank, while liable to pay its notes in specie, has under
particular emergencies been put to the necessity of purchasing
gold at a loss, in order to keep up or to repair its stock. But
generally speaking, the price of gold, being itself measured and
expressed in gold, cannot be raised or lowered by an increased
or diminished demand for it. An ounce of gold will exchange
for neither more nor less than an ounce of gold of the same
fineness, except so far as an allowance is to be made, if the one
ounce is coined or otherwise manufactured and the other is not,
for the expense of that coinage or manufacture. An ounce of
standard gold bullion will not fetch more in our market than
3*l.* 17*s.* 10½*d.*, unless 3*l.* 17*s.* 10½*d.*, in our actual currency is
equivalent to less than an ounce of gold. An increase or
diminution in the demand for gold, or what comes to the same
thing, a diminution or increase in the general supply of gold,
will, no doubt, have a material effect upon the money prices of
all other articles. An increased demand for gold, and a consequent scarcity of that article, will make it more valuable in
proportion to all other articles ; the same quantity of gold will
purchase a greater quantity of any other article than it did before : in other words, the real price of gold, or the quantity of
commodities given in exchange for it, will rise, and the money
prices of all commodities will fall ; the money price of gold
itself will remain unaltered, but the prices of all other commodities will fall. That this is not the present state of things
is abundantly manifest ; the prices of all commodities have
risen, and gold appears to have risen in its price only in common with them. If this common effect is to be ascribed to one
and the same cause, that cause can only be found in the state
of the currency of this country.

Your Committee think it proper to state still more specifically, what appear to them to be the principles which govern
the relative prices of gold in bullion and gold in coin, as well
as of paper circulating in its place and exchangeable for it.
They cannot introduce this subject more properly, than by ad-
verting to those simple principles and regulations, on which a
coinage issuing from the King's mint is founded.

The object is, to secure to the people a standard of a deter-
minate value, by affixing a stamp, under the royal authority, to
pieces of gold, which are thus-certified to be of a given weight

and fineness. Gold in bullion is the standard to which the legislature has intended that the coin should be conformed, and with which it should be identified as much as possible. And if that intention of the legislature were completely fulfilled, the coined gold would bear precisely the same price in exchange for all other commodities, as it would have borne had it continued in the shape of bullion ; but it is subject to some small fluctuations.

First, there is some expense incurred in converting bullion into coin. They who send bullion to be coined, and it is allowed to any one to send it, though they are charged with no seignorage, incur a loss of interest by the detention of their gold in the mint. This loss may hitherto have amounted to about 1*l.* per cent., but it is to be presumed that the improvements of the system of the new Mint will cause the detention and consequent loss to be much smaller. This 1*l.* per cent. has formed the limit, or nearly the limit, to the possible rise of the value of coin above that of bullion ; for to suppose that coin could, through any cause, advance much above this limit, would be to assume that there was a high profit on a transaction, in which there is no risk and every one has an opportunity of engaging.

The two following circumstances conjoined, account for the depression of the coin below the price of bullion, and will shew what must have been the limit to its extent before 1797, the period of the suspension of the cash payments of the Bank of England. First, the coin, after it had become current was gradually diminished in weight by use, and therefore if melted, would produce a less quantity of bullion. The average diminution of weight of the present current gold coin below that of the same coin when fresh from the mint, appears by the evidence to be nearly 1*l.* per cent. This evil, in more ancient times, was occasionally very great. It was particularly felt in an early period of his present Majesty's reign, and led to the reformation of the gold coin in 1773. But it is now carefully guarded against, not only by the legal punishment of every wilful deterioration of the gold coin, but also by the regulation of the statute, that guineas, of which the full weight when fresh from the mint is 5 dwts. 9$\frac{21}{32}$ grains shall not be a legal tender if worn below 5 dwts. 8 grs. ; the depreciation thus allowed being at the utmost 1. 11 per cent. A still more material cause of depression, is the difficulty under which the holders of coin have been placed when they wished to convert it into bullion. The law of this country forbids any other gold coin than that which has become light to be put into the melting pot, and, with a very questionable policy, prohibits the exportation of our gold coin, and of any gold, unless an oath is taken that it has not been produced from the coin of this realm. It appears by the evidence, that the difference between the value of gold bullion which may be sworn off for exportation, and that of the gold produced or supposed to be produced from our own coin, which by law is convertible only to domestic purposes, amounts at present to between 3*s.* and 4*s.* per ounce.

The two circumstances which have now been mentioned have unquestionably constituted, in the judgment of your Committee, the whole cause of that depression of the value of the gold coin of this country in exchange for commodities, below the value of bullion in exchange for commodities, which has occasionally arisen or could arise at those times when the Bank paid in specie, and gold was consequently obtainable in the quantity that was desired; and the limit fixed by those two circumstances conjoined, to this excess of the market price of gold above the Mint price, was therefore a limit of about 5½ per cent. The chief part of this depression is to be ascribed to that ancient, but doubtful policy of this country, which, by attempting to confine the coin within the kingdom, has served, in the same manner as permanent restrictions on the export of other articles, to place it under a disadvantage, and to give to it a less value in the market than the same article would have if subject to no such prohibition.

The truth of these observations on the causes and limits of the ordinary difference between the market and Mint price of gold, may be illustrated by a reference to the mode, explained in the evidence, of securing a fixed standard of value for the great commercial payments of Hamburgh. The payments in the ordinary transactions of life are made in a currency composed of the coins of the several surrounding states; but silver is the standard there resorted to in the great commercial payments, as gold is in England. No difference analogous to that which occurs in this country, between the Mint and market price of gold, can ever arise at Hamburgh with regard to silver, because provision is made that none of the three causes above specified [the expense of coinage, the depreciation by wear, or the obstruction to exportation] shall have any operation. The large payments of Hamburgh are effected in Bank money, which consists of actual silver of a given fineness, lodged in the Hamburgh bank by the merchants of the place, who thereupon have a proportionate credit in the bank-books, which they transfer according to their occasions. The silver being assayed and weighed with scarcely any loss of time, the first mentioned cause of fluctuation in the relative value of the current medium compared with bullion is avoided. Certain masses of it being then certified (without any stamp being affixed on the metal) to be of a given quantity and fineness, the value is transferred from individual to individual by the medium merely of the bank books, and thus the wearing of the coin being prevented, one cause of depreciation is removed. A free right is also given to withdraw, melt, and export it ; and thus the other and principal source of the occasional fall of the value of the current medium of payment, below that of the bullion which it is intended to represent, is also effectually precluded.

In this manner at Hamburgh, silver is not only the measure of all exchangeable value, but it is rendered an invariable measure, except in so far as the relative value of silver itself varies with the varying supply of that precious metal from the mines. In the same manner the usage, and at last the law, which made gold coin the usual and at last the only legal tender in large payments here, rendered that metal our measure of value : and from the period of the reformation of the gold coin down to the suspension of the Bank payments in specie in 1797, gold coin was not a very variable measure of value ; being subject only to that variation in the relative value of gold bullion which depends upon its supply from the mines, together with that limited variation, which, as above described, might take place between the market and the Mint price of gold coin.

The highest amount of the depression of the coin which can take place when the Bank pays in gold, has just been stated to be about 5¼ per cent., and accordingly it will be found, that in all the periods preceding 1797, the difference between what is called the Mint price and market price of gold never exceeded that limit.

Since the suspension of cash payments in 1797, however, it is certain, that, even if gold is still our measure of value and standard of prices, it has been exposed to a new cause of variation, from the possible excess of that paper which is not convertible into gold at will; and the limit of this new variation is as indefinite as the excess to which that paper may be issued. It may indeed be doubted, whether since the new system of Bank of England payments has been fully established, gold has in truth continued to be our measure of value : and whether we have any other standard prices than that circulating medium issued primarily by the Bank of England and in a secondary manner by the country banks, the variations of which in rela‧ tive value may be as indefinite as the possible excess of that circulating medium. But whether our present measure of value, and standard of prices, be this paper currency thus variable in its relative value, or continues still to be gold, but gold rendered more variable than it was before in consequence of being interchangeable for a paper currency, which is not at will convertible into gold, it is, in either case, most desirable for the public that our circulating medium should again be conformed, as speedily as circumstances will permit, to its real and legal standard, gold bullion.

If the gold coin of the country were at any time to become very much worn and lessened in weight, or if it should suffer a debasement of its standard, it is evident that there would be a proportionable rise of the market price of gold bullion above its Mint price: for the Mint price is the sum in coin, which is equivalent in intrinsic value to a given quantity, an ounce for example, of the metal in bullion ; and if the intrinsic value of that sum of coin be lessened, it is equivalent to a less quantity of bullion than before. The same rise of the market price of gold above its Mint price will take place, if the local currency of this particular country, being no longer convertible into gold, should at any time be issued to excess. That excess cannot be exported to other countries, and, not being convertible into specie, it is not necessarily returned upon those who issued it ; it remains in the channel of circulation, and is gradually absorbed by increasing the prices of all commodities. An increase in the quantity of the local currency of a particular country, will raise prices in that country exactly in the same manner as an increase in the general supply of precious metals raises prices all over the world. By means of the increase of quantity, the value of a given portion of that circulating medium, in exchange for other commodities, is lowered: in other words, the money prices of all other commodities are raised, and that of bullion with the rest. In this manner, an excess of the local currency of a particular country will occasion a rise of the market price of gold above its Mint price.*

---

* This is the point on which Tooke differed from the Bullion Committee. Mr. Horner, in his speech, assumed that grain was a general measure of value, as between different periods, a notion now abandoned, and the same opinion underlies this passage. Grain was dear, but, as Tooke shows, many other things were "oppressively cheap." Macleod's comment is, that they would have been much cheaper but for the depreciated currency, and that the Committee ought to have relied entirely upon the gold premium to

It is no less evident, that in the event of the prices of commodities being raised in one country by an augmentation of its circulating medium, while no similar augmentation in the circulating medium of a neighboring country has led to a similar rise of prices, the currencies of those two countries will no longer continue to bear the same relative value to each other as before. The intrinsic value of a given portion of the one currency being lessened while that of the other remains unaltered, the exchange will be computed between those two countries to the disadvantage of the former.

In this manner, a general rise of all prices, a rise in the market price of gold, and a fall of the foreign exchanges, will be the effect of an excessive quantity of circulating medium in a country which has adopted a currency, not exportable to other countries, or not convertible at will into a coin which is exportable.

II.

Your Committee are thus led to the next head of their inquiry : the present state of the exchanges between this country and the continent. And here, as under the former head, your Committee will first state the opinions which they have received from practical men, respecting the causes of the present state of the exchange.

Mr. Greffulhe, a general merchant, trading chiefly to the continent, ascribed the fall of exchange between London and Hamburgh, near 18 per cent. below par, in the year 1809, "altogether to the commercial situation of this country with the continent ; to the circumstance of the imports, and payments of subsidies, &c., having very much exceeded the exports." He stated, however, that he formed his judgment of the balance of trade in a great measure from the state of the exchange itself, though it was corroborated by what fell under his observation. He insisted particularly on the large imports from the Baltic, and the wines and brandies brought from France, in return for which no merchandise had been exported from this country. He observed on the other hand, that the export of colonial produce to the continent had increased in the last year compared with former

prove their point. He also desires to have it remembered that " excess " of currency is a relative term, and that it must be understood to mean excess relatively to the wants of commerce at the time in question,—a limitation which is to be understood as f course. (See p. 221.)

years ; and that during the last year there was an excess, to a
considerable amount, of the exports of colonial produce and
British manufactures to Holland above the imports from
thence, but not nearly equal, he thought, to the excess of imports from other parts of the world, judging from the state of
the exchange as well as from what fell generally under his observation.   He afterwards explained, that it was not strictly the
balance of trade, but the balance of payments, being unfavourable to this country, which he assigned as the principal cause
of the rate of exchange ; observing also, that the balance of
payments for the year may be against us, while the general exports exceed the imports.   He gave it as his opinion that the
cause of the present state of exchange was entirely commercial, with the addition of the foreign expenditure of government ; and that an excess of imports above exports would account for the rates of exchange continuing so high as 16 per
cent. against this country, for a permanent period of time.

It will be found in the evidence, that several other witnesses
agree in substance with Mr. Greffulhe, in this explanation of
the unfavourable state of the exchange ; particularly Mr.
Chambers and Mr. Coningham.

Sir Francis Baring stated to the Committee, that he considered the two great circumstances which affect the exchange in
its present unfavourable state, to be the restrictions upon trade
with the continent, and the increased circulation of this country in paper, as productive of the scarcity of bullion.   And he
instanced, as examples of a contrary state of things, the seven
years' war, and the American war, in which there were the same
remittances to make to the continent for naval and military expenditure, yet no want of bullion ever was felt.

The Committee likewise examined a very eminent continental merchant, whose evidence will be found to contain a variety
of valuable information.   That gentleman states, that the exchange cannot fall in any country in Europe at the present
time, if computed in coin of a definitive value, or in something
convertible into such coin, lower than the extent of the charge
of transporting it, together with an adequate profit in proportion to the risk attending such transmission.   He conceives,
that such fall of our exchange as has exceeded that extent in
the last 15 months, must certainly be referred to the circumstance of our paper currency not being convertible into specie ;
and that if that paper had been so convertible, and guineas had
been in general circulation, an unfavourable balance of trade,
could hardly have caused so great a fall in the exchange as to

the extent of 5 or 6 per cent. He explains his opinion upon the subject more specifically in the following answers, which are extracted from different parts of his evidence.

"To what causes do you ascribe the present unfavourable course of exchange?—The first great depreciation took place when the French got possession of the north of Germany, and passed severe penal decrees against a communication with this country; at the same time that a sequestration was laid upon all English goods and property, whilst the payments for English account were still to be made, and the reimbursements to be taken on this country; many more bills were in consequence to be sold than could be taken by persons requiring to make payments in England. The communication by letters being also very difficult and uncertain, middle men were not to be found, as in usual times, to purchase and send such bills to England for returns; whilst no suit at law could be instituted in the courts of justice there against any person who chose to resist payment of a returned bill, or to dispute the charges of re-exchange. Whilst those causes depressed the exchange, payments due to England only came round at distant periods; the exchange once lowered by those circumstances, and bullion being withheld in England to make up those occasional differences, the operations between this country and the continent have continued at a low rate, as it is only matter of opinion what rate a pound sterling is there to be valued at, not being able to obtain what it is meant to represent."

"The exchange against England fluctuating from 15 to 20 per cent. how much of that loss may be ascribed to the effect of the measures taken by the enemy in the north of Germany, and the interruption of intercourse which has been the result, and how much to the effect of the Bank of England paper not being convertible into cash, to which you have ascribed a part of that depreciation?—I ascribe the whole of the depreciation to have taken place originally in consequence of the measures of the enemy, and its not having recovered to the circumstance of the paper of England not being exchangeable for cash."

"Since the conduct of the enemy which you have described what other causes have continued to operate on the continent to lower the course of exchange?—Very considerable shipments from the Baltic, which were drawn for and the bills negotiated immediately on the shipments taking place, without consulting the interest of the proprietors in this country much by deferring such a negotiation till a demand should take place for such bills : The continued difficulty and uncertainty in carrying on the correspondence between this country and the continent : The curtailed number of houses to be found on the continent willing to undertake such operations, either by accepting bills for English account drawn from the various parts where shipments take place, or by accepting bills drawn from this country, either against property shipped, or on a speculative idea that the exchange either ought or is likely to rise : The length of time that is required before goods can be converted into cash, from the circuitous routes they are obliged to take : The very large sums of money paid to foreign ship owners, which in some instances, such as on the article of hemp, has amounted to nearly its prime cost in Russia: The want of middle men who as formerly used to employ great capitals in exchange operations, who, from the increased difficulties and dangers to which such operations are now subject, are at present rarely to be met with, to make combined exchange operations, which tend to anticipate probable ultimate results."

The preceding answers, and the rest of this gentleman's evidence, all involve this principle, expressed more or less distinctly, that bullion is the true regulator both of the value of a local currency and of the rate of foreign exchanges ; and that the free convertibility of paper currency into the precious metals, and the free exportation of those metals, place a limit to the fall of exchange, and not only check the exchanges from falling below that limit, but recover them by restoring the balance.

Your Committee need not particularly point out in what respects these opinions received from persons of practical detail, are vague and unsatisfactory, and in what respects they are contradictory of one another; considerable assistance, however, may be derived from the information which the evidence of these persons affords, in explaining the true causes of the present state of the exchanges.

Your Committee conceive that there is no point of trade, considered politically, which is better settled, than the subject of foreign exchanges. The par of exchange between two countries is that sum of the currency of either of the two, which, in point of intrinsic value, is precisely equal to a given sum of the currency of the other ; that is, contains precisely an equal weight of gold or silver of the same fineness. If 25 livres of France contained precisely an equal quantity of pure silver ·with 20*s.* sterling, 25 would be said to be the par of exchange between London and Paris. If one country uses gold for its principal measure of value, and another uses silver, the par between those countries cannot be estimated for any particular period, without taking into account the relative value of gold and silver at that particular period ; and as the relative value of the two precious metals is subject to fluctuation, the par of exchange between two such countries is not strictly a fixed point, but fluctuates within certain limits. An illustration of this will be found in the evidence, in the calculation of the par between London and Hamburgh, which is estimated to be 34/3½ Flemish shillings for a pound sterling. That rate of exchange, which is produced at any particular period by a balance of trade or payments between the two countries, and by a consequent disproportion between the supply and the demand of bills drawn by the one upon the other, is a departure on one side or the other from the real and fixed par. But this real par will be altered if any change takes place in the currency of one of the two countries, whether that change consists in the wear or debasement of a metallic currency below its standard, or in the discredit of a forced paper currency, or in the excess of a paper currency not convertible into specie ; a fall having taken place in the intrinsic value of a given portion of one currency, that portion will no longer be equal to the same portion, as before, of the other currency. But though the real par of the currencies is thus altered, the dealers, having little or no occasion to refer to the par, continue to reckon their course of exchanges from the former denomination of the par; and in this state of things a distinction is necessary to be made between the real and computed course of exchange. The computed course of exchange, as expressed in the tables used by the merchants, will then include, not only the real difference of exchange arising from the state of trade, but likewise the difference between the original par and the new par. Those two sums may happen to be added together in the calculation, or they may happen to be set against each other. If the country, whose currency has been depreciated in comparison with the other, has the balance of trade also against it, the computed rate of exchange will appear to be still more unfavourable than the real difference of exchange will be found to be ; and so if that same country has the balance of trade in its favour, the computed rate of exchange will appear to be much less favourable than the real difference of exchange will be found to be. Before the new coinage of our silver in King William's time, the exchange between England and Holland, computed in the usual manner according to the standard of their respective Mints, was 25 per cent. against England; but the value of the current coin of England was more than 25 per cent. below the standard value; so that if that of Holland was at its full standard, the real exchange was in fact in favour of England. It may happen in the same manner, that the two parts of the calculation may be both opposite and equal, the real exchange in favour of the country by trade being equal to the nominal exchange against it by the state of its currency; in that case, the computed exchange will be at par, while the real exchange is in fact in favour of that country. Again, the currencies of both the countries which trade together may have undergone an alteration, and that either in an equal degree, or unequally; in such a case, the question of the real state of the exchange between them becomes a little more complicated, but it is to be resolved exactly upon the same principle. Without going out of the bounds of the present inquiry, this may be well illustrated by the present state of the exchange of London with Portugal, as quoted in the tables for the 18th of May last. The exchange of London on Lisbon appears to be $67\frac{1}{2}$; $67\frac{1}{2}d$. sterling for a milree is the old established par of exchange between the two countries; and $67\frac{1}{2}$ accordingly is still said to be the par. But by the evidence of Mr. Lyne, it appears, that, in Portugal, all payments are now by law made one-half in hard money, and one-half in government paper; and that this paper is depreciated at a discount of 27 per cent. Upon all payments made in Portugal, therefore, there is a discount or loss of $13\frac{1}{2}$ per cent. and the exchange at $67\frac{1}{2}$, though nominally at. par, is in .truth $13\frac{1}{2}$ per cent. against this country. If the exchange were really at par, it would be quoted at $56\frac{65}{100}$ or apparently $13\frac{1}{2}$ per cent. in favour of London, as compared with the old par which was fixed before the depreciation of the Portuguese medium of payments. Whether this $13\frac{1}{2}$ per cent. which stands against this country by the present exchange on Lisbon, is a real difference of exchange, occasioned by the course of trade and by the remittances to Portugal on account of government, or a nominal and apparent exchange occasioned by something in the state of our own currency, or is partly real and partly nominal, may perhaps be determined by what your Committee have yet to state.

It appears to your Committee to have been long settled and understood as a principle, that the difference of exchange resulting from the state of trade and payments between two countries is limited by the expense of conveying and insuring the precious metals from one country to the other; at least, that it cannot for any considerable length of time exceed that limit. The real difference of exchange, resulting from the state of trade, and payments, never can fall lower than the amount of such expense of carriage, including the insurance. The truth of this position is so plain, and it is so uniformly agreed to by all the practical authorities, both commercial and political, that your Committee will assume it as indisputable.

It occurred, however, to your Committee that the amount of that charge and premium of insurance might be increased above what it has been in ordinary periods even of war, by the peculiar circumstances which at present obstruct the commercial intercourse between this country and the Continent of Europe ; and that as such an increase would place so much lower than usual the limit to which our exchanges might fall, an explanation might thereby be furnished of their present unusual fall. Your Committee accordingly directed their enquiries to this point.

It was stated to your Committee, by the merchant who has been already mentioned as being intimately acquainted with the trade between this country and the Continent, that the present expense of transporting gold from London to Hamburgh, independent of the premium of insurance, is from $1\frac{1}{2}$ to 2 per cent. ; that the risk is very variable from day to day, so that there is no fixed premium, but he conceived the average risk, for the fifteen months preceding the time when he spoke, to have been about 4 per cent. : making the whole cost of sending gold from London to Hamburgh for those fifteen months at such average of the risk, from $5\frac{1}{2}$ to 6 per cent.—Mr. Abraham Goldsmid stated, that in the last five or six months of the year 1809, the expense of sending gold to Holland varied exceedingly, from 4 to 7 per cent. for all charges, covering the risk as well as the costs of transportation. By the evidence which was taken before the Committees upon the Bank Affairs, in 1797, it appears that the cost of sending specie from London to Hamburgh in that time of war, including all charges as well as an average insurance, was estimated at a little more than $3\frac{1}{2}$ per cent. It is clear, therefore, that in consequence of the peculiar circumstances of the present state of the war, and the increased difficulties of intercourse with the Continent, the cost of transporting the precious metals thither from this country has not only been rendered more fluctuating than it used to be, but, upon the whole, is very considerably increased. It would appear, however, that upon an average of the risk for that period when it seems to have been highest, the last half of the last year, the cost and insurance of transporting gold to Hamburgh or to Holland did not exceed 7 per cent. It was of course greater at particular times, when the risk was above that average. It is evident also that the risk, and consequently the whole cost of transporting it to an inland market, to Paris, for example, would upon an average, be higher than that of carrying it to Amsterdam or Hamburgh. It follows, that the limit to which the exchanges, as resulting from the state of trade, might fall and continue unfavourable for a considerable length of time, has, during the period in question, been a good deal lower than in former times of war ; but it appears also, that the expense of remitting specie has not been increased so much, and that the limit, by which the depression of the exchanges is bounded, has not been lowered so much, as to afford an adequate explanation of a fall of the exchanges so great as from 16 to 20 per cent. below par. The increased cost of such remittance would explain, at those moments when the risk was greatest, a fall of something more than 7 per cent. in the exchange with Hamburgh or Holland, and a fall still greater perhaps in the exchange with Paris ; but the rest of the fall which has actually taken place, remains to be explained in some other manner.

Your Committee are disposed to think from the result of the whole evidence, contradictory as it is, that the circumstances of the trade of this country, in the course of the last year. were such as to occasion a real fall of our exchanges with the Continent to a certain extent, and perhaps at one period almost as low as the limit fixed by the expense of remitting gold from hence to the respective markets. And your Committee is inclined to this opinion, both by what is stated regarding the excess of imports from the Continent above the exports, though that is the part of the subject which is left most in doubt ; and also by what is stated respecting the mode in which the payments in our trade have been latterly effected, an advance being paid upon the imports from the Continent of Europe, and a long credit being given upon the exports to other parts of the world.

Your Committee, observing how entirely the present depression of our exchange with Europe is referred by many persons to a great excess of our imports above our exports, have called for an account of the actual value of those for the last five years ; and Mr. Irving, the Inspector General of Customs, has accordingly furnished the most accurate estimate of both that he has been enabled to form. He has also endeavoured to forward the object of the Committee. by calculating how much should be deducted from the value of goods imported, on account of articles in return for which nothing is exported. These deductions consist of the produce of fisheries, and of imports from the East and West Indies, which are of the nature of rents, profits, and capital remitted to proprietors in this country. The balance of trade in favour of this country, upon the face of the account thus made up, was:

In 1805	about	....	£ 6,616,000
" 1806	"	....	10,437,00)
" 1807	"	....	5,566,000
" 1808	"	....	12,481,000
" 1809	"	....	14,834,000

So far therefore, as any inference is to be drawn from the balance thus exhibited, the exchanges during the present year, in which many payments to this country on account of the very advantageous balances of the two former years may be expected to take place, ought to be peculiarly favourable.

Your Committee, however, place little confidence in deductions made even from the improved document which the industry and intelligence of the Inspector General has enabled him to furnish. It is defective, as Mr. Irving has himself stated, inasmuch as it supplies no account of the sum drawn by foreigners (which is at the present period peculiarly large) on account of freight due to them for the employment of their shipping, nor, on the other hand, of the sum receivable from them (and forming an addition to the value of our exported articles), on account of freight arising from the employment of British shipping. It leaves out of consideration all interest on capital in England possessed by foreigners, and on capital abroad belonging to inhabitants of Great Britain, as well as the pecuniary transactions between the governments of England and Ireland. It takes no cognizance of contraband trade, and of exported and imported bullion, of which no account is rendered at the Custom-house. It likewise omits a most important article, the variations of which, if correctly stated, would probably be found to correspond in a great degree with the fluctuations of the apparently favorable balance ; namely, the bills drawn on government for our naval, military, and other expenses in foreign parts. Your Committee had hoped to receive an account of these from the table of the House ; but there has been some difficulty and consequent delay in executing a material part of the order made for them. It appears from " An Account, as far as it could be made out, of sums paid for expenses abroad in

1793-4-5-6," inserted in the Appendix of the Lords' Report on the occasion of the Bank Restriction Bill, that the sums so paid were,

In 1793 .... £ 2,785,252
" 1794 8,335,591
" 1795 11,040,236
" 1796 10,649,916

The following is an account of the official value of our Imports and Exports with the Continent of Europe, alone, in each of the last five years :

	IMPORTS.	EXPORTS.	Balance in favor of Great Britain, reckoned in Official Value.
1805	£10,008,649	£15,465,430	£ 5,456,781
1806	8,197,256	13,216,386	5,019,130
1807	7,973,510	12,639,590	4,716,080
1808	4,210,671	11,280,490	7,069,819
1809	9,551,857	23,722,615	14,170,758

The balances with Europe alone in favour of Great Britain, as exhibited in this imperfect statement, are not far from corresponding with the general and more accurate balances before given. The favourable balance of 1809 with Europe alone, if computed according to the actual value, would be much more considerable than the value of the same year, in the former general statement. A favourable balance of trade on the face of the account of exports and imports, presented annually to Parliament, is a very probable consequence of large drafts on Government for foreign expenditure ; and augmentation of exports, and a diminution of imports, being promoted and even enforced by the means of such drafts. For if the supply of bills drawn abroad, either by the agents of Government, or by individuals, is disproportionate to the demand, the price of them in foreign money falls, until it is so low as to invite purchasers ; and the purchasers, who are generally foreigners, not wishing to transfer their property permanently to England, have a reference to the terms on which the bills on England will purchase those British commodities which are in demand, either in their own country, or in intermediate places, with which the account may be adjusted. Thus, the price of the bills being regulated in some degree by that of British commodities, and continuing to fall till it becomes so low as to be likely to afford profit on the purchase and exportation of these commodities, an actual exportation nearly proportionate to the amount of the bills drawn can scarcely fail to take place. It follows, that there cannot be, for any long period, either a highly favourable or unfavourable balance of trade; for the balance no sooner affects the price of bills, than the price of bills, by its re-action on the state of trade, promotes an equalization of commercial exports and imports. Your Committee have here considered cash and bullion as forming a part of the general mass of exported or imported articles, and as transferred according to the state both of the supply and the demand; forming, however, under certain circumstances, especially in case of great fluctuations in the general commerce, a peculiarly commodious remittance.

Your Committee have enlarged on the documents supplied by Mr. Irving, for the sake of throwing further light on the general question of the balance of trade and the exchanges, and of dissipating some very prevalent errors which have a great practical influence on the subject now under consideration.

That the real exchange against this country with the continent cannot at any time have materially exceeded the limit fixed by the cost at that time of transporting specie, your Committee are convinced upon the principles which have been already stated. That in point of fact, those exchanges have not exceeded that limit seems to receive a very satisfactory illustration from one part of the evidence of Mr. Greffulhe, who, of all the merchants examined, seemed most wedded to the opinion that the state of the balance payments alone was sufficient to account for any depression of the exchanges, however great. From what the Committee have already stated with respect to the par of exchange, it is manifest that the exchange between two countries is at its real par, when a given quantity of gold or silver in the one country is convertible at the market price into such an amount of the currency of that country, as will purchase a bill of exchange on the other country for such an amount of the currency of that other country, as will there be convertible at the market price into an equal quantity of gold or silver of the same fineness. In the same manner the real exchange is in favour of a country having money transactions with another, when a given quantity of gold or silver in the former is convertible for such an amount in the currency of that latter country, as will there be convertible into a greater quantity of gold or silver of the same fineness.

Upon these principles, your Committee desired Mr. Greffulhe to make certain calculations, which appear in his answers to the following questions, viz. :

" Supposing you had a pound weight troy of gold of the English standard at Paris, and that you wished by means of that to procure a bill of exchange upon London, what would be the amount of the bill of exchange which you would procure in the present circumstances ?—I find that a pound of gold of the British standard at the present market price of 105 francs, and the exchange at 20 livres, would purchase a bill of exchange of 59*l.* 8*s.*

" At the present market price of gold in London, how much standard gold can you purchase for 59*l.* 8*s.* ?—At the price of 4*l.* 12*s.* I find it will purchase 13 ounces of gold, within a very small fraction.

" Then what is the difference per cent. in the quantity of standard gold which is equivalent to 59*l.* 8*s.* of our currency as at Paris and in London ?—About 8½ per cent.

" Suppose you have a pound weight troy of our standard gold at Hamburgh, and that you wished to part with it for a bill of exchange upon London, what would be the amount of the bill of exchange, which, in the present circumstances, you would procure ?—At the Hamburgh price of 101, and the exchange at 29, the amount of the bill purchased on London would be 58*l.* 4*s.*

" What quantity of our standard gold, at the present price of 4*l.* 12*s.* do you purchase for 58*l.* 4*s.* ?—About 12 ounces and 3 dwts.

" Then what is the difference per cent. between the quantity of standard gold at Hamburgh and in London, which is equivalent to 58*l.* 4*s.* sterling ?—About 5½ per cent.

" Suppose you had a pound weight troy of our standard gold at Amsterdam, and wished to part with it for a bill of exchange upon London, what would be the amount sterling of the bill of exchange which you would procure ?—At the Amsterdam price of 14½, exchange 31.6, and Bank agio 1 per cent. the amount of the bill on London would be 58*l.* 18*s.*

" At the present price of 4*l.* 12*s.* what quantity of our standard gold do you purchase in London for 58*l.* 18*s.* sterling ?—12 oz. 16 dwts.

" How much is that per cent. ?—7 per cent."

Similar calculations, but made upon different assumed data,

will be found in the evidence of Mr. Abraham Goldsmid.   From
these answers of Mr. Greffulhe, it appears, that when the computed exchange with Hamburg was 29, that is, from 16 to 17
per cent. below par, the real difference of exchange, resulting
from the state of trade and balance of payments was no more
than 5½ per cent. against this country ; that when the computed
exchange with Amsterdam was 31. 6, that is about 15 per cent.
below par, the real exchange was no more than 7 per cent.
against this country ; that when the computed exchange with
Paris was 20, that is 20 per cent. below par, the real exchange
was no more than 8½ per cent. against this country.   After
making these allowances, therefore, for the effect of the balance
of trade and payments upon our exchanges with those places,
there will still remain a fall of 11 per cent. in the exchange with
Hamburgh, of above 8 per cent. in the exchange with Holland,
and 11½ per cent. in the exchange with Paris, to be explained
in some other manner.

If the same mode of calculation be applied to the more
recent statements of the exchange with the continent, it will
perhaps appear, that though the computed exchange is at present
against this country, the real exchange is in its favor.

From the foregoing reasons relative to the state of the exchanges,
if they are considered apart, your Committee find it difficult to
resist an inference, that a portion at least of the great fall which
the exchanges lately suffered must have resulted not from the
state of trade, but from a change in the relative value of our
domestic currency.   But, when this deduction is joined with
that which your Committee have stated, respecting the change
in the market price of gold, that inference appears to be dem-
onstrated.

III.

In consequence of the opinion which your Committee entertained, that, in the present artificial condition of the circulating
medium of this country, it is most important to watch the
foreign exchanges and the market price of gold, your Committee
were desirous to learn whether the Directors of the Bank of
England held the same opinion, and derived from it a practical
rule for the control of their circulation ; and particularly
whether, in the course of the last year, the great depression of
the exchanges, and the great rise in the price of gold, had suggested to the Directors any suspicion of the currency of the
country being excessive.

Mr. Whitmore, the late Governor of the Bank, stated to the Committee, that in regulating the general amount of the loans and discounts, he did "not advert to the circumstance of the exchanges; it appearing upon a reference to the amount of our notes in circulation, and the course of exchange, that they frequently have no connexion." He afterward said, "My opinion is, I do not know whether it is that of the Bank, that the amount of our paper circulation has no reference at all to the state of the exchange." And on a subsequent day, Mr. Whitmore stated, that "the present unfavourable state of exchange has no influence upon the amount of their issues, the Bank having acted precisely in the same way as they did before." He was likewise asked, Whether, in regulating the amount of their circulation, the Bank ever adverted to the difference between the market and Mint price of gold? and having desired to have time to consider that question, Mr. Whitmore, on a subsequent day, answered it in the following terms, which suggested these further questions:

In taking into consideration the amount of your notes, out in circulation, and in limiting the extent of your discounts to merchants, do you advert to the difference, when such exists, between the market and the Mint price of gold?—We do advert to that, inasmuch as we do not discount at any time for those persons who we know, or have good reason to suppose, export the gold.

"Do you not advert to it any farther than by refusing discounts to such persons?—We do advert to it, inasmuch as whenever any Director thinks it bears upon the question of our discounts, and presses to bring forward the discussion.

"The market price of gold having, in the course of the last year, risen as high as 4*l.* 10*s.* or 4*l.* 12*s.*, has that circumstance been taken into consideration by you, so as to have had any effect in diminishing or enlarging the amount of the outstanding demands?—It has not been taken into consideration by me in that view."

Mr. Pearse, now Governor of the Bank, agreed with Mr. Whitmore in this account of the practice of the Bank, and expressed his full concurrence in the same opinion.

Mr. Pearse.—"In considering this subject, with reference to the manner in which Bank notes are issued, resulting from the applications made for discounts to supply the necessary want of Bank notes, by which their issue in amount is so controlled that it can never amount to an excess, I cannot see how the amount of Bank notes issued can operate upon the price of

Bullion, or the state of the exchanges, and therefore I am individually of opinion that the price of Bullion, or the state of the exchanges, can never be a reason for lessening the amount of Bank notes to be issued, always understanding the control which I have already described.

"Is the Governor of the Bank of the same opinion, which has now been expressed by the Deputy Governor?

Mr. Whitmore.—"I am so much of the same opinion, that I never think it necessary to advert to the price of gold, or the state of the exchange, on the days on which we make our advances.

"Do you advert to these two circumstances with a view to regulate the general amount of your advances?—I do not advert to it with a view to our general advances, conceiving it not to bear upon the question."

And *Mr. Harman*, another Bank Director, expressed his opinion in these terms—"I must very materially alter my opinions before I can suppose that the exchanges will be influenced by any modifications of our paper currency."

These gentlemen, as well as several of the merchants who appeared before the Committee, placed much reliance upon an argument which they drew from the want of correspondence in point of time, observable between the amount of Bank of England notes and the state of the Hamburgh exchange during several years; and Mr. Pearse presented a paper on this subject, which is inserted in the Appendix. Your Committee would feel no distrust in the general principles which they have stated, if the discordance had been greater; considering the variety of circumstances which have a temporary effect on exchange, and the uncertainty both of the time and the degree in which it may be influenced by any given quantity of paper. It may be added, that the numerical amount of notes (supposing $1l.$ and $2l.$ notes to be excluded from the statement) did not materially vary during the period of the comparison; and that in the last year, when the general exchanges with Europe have become much more unfavourable, the notes of the Bank of England, as well as those of the country Banks, have been very considerably increased. Your Committee, however, on the whole, are not of opinion that a material depression of the exchanges has been manifestly to be traced in its amount and degree to an augmentation of notes corresponding in point of time. They conceive, that the more minute and ordinary fluctuations of exchange are generally referable to the course of our commerce; that political events, operating upon the state

of trade, may often have contributed as well to the rise as to
the fall of the exchange ; and in particular, that the first remarkable depression of it in the beginning of 1809, is to be ascribed, as has been stated in the evidence already quoted, to
commercial events arising out of the occupation of the North
of Germany by the troops of the French Emperor. The evil
has been that the exchange, when fallen, has not had the full
means of recovery under the subsisting system. And if those
occasional depressions, which arise from commercial causes,
are not after a time successively corrected by the remedy which
used to apply itself before the suspension of the cash payments of the Bank, the consequences may ultimately be exactly
similar to those which a sudden and extravagant issue of paper
would produce. The restoration of the exchange used to be
effected by the clandestine transmission of guineas, which improved it for the moment by serving as a remittance ; and unquestionably also in part, probably much more extensively, by
the reduction of the total quantity of the remaining circulating
medium, to which reduction the banks were led to contribute by
the caution which every drain of gold naturally excited. Under the present system, the former of these remedies must be
expected more and more to fail, the guineas in circulation being even now apparently so few as to form no important remittance ; and the reduction of paper seems therefore the chief,
if not the sole corrective, to be resorted to. It is only after
the Bank shall have for some time resumed its cash payments,
that both can again operate, as they did on all former occasions
prior to the restriction.

The Committee cannot refrain from expressing it to be their
opinion, after a very deliberate consideration of this part of the
subject, that it is a great practical error to suppose that the exchanges with foreign countries, and the price of Bullion, are
not liable to be affected by the amount of a paper currency,
which is issued without the condition of payment in specie at
the will of the holder. That the exchanges will be lowered,
and the price of Bullion raised, by an issue of such paper to
excess, is not only established as a principle by the most eminent authorities upon commerce and finance ; but its practical
truth has been illustrated by the history of almost every state
in modern times which has used a paper currency ; and in all
those countries, this principle has finally been resorted to by
their statesmen, as the best criterion to judge by, whether such
currency was or was not excessive.

In the instances which are most familiar in the history of

foreign countries, the excess of paper has been usually accompanied by another circumstance, which has no place in our situation at present, a want of confidence in the sufficiency of those funds upon which the paper had been issued. Where these two circumstances, excess and want of confidence, are conjoined, they will co-operate and produce their effect much more rapidly then when it is the result of the excess only of a paper of perfectly good credit ; and in both cases an effect of the same sort will be produced upon the foreign exchanges, and upon the price of bullion. The most remarkable examples of the former kind are to be found in the history of the paper currencies of the British Colonies in North America, in the early part of the last century, and in that of the assignats of the French Republic : to which the Committee have been enabled to add another, scarcely less remarkable, from the money speculations of the Austrian government in the last campaign, which will be found in the Appendix. The present state of the currency of Portugal affords, also, an instance of the same kind.

Examples of the other sort, in which the depreciation was produced by excess alone, may be gathered from the experience of the United Kingdom at different times.

In Scotland, about the end of the seven years' war, banking was carried to a very great excess ; and by a practice of inserting in their promissory notes an optional clause of paying at sight, or in six months after sight with interest, the convertibility of such notes into specie at the will of the holder was in effect suspended. These notes accordingly became depreciated in comparison with specie ; and while this abuse lasted, the exchange between London and Dumfries, for example, was sometimes four per cent. against Dumfries, while the exchange between London and Carlisle, which is not thirty miles distant from Dumfries, was at par. The Edinburgh banks, when any of their paper was brought in to be exchanged for bills on London, were accustomed to extend or contract the date of the bills they gave, according to the state of the exchange, diminishing in this manner the value of those bills, nearly in the same degree in which the excessive issue had caused their paper to be depreciated. This excess of paper was at last removed by granting bills on London at a fixed date ; for the paynent of which bills, or in other words, for the payment of which excess of paper, it was necessary in the first instance to provide, by placing large pecuniary funds in the hands of their London correspondents. In aid of such precautionary measures on the

part of the Edinburgh banks, an act of Parliament prohibited
the optional clauses, and suppressed ten and five shilling notes.
The exchange between England and Scotland was speedily restored to its natural rate : and bills on London at a fixed date
having ever since been given in exchange for the circulating
notes of Scotland, all material excess of Scottish paper above
Bank of England has been prevented, and the exchange has,
been stationary.

The experience of the Bank of England itself, within a very
short period after its first establishment, furnishes a very instructive illustration of all the foregoing principles and reasonings.   In this instance, the effects of a depreciation of the coin,
by wear and clipping, were coupled with the effect of an excessive issue of paper.*   The Directors of the Bank of England
did not at once attain a very accurate knowledge of all the
principles by which such an institution must be conducted.
They lent money not only by discount, but upon real securities,
mortgages, and even pledges of commodities not perishable ;
at the same time, the Bank contributed most materially to the
service of government for the support of the army upon the Continent.   By the liberality of these loans to private individuals, as
well as by the la ge advances to government, the quantity of
the notes of the bank became excessive, their relative value
was depreciated, and they fell to a discount of 17 per cent.
At this time there appears to have been no failure of the public confidence in the funds of the Bank ; for its stock sold for
110 per cent., though only 60 per cent. upon the subscriptions
had been paid in. By the conjoint effect of this depreciation
of the paper of the Bank from excess, and of the depreciation
of the silver coin from wear and clipping, the price of gold
bullion was so much raised, that guineas were as high as 30*s*. ; all
that had remained of good silver gradually disappeared from the
circulation ; and the exchange with Holland, which had been
before a little affected by the remittances for the army, sunk
as low as 25 per cent. under par, when the Bank † notes were

* See a short account of the Bank by Mr. Godfrey, one of the original
Directors; and a Short History of the Last Parliament, 1699, by Dr.
Drake ; both in Lord Somers' Collection of Tracts.

† Macleod (Dict. of P. E. I. 303) takes exception to this statement, and
in the form in which it stands, it is liable to be misunderstood. The history of American currency shows how much nominal convertibility may differ from actual convertibility, but notes cannot fall to 17 per cent. discount,
while the Bank offers to pay on demand. The Bank stopped payment in
May, 1696, and then its notes fell to the discount named.

at a discount of 17 per cent.   Several expedients were tried,
both by Parliament and by the Bank, to force a better silver coin
into circulation, and to reduce the price of guineas, but without effect.   At length the true remedies were resorted to : first,
by a new coinage of silver, which restored that part of the currency to its standard value, though the scarcity of money occasioned by calling in the old coin brought the Bank into
straits, and even for a time affected its credit; secondly, by
taking out of the circulation the excess of Bank notes.   This
last operation appears to have been effected very judiciously.
Parliament consented to enlarge the capital stock of the Bank,
but annexed a condition, directing that a certain proportion of
the new subscriptions should be made good in Bank notes.   In
proportion to the amount of notes sunk in this manner, the
value of those which remained in circulation began pres-
ently to rise ; in a short time the notes were at par, and the
foreign exchanges nearly so.   These details are all very fully
mentioned in authentic tracts published at the time, and the
case appears to your Committee to afford much instruction
upon the subject of their present inquiry.

Your Committee must next refer to the confirmation and
sanction which all their reasonings receive from the labours of
the Committee of this House, which was appointed in a former
Parliament to examine into the causes of the great depreciation
of the Irish exchange with England in 1804.   Most of the mercantile persons who gave evidence before that Committee, including two Directors of the Bank of Ireland, were unwilling to
admit that the fall of the exchange was in any degree to be ascribed to an excess of the paper currency arising out of the restriction of 1797 ; the whole fall in that case, as in the present, was referred to an unfavourable balance of trade or of
payments ; and it was also then affirmed, that " notes issued
only in proportion to the demand, in exchange for good and
convertible securities, payable at specific periods, could not
tend to any excess in the circulation, or to any depreciation."
This doctrine, though more or less qualified by some of the
witnesses, pervades most of the evidence given before that
Committee, with the remarkable exception of Mr. Mansfield,
whose knowledge of the effects of that over issue of Scotch
paper, which has just been mentioned, led him to deliver a
more just opinion on the subject.   Many of the witnesses before the Committee, however unwilling to acknowledge the
real nature of the evil, made important concessions, which
necessarily involved them in inconsistency.   They could not,

as practical men, controvert the truth of the general position, that "the fluctuations of exchange between two countries are generally limited by the price at which any given quantity of bullion can be purchased in the circulating medium of the debtor country, and converted into the circulating medium of the creditor country, together with the insurances and charges of transporting it from the one to the other." It was at the same time admitted, that the expense of transporting gold from England to Ireland, including insurance, was then under one per cent. ; that before the restriction, the fluctuations had never long and much exceeded this limit ; and, moreover, at the exchange with Belfast, where guineas freely circulated at the time of the investigation by that Committee was then 1¼ in favor of Ireland, while the exchange with Dublin, where only paper was in use, was 10*l.* per cent. against that country. It also appeared from such imperfect documents as it was practicable to furnish, that the balance of trade was then favourable to Ireland. Still, however, it was contended, that there was no depreciation of Irish paper, that there was a scarcity and consequent high price of gold, and that the diminution of Irish paper would not rectify the exchange. "The depreciation of Bank paper in Ireland" (it was said by one of the witnesses, a Director of the Bank of Ireland) "is entirely a relative term with respect to the man who buys and sells in Dublin by that common medium : to him it is not depreciated at all ; but to the purchaser of a bill on London, to him in that relation, and under that circumstance, there is a depreciation of 10 per cent." .By thus avoiding all comparison with a view to the point in issue between the value of their own paper and that of either the then circulating medium of this country or of gold bullion, or even of gold coin then passing at a premium in other parts of Ireland, they appear to have retained a confident opinion, that no depreciation of Irish paper had taken place.

It is further observable, that the value of a considerable quantity of dollars put into circulation by the Bank of Ireland at this period was raised to 5*s.* a dollar, for the professed purpose of rendering the new silver coin conformable to the existing state of the exchange, a circumstance on which the Committee animadverted in their Report, and which serves to show that the Irish paper currency could not stand a comparison with the standard price of silver, any more than with that of gold bullion, with gold in coin, or with the then paper currency of this kingdom.

A fact was mentioned to that Committee on the evidence

of Mr. Colville, a Director of the Bank of Ireland, which though it carried no conviction to his mind of the tendency of a limitation of paper to lower exchanges, seems very decisive on this point. He stated that in 1753 and 1754, the Dublin exchange being remarkably unfavourable, and the notes of the Dublin Bank being suddenly withdrawn, the exchange became singularly favourable. The mercantile distress produced on that occasion was great, through the suddenness of the operation, for it was effected, not by the gradual and prudential measures of the several Banks, but through the violent pressure which their unguarded issues had brought upon them. The general result, however, is not the less observable.

With a view to the further elucidation of the subject of the Irish exchanges, which so lately attracted the attention of Parliament, it may be proper to remark that Ireland has no dealings in exchange with foreign countries, except through London, and that the payments from Ireland to the Continent are consequently converted into English currency, and then into the currency of the countries to which Ireland is indebted. In the spring of 1804 the Exchange of England with the Continent was above par, and the Exchange of Ireland was in such a state that 118*l.* 10*s.* of the notes of the Bank of Ireland would purchase only 100*l.* of those of the Bank of England. Therefore, if the notes of the Bank of Ireland were not depreciated, and it was so maintained, it followed that the notes of the Bank of England were at more than 10 per cent. premium above the standard coin of the two countries.

The principles laid down by the Committee of 1804, had probably some weight with the Directors of the Bank of Ireland ; for between the period of their Report (June, 1804) and January, 1806, the circulation of the notes of the Bank of Ireland was gradually (though with small occasional fluctuations) reduced from about three millions to 2,410,000*l.*, being a diminution of nearly one-fifth ; at the same time, all the currency which had been issued under the name of silver tokens, was by law suppressed. The paper currency, both of the Bank of England and of the English country Banks, seems during the same period to have gradually increased. The combination of these two causes is likely to have had a material effect in restoring to par the Irish exchange with England.

The Bank of Ireland has again gradually enlarged its issues to about 3,100,000*l.*, being somewhat higher than they stood in 1804, an increase probably not disproportionate to that which has occurred in England within the same period. Perhaps, however, it ought not to be assumed, that the diminution of issues of the Bank of Ireland between 1804 and 1806, would produce a corresponding reduction in the issues of private Banks in Ireland, exactly in the same manner in which a diminution of Bank of England paper produces that effect on the country banks in Great Britain; because the Bank of Ireland does not possess the same exclusive power of supplying any part of that country with a paper currency, which the Bank of England enjoys in respect to the metropolis of the empire. The Bank of England, by restricting the quantity of this necessary article in that important quarter, can more effectually secure the improvement of its value; and every such improvement must necessarily lead, by a corresponding diminution in amount, to a similar augmentation of the value of country Bank paper exchangeable for it. That the same diminution of the circulation of private Banks took place in Ireland is more than probable, for the private Banks in Ireland are accustomed to give Bank of Ireland paper for their own circulating notes when required to do so, and therefore could not but feel the effect of any new limitation of that paper for which their own was exchangeable.

It is due, however, in justice to the present Directors of the Bank of England, to remind the House that the suspension of their cash payments, though it appears in some degree to have originated in a mistaken view taken by the Bank of the peculiar difficulties of that time was not a measure sought for by the Bank, but imposed upon it by the Legislature for what were held to be urgent reasons of state policy and public expediency. And it ought not to be urged as matter of charge against the Directors, if in this novel situation in which their commercial company was placed by the law, and entrusted with the regulation and control of the whole circulating medium of the country, they were not fully aware of the principles by which so delicate a trust should be executed, but continued to conduct their business of discounts and advances according to their former routine.

It is important at the same time, to observe, that under the former system, when the Bank was bound to answer its notes in specie upon demand, the state of the foreign exchanges and the price of gold did most materially influence its conduct in the issue of those notes, though it was not the practice of the Directors systematically to watch either the one or the other. So long as gold was demandable for their paper, they were speedily apprised of a depression of the exchange, and a rise in the price of gold, by a run upon them for that article. If at any time they incautiously exceeded the proper limit of their advances and issues, the paper was quickly brought back to them, by those who were tempted to profit by the market price of gold or by the rate of exchange. In this manner the evil soon cured itself. The Directors of the Bank having their apprehensions excited by the reduction of their stock of gold, and being able to replace their loss only by reiterated purchases of bullion at a very losing price, naturally contracted their issues of paper, and thus gave to the remaining paper, as well as to the coin for which it was interchangeable, an increased value, while the clandestine exportation either of the coin, or the gold produced from it, combined in improving the state of the exchange and in producing a corresponding diminution of the difference between the market price and Mint price of gold, or of paper convertible into gold.

Your Committee do not mean to represent that the manner in which this effect resulted from the conduct which they have described, was distinctly perceived by the Bank Directors. The fact of limiting their paper as often as they experienced any great drain of gold, is, however, unquestionable. Mr. Bosanquet stated, in his evidence before the secret Committee of the House of Lords, in the year 1797, that in 1783, when the Bank experienced a drain of cash, which alarmed them, the Directors took a bold step and refused to make the advances on the loan of that year. This, he said, answered the purpose of making a temporary suspension in the amount of the drain of their specie. And all the three Directors who have been examined before your Committee, represent some restriction of the Bank issues as having usually taken place at those periods antecedent to this suspension of the cash payments of the Bank when they experienced any material run. A very urgent demand for guineas, though arising not from the high price of gold and the state of the exchange, but from a fear of invasion, occurred in 1793, and also in 1797, and in each of these periods the Bank restrained their discounts, and consequently also the amount of their notes, very much below the demands of the merchants. Your Committee question the policy of thus limiting the accommodation in a period of alarm, unaccompanied with an unfavorable exchange and high price of bullion ; but they consider the conduct of the Bank at the two last mentioned periods, as affording illustration of their general disposition, antecedently to 1797, to contract their loans and their paper, when they found their gold to be taken from them.

It was a necessary consequence of the suspension of cash payments, to exempt the Bank from that drain of gold, which, in former times, was sure to result from an unfavorable exchange and a high price of bullion. And the Directors, released from all fears of such a drain, and no longer feeling any inconvenience from such a state of things, have not been prompted to restore the exchanges and the price of gold to their proper level by a reduction of their advances and issues. The Directors, in former times, did not perhaps perceive and acknowledge the principle more distinctly than those of the present day, but they felt the inconvenience, and obeyed its impulse ; which practically established a check and limitation to the issue of paper. In the present times the inconvenience is not felt ; and the check, accordingly, is no longer in force.

But your Committee beg leave to report it to the House as their most clear opinion, that so long as the suspension of cash payments is permitted to subsist, the price of gold bullion and the general course of exchange with foreign countries, taken for any considerable period of time, form the best general criterion from which any inference can be drawn, as to the sufficiency or excess of paper currency in circulation ; and that the Bank of England cannot safely regulate the amount of its issues, without having reference to the criterion presented by these two circumstances. And upon a review of all the facts and reasonings which have already been stated, your Committee are further of opinion, that, although the commercial state of this country, and the political state of the continent, may have had some influence on the high price of gold bullion and the unfavourable course of exchange with foreign countries, this price, and this depreciation, are also to be ascribed to the want of a permanent check, and a sufficient limitation of the paper currency in this country.

In connection with the general subject of this part of their report, the policy of the Bank of England respecting the amount of their circulation, your Committee have now to call the attention of the House to another topic, which was brought under their notice in the course of their inquiry, and which in their judgment demands the most serious consideration. The Bank Directors, as well as some of the merchants who have been examined, shewed a great anxiety to state to your Committee a doctrine, of the truth of which they professed themselves to be most thoroughly convinced, that there can be no possible excess in the issue of Bank of England paper, so long as the advances in which it is issued are made upon the principles which at present guide the conduct of the Directors, that is, so long as the discount of mercantile bills are confined to paper of undoubted solidity, arising out of real commercial transactions, and payable at short and fixed periods. That the discounts should be made only upon bills growing out of real commercial transactions, and falling due in a fixed and short period, are sound and well-established principles. But that, while the Bank is restrained from paying in specie, there need be no other limit to the issue of their paper than what is fixed by such rules of discount, and that during the suspension of cash payments the discount of good bills falling due at short periods cannot lead to any excess in the amount of bank paper in circulation, appears to your Committee to be a doctrine wholly erroneous in principle, and pregnant with dangerous consequences in practice.

But before your Committee proceed to make such observations upon this theory as it appears to them to deserve, they think it right to shew from the evidence, to what extent it is entertained by some of those individuals who have been at the head of the affairs of the Bank. The opinions held by those individuals are likely to have an important practical influence; and appeared to your Committee, moreover, the best evidence of what has constituted the actual policy of that establishment in its corporate capacity.

Mr. Whitmore, the late Governor of the Bank, expressly states, "The Bank never force a note in circulation, and there will not remain a note in circulation more than the immediate wants of the public require; for no banker, I presume, will keep a larger stock of bank notes by him than his immediate payments require, as he can at all times procure them." The reason here assigned is more particularly explained by Mr. Whitmore, when he says, "The Bank notes would revert to us if there was a redundancy in circulation, as no one would pay interest for a bank note that he did not want to make use of." Mr. Whitmore further states, "The criterion by which I judge of the exact proportion to be maintained between the occasions of the public, and the issues of the Bank, is by avoiding as much as possible to discount what does not appear to be legitimate mercantile paper." And further when asked, What measure the court of Directors has to judge by, whether the quantity of bank notes out in circulation is at any time excessive? Mr. Whitmore states, that their measure of the security or abundance of bank notes is certainly by the greater or less application that is made to them for the discount of good paper.

Mr. Pearse, late Deputy-Governor, and now Governor of the Bank, stated very distinctly his concurrence in opinion with Mr. Whitmore upon this particular point.   He referred "to the manner in which bank notes are issued, resulting from the applications made for discounts to supply the necessary want of bank notes, by which their issue in amount is so controlled that it can never amount to an excess."   He considers "the amount of the bank notes in circulation as being controlled by the occasions of the public, for internal purposes," and that, "from the manner in which the issue of bank notes is controlled, the public will never call for more than is absolutely necessary for their wants."

Another Director of the Bank, Mr. Harman, being asked, If he thought that the sum total of discounts applied for, even though the accommodation afforded should be on the security of good bills to safe persons, might be such as to produce some excess in the quantity of the Bank issues, if fully complied with ? he answered, " I think if we discount only for solid persons, and such paper as is for real *bonâ-fide* transactions, we cannot materially err."   And he afterwards states, that what he should consider as the test of a superabundance would be, "money being more plentiful in the market."

It is material to observe, that both Mr. Whitmore and Mr. Pearse state that " the Bank does not comply with the whole demand upon them for discounts, and that they are never induced, by a view to their own profit, to push their issues beyond what they deem consistent with the public interest."

Another very important part of the evidence of these gentlemen upon this point, is contained in the following extract :

" Is it your opinion that the same security would exist against any excess in the issues of the Bank, if the rate of the discount were reduced from 5*l.* to 4*l.* per cent. ? "   Answer.—" The security of an excess of issue would be, I conceive, precisely the same."   Mr. *Pearse.*—" I concur in that answer."

" If it were reduced to 3*l.* per cent. ? "—Mr. *Whitmore.*—" I conceive there would be no difference if our practice remained the same as now, of not forcing a note into circulation."   Mr. *Pearse.*—" I concur in that answer."

Your Committee cannot help again calling the attention of the House to the view which this evidence presents, of the consequences which have resulted from the peculiar situation in which the Bank of England was placed by the suspension of cash payments.   So long as the paper of the Bank was convertible into specie at the will of the holder, it was enough, both for the safety of the Bank and for the public interest in what regarded its circulating medium, that the Directors attended only to the character and quality of the bills discounted, as real ones and payable at fixed and short periods. They could not much exceed the proper bounds in respect of the quantity and amount of bills discounted, so as thereby to produce an excess of their paper in circulation, without quickly finding that the surplus returned upon themselves in demand for specie. The private interest of the Bank to guard themselves against a continued demand of that nature, was a sufficient protection for the public against any such excess of Bank paper as would occasion a material fall in the relative value of the circulating medium. The restriction of cash payments, as has already been shown, having rendered the same preventive policy no longer necessary to the Bank, has removed that check upon its issues which was the public security against an excess. When the Bank Directors were no longer exposed to the inconvenience of a drain upon them for gold, they naturally felt that they had no such inconvenience to guard against by a more restrained system of discounts and advances ; and it was very natural for them to pursue, as before (but without that sort of guard and limitation which was now become unnecessary to their own security), the same liberal and prudent system of commercial advances from which the prosperity of their own establishment had resulted, as well as in a great degree the commercial prosperity of the whole country. It was natural for the Bank Directors to believe, that nothing but benefit could accrue to the public at large, while they saw the growth of Bank profits go hand in hand with the acommodations granted to the merchants. It was hardly to be expected of the Directors of the Bank, that they should be fully aware of the consequences that might result from their pursuing, after the suspension of cash payments, the same system which they had found a safe one before. To watch the operation of so new a law, and to provide against the injury which might result from it to the public interests, was the province, not so much of the Bank as of the Legislature : and, in the opinion of your Committee, there is room to regret that this House has not taken earlier notice of all the consequences of that law.

By far the most important of those consequences is, that while the convertibility into specie no longer exists as a check to an overissue of paper, the Bank Directors have not perceived that the removal of that check rendered it possible that such an excess might be issued by the discount of perfectly good bills. So far from perceiving this, your Committee have shown that they maintain the contrary doctrine with the utmost confidence, however it may be qualified occasionally by some of their expressions. That this doctrine is a very fallacious one, your Committee cannot entertain a doubt. The fallacy, upon which it is founded, lies in not distinguishing between an advance of capital to merchants, and an addition of supply of currency to the general mass of circulating medium. If the advance of capital only is considered, as made to those who are ready to employ it in judicious and productive undertakings, it is evident there need be no other limit to the total amount of advances than what the means of the lender, and his prudence in the selection of borrowers, may impose. But in the present situation of the Bank, intrusted as it is with the function of supplying the public with that paper currency which forms the basis of our circulation, and at the same time not subjected to the liability of converting the paper into specie, every advance which it makes of capital to the merchants in the shape of discount, becomes an addition also to the mass of circulating medium. In the first instance, when the advance is made by notes paid in discount of a bill, it is undoubtedly so much capital, so much power of making purchases, placed in the hands of the merchant who receives the notes; and if those hands are safe, the operation is so far, and in this its first step, useful and productive to the public. But as soon as the portion of circulating medium in which the advance was thus made performs in the hands of him to whom it was advanced this its first operation as capital, as soon as the notes are exchanged by him for some other article which is capital, they fall into the channel of circulation as so much circulating medium, and form an addition to the mass of currency. The necessary effect of every such addition to the mass is to diminish the relative value of any given portion of that mass in exchange for commodities. If the addition were made by notes convertible into specie, this diminution of the relative value of any given portion of the whole mass would speedily bring back upon the Bank which issued the notes as much as was excessive. But if by law they are not so convertible, of course this excess will not be brought back, but will remain in the channel of circulation, until paid in again to the Bank itself in discharge of the bills which were originally discounted. During the whole time they remain out, they perform all the functions of circulating medium; and before they come to be paid in discharge of those bills, they have already been followed by a new issue of notes in a similar operation of discounting. Each successive advance repeats the same process. If the whole sum of discounts continues outstanding at a given amount, there will remain permanently out in circulation a corresponding amount of paper; and if the amount of discounts is progressively increasing, the amount of paper, which remains out in circulation over and above what is otherwise wanted for the occasions of the public, will progressively increase also, and the money prices of commodities will progressively rise. This progress may be as indefinite, as the range of speculation and adventure in a great commercial country.

It is necessary to observe, that the law, which in this country limits the rate of interest, and of course the rate at which the Bank can legally discount, exposes the Bank to still more extensive demands for commercial discounts. While the rate of commercial profit is very considerably higher than five per cent., as it has lately been in many branches of our foreign trade, there is in fact no limit to the demands which merchants of perfectly good capital, and of the most prudent spirit of enterprise, may be tempted to make upon the Bank for accommodation and facilities by discount. Nor can any argument or illustration place in a more striking point of view the extent to which such of the Bank Directors as were examined before the Committee, seem to have in theory embraced that doctrine upon which your Committee have made these observations, as well as the practical consequences to which that doctrine may lead in periods of a high spirit of commercial adventure, than the opinion which Mr. Whitmore and Mr. Pearse have delivered; that the same complete security to the public against any excess in the issues of the Bank would exist if the rate of discount were reduced from five to four, or even to three per cent. From the evidence, however, of the late Governor and Deputy Governor of the Bank it appears, that though they state the principle broadly, that there can be no excess of their circulation if issued according to their rules of discount, yet they disclaim the idea of acting up to it in its whole extent; though they stated the applications for the discount of legitimate bills to be their sole criterion of abundance or scarcity, they gave your Committee to understand that they do not discount to the full extent of such applications. In other words, the Directors do not act up to the principle which they represent as one perfectly sound and safe, and must be considered, therefore, as possessing no distinct and certain rule to guide their discretion in controlling the amount of their circulation.

The suspension of cash payments has had the effect of committing into the hands of the Directors of the Bank of England, to be exercised by their sole discretion, the important charge of supplying the country with that quantity of circulating medium which is exactly proportioned to the wants and occasions of the public. In the judgment of the Committee, that is a trust which it is unreasonable to expect that the Directors of the Bank of England should ever be able to discharge. The most detailed knowledge of the actual trade of the country, combined with the profound science in all the principles of money and circulation, would not enable any man or set of men to adjust, and keep always adjusted, the right proportion of circulating medium in a country to the wants of trade. When the currency consists entirely of the precious metals, or of paper convertible at will into the precious metals, the natural process of commerce, by establishing exchanges among all the different countries of the world, adjust, in every particular country, the proportion of circulating medium to its actual occasions, according to that supply of the precious metals which the mines furnish to the general market of the world. The proportion which is thus adjusted and maintained by the natural operation of commerce, cannot be adjusted by any human wisdom or skill. If the natural system of currency and circulation be abandoned, and a discretionary issue of paper money substituted in its stead, it is vain to think that any rules can be devised for the exact exercise of such discretion ; though some cautions may be pointed out to check and control its consequences, such as are indicated by the effect of an excessive issue upon exchanges and the price of gold. The Directors of the Bank of England, in the judgment of your Committee, have exercised the new and extraordinary discretion reposed in them since 1797, with an integrity and a regard to the public interest according to their conceptions of it, and indeed a degree of forbearance in turning it less to the profit of the Bank than it would easily have admitted of, that merit the continuance of that confidence which the public has so long and so justly felt in the integrity with which its affairs are directed, as well as in the unshaken stability and ample funds of that great establishment. That their recent policy involves great practical errors, which it is of the utmost public importance to correct, your Committee are fully convinced ; but those errors are less to be imputed to the Bank Directors than to be stated as the effect of a new system, of which, however it originated or was rendered necessary as a temporary expedient, it might have been well if Parliament had sooner taken into view all the consequences. When your Committee consider that this discretionary power of supplying the kingdom with circulating medium has been exercised under an opinion that the paper could not be issued to excess if advanced in discounts to merchants in good bills payable at stated periods, and likewise under an opinion that neither the price of bullion nor the course of exchanges need be adverted to, as affording any indication with respect to the sufficiency or excess of such paper, your Committee cannot hesitate to say that these opinions of the Bank must be regarded as in a great measure the operative cause of the continuance of the present state of things.

IV.

Your Committee will now proceed to state from the information which has been laid before them what appears to have been the progressive increase, and to be the present amount of the paper circulation of this country, consisting primarily of the notes of the Bank of England not at present convertible into specie ; and, in a secondary manner, of the notes of the country bankers which are convertible, at the option of the holder, into Bank of England paper. After having stated the amount of Bank of England paper, your Committee will explain the reasons which induce them to think that the numerical amount of that paper is not alone to be considered as decisive of the question as to its excess : and before stating the amount of country bank paper, so far as that can be ascertained, your Committee will explain their reasons for thinking that the amount of the country bank circulation is limited by the amount of that of the Bank of England.

1. It appears from the accounts laid before the Committees upon the Bank affairs in 1797, that for several years previous to the year 1796, the average amount of bank notes in circulation was between 10,000,000*l.* and 11,000,000*l.*, hardly ever falling below 9,000,000*l.*, and not often exceeding to any great amount 11,000,000*l.*

The following abstract of the several accounts referred to your Committee, or ordered by your Committee from the Bank, will show the progressive increase of the notes from the year 1798 to the end of the last year.

Average amount of Bank of England Notes in circulation in each of the following years :

	Notes of £5 and upwards, including Bank Post Bills.	Notes under £5.	Total.
	£	£	£
1798................	11,527,250	1,807,502	13,334,752
1799................	12,408,522	1,653,805	14,062,327
1800....	13,598,666	2,243,266	15,841,932
1801...............	13,454,367	2.715,132	16,169,594
1802..............	13,917,977	3,136,477	17,054,454
1803.............	12,953,477	3,064,045	16,847,522
1804..............	12,621,348	4,723,672	17,345,020
1805................	12,697,352	4,544,580	17.241,932
1806..............	12,844,170	4,291,230	17,135,400
1807...............	13,221,988	4,183,013	17,405,001
1808..............	13,402,160	4,132,420	17,534,580
1809..............	14,133,615	4,863,275	19,001,890

Taking from the accounts the last half of the year 1809, the average will be found higher than for the whole year, and amounts to 19,880,310.

The accounts in the Appendix give very detailed returns for the first four months of the present year, down to the 12th May, from which it will be found that the amount was then increasing, particularly in the smaller notes. The whole amount of bank notes in circulation, exclusive of 939,990*l.* of bank post bills, will be found on the average of the two returns for the 5th and 12th May last, to be 14,136,610*l.* in notes of 5*l.* and upwards, and 6,173,380*l.* in notes under 5*l.* making the sum of 20,309,990*l.* and, including the bank post bills, the sum of 21,249,980*l.*

By far the most considerable part of this increase since 1798, it is to be observed, has been in the article of small notes, part of which must be considered as having been introduced to supply the place of the specie which was deficient at the period of the suspension of cash payments. It appears, however, that the first supply of small notes, which was thrown into circulation after that event, was very small in comparison of their present amount ; a large augmentation of them appears to have taken place from the end of the year 1799 to that of the year 1802, and a very rapid increase has also taken place since the month of May in the last year to the present time ; the augmentation of these small notes from 1st May, 1809, to the 5th of May, 1810, being from the sum of 4,509,470*l.* to the sum of 6,161,020*l.*

The notes of the Bank of England are principally issued in advances to government for the public service, and in advances to the merchants upon the discount of their bills.

Your Committee have had an account laid before them, of advances made by the Bank to government on land and malt, Exchequer Bills, and other securities, in every year since the suspension of cash payments; from which, as compared with the accounts laid before the Committees of 1797, and which were then carried back for twenty years, it will appear that the yearly advances of the Bank to government have upon an average, since the suspension, been considerably lower in amount than the average amount of advances prior to that event, and the amount of those advances in the last two years, though greater in amount than those of some years immediately preceding, is less than it was for any of the six years preceding the restriction of cash payments.

With respect to the amount of commercial discounts, your Committee did not think it proper to require from the Directors of the Bank a disclosure of their absolute amount, being a part of their private transactions as a commercial company, of which, without urgent reason, it did not seem right to demand a disclosure. The late Governor and Deputy Governor however, at the desire of your Committee, furnished a comparative scale, in progressive numbers, showing the increase of the amount of their discounts from the year 1790 to 1809, both inclusive. They made a request, with which your Committee have thought it proper to comply, that this document might not be made public; the Committee, therefore, have not placed it in the Appendix to the present report but have returned it to the Bank. Your Committee, however, have to state in general terms, that the amount of discounts has been progressively increasing since the year 1796; and that their amount in the last year (1809) bears a very high proportion to their largest amount in any year preceding 1797. Upon this particular subject, your Committee are only anxious to remark, that the largest amount of mercantile discounts by the Bank, if it could be considered by itself, ought never, in their judgment, to be regarded as any other than a great public benefit, and that it is only the excess of paper currency thereby issued, and kept out in circulation, which is to be considered as the evil.

But your Committee must not omit to state one very impor-

tant principle, t' at the mere numerical return of the amount of
bank notes out in circulation, cannot be considered as at all
deciding the question whether such paper is or is not excessive.
It is necessary to have recourse to other tests. The same
amount of paper may at one time be less than enough, and at
another time more. The quantity of currency required will
vary in some degree with the extent of trade ; and the increase
of our trade, which has taken place since the suspension, must
have occasioned some increase in the quantity of our currency.
But the quantity of currency bears no fixed proportion to the
quantity of commodities ; and any inferences proceeding upon
such a supposition would be entirely erroneous. The effective
currency of the country depends upon the quickness of circulation, and the number of exchanges performed in a given time,
as well as upon its numerical amount ; and all the circumstances, which have a tendency to quicken or to retard the rate of
circulation, render the same amount of currency more or less
adequate to the wants of trade. A much smaller amount is
required in a high state of public credit, than when alarms
make individuals call in their advances, and provide against accidents by hoarding ; and in a period of commercial security
and private confidence, than when mutual distrust discourages
pecuniary arrangements for any distant time. But, above all,
the same amount of currency will be more or less adequate, in
proportion to the skill which the great money dealers possess in
managing and economizing the use of the circulating medium.
Your Committee are of opinion, that the improvements which
have taken place of late years in this country, and particularly
in the district of London, with regard to the use and economy
of money among bankers, and in the mode of adjusting commercial payments, must have had a much greater effect than
has hitherto been ascribed to them, in rendering the same sum
adequate to a much greater amount of trade and payments
than formerly. Some of those improvements will be found detailed in the evidence : they consist principally in the increased
use of bankers' drafts in the common payments of London ; the
contrivance of bringing all such drafts daily to a common re-
ceptacle, where they are balanced against each other ; the intermediate agency of bill-brokers ; and several other changes
in the practice of London bankers, are to the same effect, of
rendering it unnecessary for them to keep so large a deposit of
money as formerly. Within the London district, it would certainly appear, that a smaller sum of money is required than
formerly, to perform the same number of exchanges and amount

of payments, if the rate of prices had remaine the same. It is material also to observe, that both the policy of the Bank of England itself, and the competition of the country bank paper have tended to compress the paper of the Bank of England, more and more, within London and the adjace t district. All these circumstances must have co-operated to render a smaller augmentation of Bank of England paper necessary to supply the demands of our increased trade than might otherwise have been required ; and shew how impossible it is, from the numerical amount alone of that paper, to pronounce whether it is excessive or not : a more sure criterion must be resorted to ; and such a criterion, your Committee have already shewn, is only to be found in the state of the exchanges, and the price of gold bullion.

The particular circumstances of the two years which are so remarkable in the recent history of our circulation, 1793 and 1797, throw great light upon the principle which your Committee have last stated.

In the year 1793, the distress was occasioned by a failure of confidence in the country circulation, and a consequent pressure upon that of London. The Bank of England did not think it advisable to enlarge their issues to meet this increased demand, and their notes, previously issued, circulating less freely in consequence of the alarm that prevailed, proved insufficient for the necessary payments. In this crisis, Parliament applied a remedy, very similar, in its effect, to an enlargement of the advances and issues of the bank ; a loan of exchequer bills was authorized to be made to as many mercantile persons, giving good security, as should apply for them ; and the confidence which this measure diffused, as well as the increased means which it afforded of obtaining bank notes through the sale of the exchequer bills, speedily relieved the distress both of London and of the country. Without offering an opinion upon the expediency of the particular mode in which this operation was effected, your Committee think it an important illustration of the principle, that an enlarged accommodation is the true remedy for that occasional failure of confidence in the country districts, to which our system of paper credit is unavoidably exposed.

The circumstances which occurred in the beginning of the year 1797, were very similar to those of 1793 ;—an alarm of invasion, a run upon the country banks for gold. the failure of some of them, and a run upon the Bank of England, forming a crisis like that of 1793, for which, perhaps, an effectual rem-

edy might have been provided, if the Bank of England had
had courage to extend instead of restricting its accommodations
and issue of notes.　Some few persons, it appears from the Report of the Secret Committee of the Lords, were of this opinion at the time ; and the late Governor and Deputy Governor of
the Bank stated to your Committee, that they, and many of the
Directors, are now satisfied from the experience of the year
1797, that the diminution of their notes in that emergency increased the public distress : an opinion in the correctness of
which your Committee entirely concur.

It appears to your Committee, that the experience of the
Bank of England in the years 1793 and 1797, contrasted with
the facts which have been stated in the present report, suggests
a distinction most important to be kept in view, between that
demand upon the Bank for gold for the supply of the domestic
channels of circulation, sometimes a very great and sudden
one, which is occasioned by a temporary failure of confidence,
and that drain upon the Bank for gold which grows out of an
unfavourable state of the foreign exchanges.　The former,
while the Bank maintains its high credit, seems likely to be best
relieved by a judicious increase of accommodation to the country ; the latter, so long as the Bank does not pay in specie,
ought to suggest to the Directors a question, whether their issues may not be already too abundant.

Your Committee have much satisfaction in thinking that the
Directors are perfectly aware that they may err by a too scanty
supply in a period of stagnant credit.　And your Committee
are clearly of opinion, that although it ought to be the general
policy of the Bank Directors to diminish their paper in the
event of the long continuance of a high price of bullion and a
very unfavourable exchange, yet it is essential to the commercial interests of this country, and to the general fulfilment of
those mercantile engagements which a free issue of paper may
have occasioned, that the accustomed degree of accommodation to the merchants should not be suddenly and materially
reduced ; and that if any general and serious difficulty or ap-
prehension on this subject should arise, it may, in the judgment of your Committee, be counteracted without danger, and
with advantage to the public, by a liberality in the issue of
Bank of England paper proportioned to the urgency of the
particular occasion.　Under such circumstances, it belongs to
the Bank to take likewise into their own consideration, how far
it may be practicable, consistently with a due regard to the immediate interests of the public service, rather to reduce their

paper by a gradual reduction of their advances to government, than by too suddenly abridging the discounts to the merchants.

2. Before your Committee proceed to detail what they have collected with respect to the amount of country bank paper, they must observe, that so long as the cash payments of the Bank are suspended, the whole paper of the country bankers is a superstructure raised upon the foundation of the paper of the Bank of England. The same check, which the convertibility into specie, under a better system, provides against the excess of any part of the paper circulation is, during the present system, provided against an excess of country bank paper, by its convertibility into Bank of England paper. If an excess of paper be issued in a country district, while the London circulation does not exceed its due proportion, there will be a local rise of prices in that country district, but prices in London will remain as before. Those who have the country paper in their hands will prefer buying in London where things are cheaper, and will therefore return that country paper upon the banker who issued it, and will demand from him Bank of England notes or bills upon London ; and thus, the excess of country paper being continually returned upon the issuers for Bank of England paper, the quantity of the latter necessarily and effectually limits the quantity of the former. This is illustrated by the account which has been already given of the excess, and subsequent limitation, of the paper of the Scotch banks, about the year 1763. If the Bank of England paper itself should at any time, during the suspension of cash payments, be issued to excess, a corresponding excess may be issued of country Bank paper which will not be checked ; the foundation being enlarged, the superstructure admits of a proportionate extension. And thus, under such a system, the excess of Bank of England paper will produce its effect upon prices not merely in the ratio of its own increase, but in a much higher proportion.

It has not been in the power of your Committee to obtain such information as might enable them to state, with anything like accuracy, the amount of country bank paper in circulation. But they are led to infer from all the evidence they have been able to procure on this subject, not only that a great number of new country banks has been established within these last two years, but also that the amount of issues of those which are of an older standing has in general been very considerably increased : whilst on the other hand, the high state of mercantile and public credit, the proportionate facility of converting at short notice all public and commercial securities into Bank of England paper, joined to the preference generally given within the limits of its own circulation to the paper of a well-established country bank over that of the Bank of England, have prob ably not rendered it necessary for them to keep any large permanent deposits of Bank of Eng'and paper in their hands. And it seems reasonable to believe that the total amount of the unproductive stock of all the country banks, consisting of specie and Bank of England paper, is much less, at this period, under a circulation vastly increased in extent, than it was before the restriction of 1797. The temptation to establish country banks, and issue promissory notes, has therefore greatly increased. Some conjecture as to the probable total amount of those issues, or at least as to their recent increase, may be formed, as your Committee conceive, from the amount of the duties paid for stamps on the reissuable notes of country banks in Great Britain. The total amount of these duties for the year ended on the 10th of October, 1808, appears to have been 60,522*l.* 15*s.* 3d., and for the year ended on the 10th of October, 1809, 175,129*l.* 17*s.* 7*d.* It must, however, be observed, that on the 10th of October, 1808, these duties experienced an augmentation somewhat exceeding one-third ; and that some regulations were made, imposing limitations with respect to the reissue of all notes not exceeding 2*l.* 2*s.*, the effect of which has been to produce a much more than ordinary demand for stamps or notes of this denomination within the year 1809. Owing to this circumstance, it appears impossible to ascertain what may have been the real increase in the circulation of the notes, not exceeding 2*l.* 2*s.*, within the last year ; but with respect to the notes of a higher value, no alteration having been made in the law as to their reissue, the following comparison affords the best statement that can be collected from the documents before the Committee, of the addition made in the year 1809, to the number of those notes.

Number of Country Bank Notes exceeding 2*l.* 2*s.* each, stamped in the years ended the 10th of October, 1808, and 10th of October, 1809, respectively :

	1808. No.	1809. No.
Exceeding £2 2, and not exceeding £5 5........	666,071	922,073
Exceeding £5 5, and not exceeding £20	198,473	380,006
Exceeding £20, and not exceeding £30.........		2,425
Exceeding £30, and not exceeding £50.........		674
Exceeding £50, and not exceeding £100........		**2,611**

Assuming that the notes in the first two of these classes, were all issued for the lowest denomination to which the duties respectively attach, and such as are most commonly met with in the circulation of country paper, viz., notes of 5*l.* and 10*l.* [although in the second class there is a considerable number of 20*l.*] and even omitting altogether from the comparison the notes of the three last classes, the issue of which your Committee understands is in fact confined to the chartered banks of Scotland, the result would be, that, exclusive of any increase in the number of notes under 2*l.* 2*s.* the amount of country bank paper stamped in the year ended the 10th of October, 1809, has exceeded that of the year ended on the 10th of October, 1808, in the sum of 3,095,340*l.* Your Committee can form no positive conjecture as to the amount of country bank paper cancelled and withdrawn from circulation in the course of the last year. But considering that it is the interest and practice of the country bankers to use the same notes as long as possible ; that, as the law now stands, there is no limitation of time to the re-issuing of those not exceeding 2*l.* 2*s.*; and that all above that amount are reissuable for three years from the date of their first issuing ; it appears difficult to suppose that the amount of notes above 2*l.* 2*s.* cancelled in 1809, could be equal to the whole amount stamped in 1808 : but even upon that supposition, there would still be an increase for 1809 in the notes of 5*l.* and 10*l.* alone, to the amount above specified of 3,095,340*l.* to which must be added an increase within the same period of Bank of England notes to the amount of about 1,500,000*l.* making in the year 1809, an addition in the whole of between four and five millions to the circulation of Great Britain alone, deducting only the gold which may have been withdrawn in the course of that year from actual circulation, which cannot have been very considerable, and also making an allowance for some increase in the amount of such country paper, as, though stamped, may not be in actual circulation. This increase in the general paper currency in last year, even after these deductions, would probably be little short of the amount which in almost any one year, since the discovery of America, has been added to the circulating coin of the whole of Europe. Although, as your Committee has already had occasion to observe, no certain conclusion can be drawn from the numerical amount of paper in circulation, considered abstractedly from all other circumstances, either as to such paper being in excess, or still less as to the proportion of such excess ; yet they must remark, that the fact of any very great and rapid increase in that amount

when coupled and attended with all the indications of a depreciated circulation, does afford the strongest confirmatory evidence, that from the want of some adequate check, the issues
of such paper have not been restrained within their proper
limits.

Your Committee cannot quit this part of the subject without
further observing, that the addition of between four and five millions sterling to the paper circulation of this country, has doubtless
been made at a very small expense to the parties issuing it,
only about 100,000*l.* having been paid thereupon in stamps to
the revenue, and probably for the reasons already stated, no
corresponding deposits of gold or Bank of England notes being
deemed by the country banks necessary to support their additional issues. These parties, therefore, it may be fairly stated,
have been enabled under the protection of the law, which vir-
tually secures them against such demands, to create within the
last year or fifteen months, at a very trifling expense, and in a
manner almost free from all present risk to their respective
credits as dealers in paper money, issues of that article to the
amount of several millions, operating, in the first instance and
in their hands, as capital for their own benefit, and when used
as such by them, falling into and in succession mixing itself with
the mass of circulation of which the value in exchange for all
other commodities is gradually lowered in proportion as that
mass is augmented. If your Committee could be of opinion
that the wisdom of Parliament would not be directed to apply
a proper remedy to a state of things so unnatural, and teeming,
if not corrected in time, with ultimate consequences, so preju-
dicial to the public welfare, they would not hesitate to declare
an opinion, that some mode ought to be derived of enabling
the state to participate much more largely in the profits accru-
ing from the present system ; but as this is by no means the
policy they wish to recommend, they will conclude their observations on this part of the subject, by observing that in proportion as they most fully agree with Dr. Adam Smith and all the
most able writers and statesmen of this country, in considering
a paper circulation constantly convertible into specie, as one
of the greatest practical improvements which can be made in
the political and domestic economy of any state ; and in viewing
the establishment of the country banks issuing such paper as a
most valuable and essential branch of that improvement in this
kingdom ; in the same proportion is your Committee anxious
to revert as speedily as possible to the former practice
and state of things in this respect: convinced on the one

hand, that anything like a permanent and systematic departure from that practice must ultimately lead to results, which among other attendant calamities, would be destructive of the system itself; and on the other, that such an event would be the more to be deprecated, as it is only in a country like this, where good faith, both public and private, is held so high, and where, under the happy union of liberty and law, property and the securities of every description by which it is represented, are equally protected against the encroachments of power and the violence of popular commotion, that the advantages of this system, unaccompanied with any of its dangers, can be permanently enjoyed, and carried to their fullest extent.

Upon a review of all the facts and reasonings, which have been submitted to the consideration of your Committee in the course of their inquiry, they have formed an opinion, which they submit to the House :—That there is at present an excess in the paper circulation of this country, of which the most unequivocal symptom is the very high price of bullion, and next to that, the low state of the continental exchanges; that this excess is to be ascribed to the want of a sufficient check and control in the issues of paper from the Bank of England; and originally to the suspension of cash payments, which removed the natural and true control. For upon a general view of the subject, your Committee are of opinion, that no safe, certain, and constantly adequate, provision against an excess of paper currency, either occasional or permanent, can be found, except in the convertibility of all such paper into specie. Your Committee cannot, therefore, but see reason to regret, that the suspension of cash payments, which, in the most favourable light in which it can be viewed, was only a temporary measure, has been continued so long; and particularly, that by the manner in which the present continuing act is framed, the character should have been given to it of a permanent war measure.

Your Committee conceive that it would be superfluous to point out, in detail, the disadvantages which must result to the country, from any such general excess of currency as lowers its relative value. The effect of such an augmentation of prices upon all money transactions for time; the unavoidable injury suffered by annuitants, and by creditors of every description, both private and public; the unintended advantage gained by government and all other debtors; are consequences too obvious to require proof, and too repugnant to justice to be left without remedy. By far the most important portion of this effect it ap-

pears to your Committee to be that which is communicated to
the wages of common country labor, the rate of which, it is well
known, adapts itself more slowly to the changes which happen in
the value of money, than the price of any other species of labor
or commodity.   And it is enough for your Committee to allude
to some classes of the public servants, whose pay, if once
raised in consequence of a depreciation of money, cannot so
conveniently be reduced again to its former rate, even after
money shall have recovered its value.   The future progress of
these inconveniences and evils, if not checked, must at no
great distance of time work a practical conviction upon the
minds of all those who may still doubt their existence ; but even
if their progressive increase were less probable than it appears
to your Committee, they cannot help expressing an opinion,
that the integrity and honor of Parliament are concerned, not
to authorize longer than is required by imperious necessity, the
continuance in this great commercial country of a system of
circulation, in which that natural check or control is absent
which maintains the value of money, and by the permanency
of that common standard of value, secures the substantial justice and faith of moneyed contracts and obligations between man
and man.

Your Committee moreover beg leave to advert to the temptation to resort to a depreciation even of the value of the gold
coin by an alteration of the standard, to which Parliament itself
might be subjected by a great and long-continued excess of
paper.   This has been the resource of many governments
under such circumstances, and is the obvious and most easy
remedy to the evil in question.   But it is unnecessary to dwell
on the breach of public faith and dereliction of a primary duty
of government, which would manifestly be implied in preferring
the reduction of the coin down to the standard of the paper, to
the restoration of the paper to the legal standard of the coin.

Your Committee therefore, having very anxiously and de-
liberately considered this subject, report it to the House as
their opinion, that the system of the circulating medium of this
country ought to be brought back, with as much speed as is
compatible with a wise and necessary caution, to the original
principle of cash payments at the option of the holder of Bank
paper.

Your Committee have understood that remedies, or palliatives,
of a different nature, have been projected ; such as, a compulsory limitation of the amount of Bank advances and discounts,
during the continuance of the suspension ; or, a compulsory

limitation during the same period, of the rate of Bank profits and dividends, by carrying the surplus of profits above that rate to the public account. But, in the judgment of your Committee, such indirect schemes, for palliating the possible evils resulting from the suspension of cash payments, would prove wholly inadequate for that purpose, because the necessary proportion could never be adjusted, and if once fixed, might aggravate very much the inconveniences of a temporary pressure ; and even if their efficacy could be made to appear, they would be objectionable as a most hurtful and improper interference with the rights of commercial property.

According to the best judgment your Committee has been enabled to form, no sufficient remedy for the present, or security for the future, can be pointed out, except the repeal of the law which suspends the cash payments of the Bank of England.

In effecting so important a change, your Committee are of opinion that some difficulties must be encountered, and that there are some contingent dangers to the Bank, against which it ought most carefully, and strongly to be guarded. But all those may be effectually provided for, by entrusting to the discretion of the Bank itself the charge of conducting and completing the operation, and by allowing to the Bank so ample a period of time for conducting it, as will be more than sufficient to effect its completion. To the discretion, experience, and integrity of the Directors of the Bank, your Committee believe that Parliament may safely entrust the charge of effecting that which Parliament may in its wisdom determine upon as necessary to be effected ; and that the Directors of that great institution, far from making themselves a party with those who have a temporary interest in spreading alarm, will take a much longer view of the permanent interests of the Bank, as indissolubly blended with those of the public. The particular mode of gradually effecting the resumption of cash payments ought therefore, in the opinion of your Committee, to be left in a great measure to the discretion of the Bank, and Parliament ought to do little more than to fix definitely the time at which cash payments are to become, as before, compulsory. The period allowed ought to be ample, in order that the Bank Directors may feel their way, and that, having a constant watch upon the varying circumstances that ought to guide them, and availing themselves only of favourable circumstances, they may tread back their steps slowly, and may preserve both the course of their own affairs as a company, and that of public and commercial credit, not only safe, but unembarrassed.

With this view, your Committee would suggest, that the restriction on cash payments cannot safely be removed at an earlier period than two years from the present time ; but your Committee are of opinion, that early provision ought to be made by Parliament for terminating, by the end of that period, the operation of the several statutes which have imposed and continued that restriction.

In suggesting this period of two years, your Committee have not overlooked the circumstance, that, as the law stands at present, the Bank would be compelled to pay in cash at the end of six months after the ratification of a definitive treaty of peace ; so that if peace were to be concluded within that period, the recommendation of your Committee might seem to have the effect of postponing, instead of accelerating the resumption of payments. But your Committee are of opinion, that if peace were immediately to be ratified, in the present state of our circulation, it would be most hazardous to compel the Bank to pay cash in six months, and would be found wholly impracticable. Indeed, the restoration of peace, by opening new fields of commercial enterprise, would multiply instead of abridging the demands upon the Bank for discount, and would render it peculiarly distressing to the commercial world if the Bank were suddenly and materally to restrict their issues. Your Committee are therefore of opinion, that even if peace should intervene, two years should be given to the Bank for resuming its payments ; but that even if the war should be prolonged, cash payments should be resumed by the end of that period.

Your Committee have not been indifferent to the consideration of the possible occurrence of political circumstances, which may be thought hereafter to furnish an argument in favor of some prolongation of the proposed period of resuming cash payments, or even in favor of a new law for their temporary restriction after the Bank shall have opened. They are, however, far from anticipating a necessity, even in any case, of returning to the present system. But if occasion for a new measure of restriction could be supposed at any time to arise, it can in no degree be grounded, as your Committee think, on any state of the foreign exchanges (which they trust that they have abundantly shown the Bank itself to have the general power of controlling), but on a political state of things producing, or likely very soon to produce, an alarm at home, leading to so indefinite a demand for cash for domestic uses as it must be impossible for any banking establishment to provide against. A return to the ordinary system of banking is, on the very ground of the late extravagant fall of the exchanges and high price of gold, peculiarly requisite. That alone can effectually restore general confidence in the value of the circulating medium of the kingdom; and the serious expectation of this event must enforce a preparatory reduction of the quantity of paper, and all other measures which accord with the true principles of banking. The anticipation of the time when the Bank will be constrained to open, may also be expected to contribute to the improvement of the exchanges; whereas a postponement of this era, so indefinite as that of six months after the termination of the war, and especially in the event of an exchange continuing to fall (which more and more would generally be perceived to arise from an excess of paper, and a consequent depreciation of it), may lead, under an unfavourable state of public affairs, to such a failure of confidence (and especially among foreigners), in the determination of Parliament to enforce a return to the professed standard of the measure of payments, as may serve to precipitate the further fall of the exchanges, and lead to consequences at once the most discreditable and disastrous.

Although the details of the best mode of returning to cash payments ought to be left to the discretion of the Bank of England, as already stated, certain provisions would be necessary, under the authority of Parliament, both for the convenience of the Bank itself, and for the security of the other banking establishments in this country and in Ireland.

Your Committee conceive it may be convenient for the Bank to be permitted to issue notes under the value of 5*l.* for some little time after it had resumed payments in specie.

It will be convenient, also, for the chartered Banks of Ireland and Scotland, and all the country banks, that they should not be compelled to pay in specie until some time after the resumption of payments in cash, by the Bank of England; but that they should continue for a short period upon their present footing, of being liable to pay their own notes on demand, in Bank of England paper.

COSIMO-on-DEMAND

COSIMO is an innovative publisher of books and publications that inspire, inform and engage readers worldwide. Our titles are drawn from a range of subjects including health, business, philosophy, history, science and sacred texts. We specialize in using print-on-demand technology (POD), making it possible to publish books for both general and specialized audiences and to keep books in print indefinitely. With POD technology new titles can reach their audiences faster and more efficiently than with traditional publishing.

> ➢ **Permanent Availability:** Our books & publications never go out-of-print.

> ➢ **Global Availability:** Our books are always available online at popular retailers and can be ordered from your favorite local bookstore.

COSIMO CLASSICS brings to life unique, rare, out-of-print classics representing subjects as diverse as *Alternative Health, Business and Economics, Eastern Philosophy, Personal Growth, Mythology, Philosophy, Sacred Texts, Science, Spirituality* and much more!

COSIMO-on-DEMAND publishes your books, publications and reports. If you are an Author, part of an Organization, or a Benefactor with a publishing project and would like to bring books back into print, publish new books fast and effectively, would like your publications, books, training guides, and conference reports to be made available to your members and wider audiences around the world, we can assist you with your publishing needs.

Visit our website at www.cosimobooks.com to learn more about Cosimo, browse our catalog, take part in surveys or campaigns, and sign-up for our newsletter.

And if you wish please drop us a line at info@cosimobooks.com. We look forward to hearing from you.